Penguin University Books
Fundamental Questions of Philosophy

Stephan Körner

FUNDAMENTAL QUESTIONS OF PHILOSOPHY

One Philosopher's Answers

Penguin Books

Penguin Books Ltd, Harmondsworth,
Middlesex, England
Penguin Books Inc., 7110 Ambassador Road,
Baltimore, Maryland 21207, U.S.A.
Penguin Books Australia Ltd, Ringwood,
Victoria, Australia

First published by Allen Lane The Penguin Press 1969
Published in Penguin University Books 1971

Copyright © Stephan Körner, 1969

Made and printed in Great Britain by
Fletcher & Son Ltd, Norwich
Set in Monotype Plantin

To Richard Bevan Braithwaite

Contents

Contents

'. . . it is the mark of an educated mind to expect that amount of exactness in each kind which the nature of the particular subject admits.'

ARISTOTLE (*Nicomachean Ethics*, Book I, 1094 b 25)

'But there is yet another consideration which is more philosophical and *architectonic* in character; namely to grasp the *idea of the whole* correctly and thence to view all . . . parts in their mutual relations. . . .'

KANT (Preface to the *Critique of Practical Reason*)

Preface

A book on the nature of philosophy which is to be intelligible to laymen and useful to beginners might take many different forms. I shall therefore briefly indicate some of the aims which I have tried to achieve, and the manner in which I have attempted to strike a balance between them.

The life and development of philosophy, like that of other disciplines, depends on discussion, criticism and controversy. I have tried to illustrate the diversity of philosophical positions, without at the same time sacrificing the unity of presentation. If such unity is to be genuine, it must derive from a point of view of one's own. Instead of resting content with a catalogue of various approaches to a problem, I have not hesitated to approach it also from my own position and, in doing so, to draw on my previous writings.

The problems of philosophy are closely connected with each other, as well as with problems belonging to other disciplines. The network of these connexions is one of the most attractive features, intellectually and aesthetically, of philosophy, and I have tried to exhibit some strands of the net. In selecting them I have naturally had to follow my own inclinations and interests. To trace them all is in any case beyond the capacities of any one man.

In order to illustrate the vitality of the classical traditions and the power of philosophical thinking to progress beyond them, it was neither necessary to strive after historical completeness, nor to examine every single view which has been defended in this century. I have, in particular, avoided any evaluation of the works by my contemporaries. A reasoned appraisal of their contributions would have required another book, while stray statements of approval or disapproval would have been as worthless as are expressions of a merely personal bias.

I have tried to write simply and clearly. But I have never deliberately misrepresented a point or an argument in order to create the agreeable impression of a lucid literary style. To do so would have been dishonest. It would also have been imprudent, since all my points and arguments will be – and should be – exposed to expert scrutiny and criticism.

Intelligent laymen and beginners are not equally knowledgeable in all fields, so that the various parts of the book will require different degrees of attention from different groups of readers. Part 2 demands close reading from those who have little acquaintance with mathematical reasoning, Part 4 from those who are not accustomed to fairly abstract thinking. But the effort is no greater than that which they would be required to make in reading an introduction to, say, mathematics or any of the natural sciences. The purpose of Part 5 is not so much to present a historical survey as to give some indication of the role played by philosophy in the history of ideas.

The footnotes are not essential to an understanding of the text. They contain, for the most part, references to the first or standard editions of the works mentioned. (Most other editions and translations either contain marginal references to the pagination of the quoted editions, or else preserve their division into chapters, sections, paragraphs, etc.) The dates of the authors mentioned in the text are found in the Index of Persons. I have added a selective bibliographical appendix of recent books, which should help readers to find their way through the literature.

I should like to thank my friend and colleague Dr C. J. F. Williams for reading the penultimate draft of the book. I have accepted most of his criticisms; and in the rare cases in which I did not accept them, I have tried to express my views more clearly. He is, of course, not responsible for my mistakes and must not be assumed to agree with my general philosophical position. Messrs T. Honderich and R. Hutchison, who read the final draft for the publishers, also made some helpful suggestions.

Part I

PHILOSOPHICAL PROBLEMS AND PHILOSOPHICAL METHODS

Introduction

Ideally, the definition of a theoretical discipline would consist in a sharp demarcation of its solved and unsolved problems and of the methods used in achieving or attempting their solution. For fairly obvious reasons such a definition is rarely possible or useful. Most theoretical disciplines, such as mathematics, physics and in particular philosophy, continually change as they face new problems, discard old ones and modify their methods. Again, the problems and methods of different disciplines may overlap: for example, when an old science gives birth to a new or when it turns out that a problem is unsolvable in one discipline, but can be solved or brought nearer to a solution in another. Sharp demarcation lines may also lead to barren demarcation-disputes and to the impression that it is less important to solve a problem than to decide to which theoretical discipline it belongs. Lastly, the notions of problem and method admit of gradations which are easily lost sight of in attempts at rigid definitions. Problems in any theoretical discipline may be almost indistinguishable from vague misgivings, which in turn merge into a perplexed groping for as yet unformulated questions. Problems which can be formulated in the form of clear questions range from questions which seem, or are, unanswerable by all available methods to questions which may be fairly set at an examination. The notion of method similarly covers a wide spectrum, ranging from instinctively followed procedures to explicitly formulated rules of thumb.

All this suggests that we should approach our topic by way of exemplification rather than definition. The illustrations of philosophical problems and methods contained in the following two chapters are meant to convey something of the manner and flavour of philosophical investigation and thereby to serve as an introduction to a systematic inquiry into particular clusters of philosophical problems.

1. Philosophical Problems

For the ancient Greeks 'philosophy' meant any attempt to solve theoretical problems by theoretical methods. 'It is through wonder', says Aristotle in the first book of the *Metaphysics*,

that men now begin and originally began to philosophize; wondering in the first place at obvious perplexities; and then by gradual progression raising questions about the greater matters too, e.g. about the changes of the moon and of the sun, about the stars and about the origin of the universe.[1]

Of the questions about 'the greater matters' mentioned by Aristotle, only the last is still partly philosophical, and even here much of what used to be philosophical cosmology has moved into physics, albeit into what is a rather speculative branch of it. Yet many problems which the ancient Greek thinkers regarded as philosophical and which engaged the attention of the thinkers of other ancient civilizations have remained philosophical problems until today; and some of these are likely to remain so for a long time.

In setting down some examples of philosophical problems for preliminary discussion I have naturally tried to choose

[1] *Metaphysics* 982b10. Most editions of Aristotle's works refer in the margin to the pagination of Bekker's edition (Berlin 1831f.)

4

problems which would be likely to arouse at least a slight degree of curiosity; which would jointly be representative of a wide variety of philosophical interests; and which would also serve as fixed points of reference in the later discussions. Two considerations, however, have been uppermost in my mind: first that the problems should be capable of being stated briefly, and second that they should have proved, and be likely to continue to prove, intellectually fertile by suggesting new insights and new lines of philosophical or non-philosophical inquiry. The first consideration excludes, for example, the problem 'whether several angels can simultaneously occupy the same place'.[1] Only a long exposition of the unfamiliar context in which it arose could show that it leads to interesting questions, which are far from being inane and are not necessarily connected with a belief in the existence of angels. The second consideration excludes, for example, the question whether if a cow moves around a tree the tree also moves round the cow. A person who is perplexed by it should consult an intelligent schoolboy taking physics. To philosophize is not to be perplexed by the unperplexing, to cultivate perplexity for perplexity's sake or, even worse, to adopt the pose of being eternally perplexed. Perplexity is often not only the beginning but also the end of serious thought. It is not its aim.

Each of the following examples of a philosophical problem belongs to a group of closely interrelated problems which together form the whole or a substantial part of a special branch of philosophical inquiry: logic, philosophy of mathematics, philosophy of science, ethics, etc. They each present a different type of difficulty and are thus unlikely to appear equally attractive, or forbidding, to everybody. The examples are on the whole arranged in order of decreasing abstractness of the concepts involved, and not in any particular order of philosophical importance, whatever that might be. The opening two examples, especially the first, make the greatest demands on one's powers of abstraction. They exemplify problems which for a

[1] Thomas Aquinas, *Summa Theologica*, Pars I, Q. LII, Art. III. (Leonine edition, Rome 1882 and onwards)

5

very long time have been shared by philosophers and mathematicians and bear the imprint of both philosophical and mathematical thought. The omission of these or similar problems would, I believe, have been tantamount to misrepresentation. The intention of the brief comments on each problem is to point to the visible part of an iceberg, not to chart its whole extent. Yet much that will be unclear initially will become clear in the further course of the discussion.

THE PROBLEM OF CLASS-EXISTENCE

All thinking involves explicit or implicit classifications. To state that Socrates is a man is to put an individual into a class of individuals. It is to state that Socrates is an element (a member) of the class of men. To state that man is an animal is to classify a class: the class of men is a subclass (species) of the class (genus) of animals. To state that no man is a donkey is to state that the class of men and the class of donkeys are mutually exclusive (have no common member). A class may be a member of a class. For example, a learned society, such as the class of all egyptologists who have fulfilled certain formalities, may be a member of the class of learned societies, which has only societies, *qua* societies, as members. A class is determined either by enumerating its members or by indicating a property which all, and only, its members possess. Enumeration is impossible in the case of infinite classes and impracticable in the case of large finite classes. The class of all men is the class of those, and only those, entities which have the property of being a man. The universal class (the highest genus) is the class of all entities which have the property of being entities, i.e. the class of all entities. It can also be defined as the class of those, and only those, entities which have the property of being identical with themselves. The 'empty class' (the null-class) is the class which has no members. It can be defined as the class of all entities which possess a self-contradictory property, e.g. the class of those, and only those, entities which have the property of being animals and non-animals or of not being self-identical.

Our first problem can now be formulated as a question. Is it possible to assume of every class – determined by an enumeration or the indication of a property – that it exists? More precisely, can the assumption that it exists imply a logical contradiction? The natural inclination of many people, including eminent logicians of all epochs, has been to say that it cannot. Yet already Aristotle[1] argued that the existence of the universal class, i.e. the class of all entities, is logically impossible. I omit exposition of his rather condensed argument in order to avoid problems of exegesis and controversy about the extent to which it anticipates modern developments. Instead I shall briefly explain the famous paradox of Russell from which it seems to follow that certain classes cannot exist.

Let us call a class 'normal' if, and only if, it is not an element of itself. The zoologist's classes are all normal since, e.g., the class of all vertebrates is not a member of itself, i.e. is not itself a vertebrate. Indeed most classes which normally concern us are 'normal'. On the other hand the universal class is abnormal since it contains all entities as members, and consequently includes itself. Again the class of all classes is abnormal because it is itself a class and thus a member of itself. I now define Russell's class by the property of being a normal class, i.e. as the class which contains all, and only, normal classes as its members. Is Russell's class normal or abnormal? If it is normal then, since it is the class of all normal classes, it is a member of itself, i.e. abnormal. If it is abnormal then, since it is the class of all normal classes, it is not a member of itself, i.e. normal. To assume the existence of Russell's class implies a logical contradiction. Some properties, e.g. the property of being a normal class, do not determine classes. The conclusion seems unavoidable. It seemed so to Russell, who avoided the contradiction by (i) distinguishing between different types of entities, namely individuals, classes of individuals, classes of classes of individuals, etc., and (ii) laying down conditions under which

---

[1] *Metaphysics* 998b22. Compare I. M. Bochenski, *A History of Formal Logic* (Notre Dame University 1961), page 54

an entity of a certain type can be an element of an entity of another type. Russell's theory of types was later simplified by F. P. Ramsey[1].

But there is at least one other way of dealing with the problem of class-existence. It is to question the assumption made by Russell and his predecessor Frege that every class is – like the society of egyptologists – both a plurality and an individual capable of membership in a class. A theory based on a suitable distinction between mere pluralities and pluralities which are also individuals is as successful as a theory of types in avoiding Russell's and other paradoxes. Such a theory was explicitly developed by the mathematician J. von Neumann.[2] It is of some interest to note that neither Russell's theory of types nor von Neumann's theory admits the existence of a universal class as a plurality and an individual capable of class-membership, although the latter theory admits it as a plurality. In a sense they thus side with Aristotle who denied the existence of a highest genus. Between Aristotle's and our own day the problem of class-existence has stimulated much philosophical and logico-mathematical thought. To regard its apparent abstractness and abstruseness as a symptom of intellectual sterility would, as I have tried to show, be a mistake.

It might perhaps be objected that Russell and von Neumann by making arbitrary stipulations avoid the problem rather than solve it. But in order to justify this charge one would have to show that no stipulation is needed. An analogy might help to clarify the position: if a legal expert argues that a law, which is intended to fill a gap or remove an apparent contradiction in a legal system, is not needed, he will have to shoulder the burden of showing that there is no gap or contradiction in the system. A mere expression of uneasiness about a stipulation does not amount to a demonstration of its being superfluous or inappropriate.

[1] Russell and Whitehead, *Principia Mathematica*, 2nd edition (Cambridge 1925), Introduction
[2] 'Die Axiomatisierung der Mengenlehre', *Math. Zeitschrift*, volume 27 (1928)

THE PROBLEM OF ZENO'S DICHOTOMY

This problem is less abstract than the problem of class-existence, because the notions involved in stating it are not as all-pervasive as the notion of class and thing. Even though the problem was probably meant to suggest that sense-experience is illusory, it at least appeals to such experience. In Aristotle's terse formulation[1] it 'declares movement to be impossible because, however near the mobile is to any given point, it will always have to cover the half, and then the half of that, and so on without limit before it gets there'. Let us assume that a ball rolls along a yard-stick. Before it has travelled a yard it will have to travel half of a yard, before it has travelled half of a yard it will have to travel a quarter of a yard, etc. The division can proceed *ad infinitum* so that (it would seem) the yard-stick is divided into an infinite number of small bits. To traverse each bit takes a finite time. The journey through an infinite number of bits, each taking a finite time, takes an infinite time and the ball will never arrive. The argument does not, of course, depend on the distance's being one yard. Any distance, however small, would do. If Zeno's argument is correct, no body can move even the smallest distance and motion is indeed impossible. Yet bodies obviously do move. So there is something wrong with the argument. But what? The list of thinkers who have tried to supply an answer includes many of the great names in philosophy and mathematics and some of the great names in physics.

In putting forward this and other arguments against the possibility of motion Zeno intended to support the metaphysical doctrines of his teacher Parmenides that reality is an indivisible, continuous, homogeneous and changeless whole, and that consequently all appearance to the contrary, even all sense-experience to the contrary, is mere appearance or illusion. That of which the description is internally contradictory does not exist. A sphere described as being at the same time an inch and a yard in diameter cannot exist. Zeno wishes to show that any

[1] *Physics*, 6, 239b10

description of motion is similarly contradictory, and that motion therefore is not real. His argument is the prototype of many metaphysical attempts to use logical analysis, not in the service of the familiar distinction between reliable and illusory perceptions, but in order to prove that all perception is illusory. It has been adopted and adapted by many metaphysicians.

Aristotle's attempt to resolve Zeno's paradox is based, among other things, on his rejection of Zeno's assumption that if a process can be continued *ad infinitum* there exists the infinite set of all its phases. He rejects as spurious and self-contradictory the notion of a so-called actual infinity, e.g. the existence of the totality of all positive integers 1, 2, 3 . . . and only admits so-called potential infinities, e.g. the possibility of conceiving of an ever-increasing sequence of positive integers. A finite class can be actually given or actual in the sense that its members are all available for separate identification and complete enumeration. In the case of an infinite class any process of separately identifying and enumerating its members must remain incomplete.

The problem of infinity is part of the problem of continuity. Consider the infinite number of points on the segment of a line between 1 and 2 units. If all the points are to be represented, we must – as the Greeks already knew – in addition to the fractions, make use of irrational numbers which (like e.g. $\sqrt{2}$) cannot be represented by fractions. Only then will the representation of the points by the numbers be 'continuous'. What precisely does the notion of continuity mean in this and similar contexts? It would be wrong, or at least controversial, to say that the problems of the nature of infinity and continuity have been solved either by philosophers or by pure mathematicians. About their vitality and intellectual fruitfulness for over two and a half thousand years there can, however, be little doubt.

If one makes the assumption that we nowadays possess an internally consistent mathematical theory of continuity there arises the further important question of its relation to perceptually given continuous expanses, durations and motions. Does the mathematical concept of a continuum – and for that matter does any mathematical concept – describe perceptual phenomena and, if so, does it perhaps describe their structure or form rather than their sensory content or matter? Does the concept perhaps describe some objective reality of which perceptual phenomena are only blurred and imprecise copies? Or is the mathematical concept of a continuum merely a usefully simplified description of the objects of sense-experience? Thus at least one aspect of Zeno's paradox forms part of the philosophical problem of the nature of the application of mathematics to sense-experience and consequently also of the role of mathematics in the natural sciences. Indeed one reason for the intellectual perplexity caused by the paradox is the impression of a head-on collision between apparently flawless mathematical reasoning and the apparently unimpeachable testimony of the senses.

THE PROBLEM OF THE ANTICIPATION OF NATURE

As this problem has in modern times been most forcefully put by Hume it might also be called Hume's challenge. This is how he formulates it:

These two propositions are far from being the same, *I have found that such an object has always been attended with such an effect*, and *I foresee, that other objects, which are in appearance similar, will be attended with similar effects*. I shall allow if you please, that one proposition may justly be inferred from the other: I know in fact that it is always inferred. But if you insist that the inference is made by a chain of reasoning, I desire you to produce that reasoning. The connexion between these propositions is not intuitive. There is required a medium, which may enable the mind to draw such an inference, if indeed it be drawn by reasoning and argument. What that medium is, I must confess, passes my comprehension; and it is incumbent on those to produce it, who assert that it really exists, and is the origin of all our conclusions concerning matters of fact.[1]

[1] *Philosophical Essays* (later *Enquiry*) *Concerning Human Understanding* (London 1748), section IV, part II

Hume does not doubt that everybody 'but a fool or madman' makes inductions of the form described by him from retrospective statements about natural phenomena to forward-looking generalizations about them. But he requires a philosophical justification and implies that this cannot be given.

The challenge raises a number of important questions about the nature of induction, e.g. whether all or some people implicitly employ rules by reference to which correct inductions can be distinguished from incorrect ones and, if so, whether these rules could be clearly exhibited and systematized as a theory or logic of induction; whether, apart from minor flaws, such a logic already exists, say under the name of statistics, or whether it is in principle impossible. It raises the further question as to what would be the nature of a justification of induction, since what might be acceptable as a justification to some people might not be acceptable to others. Hume's challenge – whether or not it can be satisfactorily answered – naturally leads to more general questions about the nature of empirical prediction, of the role of scientific theories in it and of the relation between scientific theories and experience. It is central to the so-called theory of knowledge and the philosophy of science.

THE PROBLEM OF THE RELATION
BETWEEN MENTAL AND PHYSICAL PHENOMENA

At least one important aspect of this problem becomes clear by considering the following assertions by Leibniz: 'It must be confessed that *perception* and that which depends on it are *inexplicable on mechanical grounds*, that is to say, by means of figures and motions. And supposing there were a machine, so constructed as to think, feel and have perception, it might be conceived as increased in size, while keeping the same proportions, so that one might go into it as into a mill. That being so, we should, on examining its interior, find only parts which work upon one another, and never anything by which to explain a perception.' He concludes 'that it is in a simple substance, and not in a compound or in a machine, that perception must be sought for'.[1] It may, I think, be safely assumed that had electro-magnetic phenomena been familiar in Leibniz's day he would have added that perception is not explicable on electro-magnetic grounds either. It should further be noted that he does not deny, and is not even concerned with, the possibility of constructing a thinking, feeling and perceiving artefact or an artificial man. His problem is the nature of mental phenomena and their relation to physical ones.

Before one can agree, or disagree, with these statements of Leibniz one would first of all have to attempt to find some way of demarcating the class of mental and, thus, the class of physical phenomena, or, more precisely, the class of apparently mental and apparently physical phenomena. For even if all apparently physical entities and phenomena should turn out to be 'reducible' to mental ones, or all apparently mental entities and phenomena to physical ones, one would, at least at the outset, have to acknowledge the apparent existence of two different classes of entities and phenomena. One cannot 'reduce' a thing to itself, except in some technical sense of the term which would be irrelevant in the present context. Next, one would have to explain the nature of the reduction. Thus a mere correlation between mental and physical phenomena would not be sufficient, e.g. a correlation between a certain type of physical event in a person's body and his perception of a red circular surface.

Of the host of other questions which the quoted statements suggest I shall mention only one. 'Supposing', as Leibniz does, 'there were a machine so constructed as to think, feel and have perception', how could we ever know this? We are from our own experience, including that of our interaction with our surroundings, aware of our own thinking, perceiving and feeling, in a way in which (at least *prima facie*) we are not aware of the thinking, perceiving and feeling of other beings. What then are the criteria by which we come to know or believe that the external behaviour of other beings embodies, or is symptomatic

[1] *La Monadologie* (1714), section 17

of, their thinking, perceiving and feeling; or more generally, what is the relation between external behaviour and the mental phenomena which, as it were, are gauged from them? It may, of course, be that the science of psychology has answered these questions or shown that they are confused. But then one would have to examine its claim to have done so very carefully, especially as in this region of thought dubious metaphysics not infrequently masquerades as scientific discovery.

THE PROBLEM OF MORAL DISAGREEMENT

The next four examples of philosophical problems are perhaps the most familiar ones. That they are a frequent subject matter of superficial talk around many a coffee-table does not detract from their interest and difficulty. The problem of moral disagreement can be partly formulated by asking the question 'What is moral disagreement about?' When two people disagree in their beliefs about the height of the Eiffel Tower, the date of Napoleon's death or the half-life of a radium atom, at least one of them must be wrong and at most one of them can be right. In all these cases something exists independently of their belief, in virtue of which the belief is true, if it is true, and false, if it is false. On the other hand when two people disagree in their attitudes, e.g. if one of them likes eating spinach, while the other dislikes it, there is no one fact about which they disagree: they simply have, and express, different attitudes. This is so even when the disagreement is expressed in a context in which one, or both of them, is trying to change the attitude of the other. Are moral disagreements about actions, e.g. the moral rightness or wrongness of a white or black lie, and states of affairs, e.g. racial segregation, disagreements in belief or in attitude, or are they unlike either? More generally what is the correct analysis of a moral judgement?

THE PROBLEM OF AESTHETIC DISAGREEMENT

In its general form this problem is similar to the preceding one.

It makes itself felt for example in the attitude of a lover of classical music, who holds that *de gustibus non est disputandum* and yet harbours – and wishes to explain – the suspicion that Bach's concertos are in some important sense aesthetically more valuable than the overtures to Offenbach's operettas, even though he may like the latter a great deal. Both this man and a person who rejects the suspicion as groundless will have to attempt an analysis of the general nature of aesthetic judgements, if they wish to justify their convictions.

THE PROBLEM OF A JUST SOCIETY

This problem has been posed again and again by philosophers. It is one of the main topics of Plato's *Republic* and is well expressed in the first sentence of the first book of Rousseau's *Social Contract*[1]: 'I mean to inquire if, in the civil order, there can be any sure and legitimate rule of administration, men being as they are and laws as they might be.' Since by a 'legitimate rule' Rousseau means a moral rule he seems to raise the question of applying morality to social life – a question of applied ethics, as it were. However, if morality is itself essentially a social phenomenon we would, by regarding politics as applied ethics, put the cart before the horse. This is indeed Rousseau's own view. It is shared by many Greek thinkers for whom politics and ethics were one branch of philosophical inquiry and by some modern thinkers who hold that by cutting itself off from social anthropology ethics condemns itself to intellectual barrenness.

THE PROBLEM OF GOD AND EVIL

In reflecting on the content of the main Western and of some Eastern religions one is soon faced with the following paradox: there exists an omnipotent, omniscient and wholly benevolent God *and* there exists much suffering and wickedness in the world. From a purely logical point of view the paradox could

[1] First published in 1762

be removed in a number of ways, e.g. (*a*) by denying the existence of God or by limiting his power, knowledge or benevolence, (*b*) by denying the 'reality' of suffering and wickedness, (*c*) by providing or hinting at a description of the universe from which the compatibility of the two apparently contradictory propositions would follow. In all ages philosophers of religion have tried to defend one or other of these solutions by arguments. In some cases the substance, form and subtlety of their arguments have influenced philosophical and non-philosophical thinking far beyond the scope of the problem towards which they were directed.

THE PROBLEM OF CONCEPTUAL OR LINGUISTIC IMPRISONMENT

In drawing attention to the problem of class-existence I pointed out that all thinking involves classification and that e.g. the class of all men corresponds to the property of being a man. As well as properties, thinking also employs relations connecting two or more individuals. The relation 'greater than', for example, connects two, the relation 'between' three individuals. By writing 'x is greater than y' for the first and 'x lies between y and z' for the second, one indicates not only the number of individuals which are connected by a relation but also the order in which they occur in it. The attributes – to use a common name for properties and relations – which a person employs in describing, interpreting and evaluating his surroundings, determine the world as apprehended by him. Is there another non-conceptual, perhaps mystical, way of apprehending the world as it is without the interposition of attributes; and, if so, how could one be sure that this non-conceptual apprehension was not illusory? If there is not, then the thinker's world is bounded by the attributes which he uses and the language which embodies his use. '*The limits of my language*', as Wittgenstein puts it, would then 'mean the limits of my world'.[1]

[1] *Tractatus Logico-Philosophicus* (London 1922), No. 5. 6

Not all the attributes which together form, as it were, a person's conceptual prison seem equally fundamental and clearly some reconstruction work is usually going on. Examples of familiar replacements of some attributes by others would be the reclassification of a genus or species of animals or plants or the modification of a person's concepts in the course of his mathematical, scientific or literary education or simply in the process of his intellectual growth and decline. But are there some attributes, e.g. the Aristotelian or Kantian categories, which are indispensable to all thinking; and if so, can their indispensability be demonstrated in any way? Or could one on the contrary argue that not even logic and arithmetic are immune from conceptual change? Questions of this kind have engaged the minds of philosophers from Aristotle to Wittgenstein and beyond.

THE PROBLEM OF FREEDOM
AND NATURAL DETERMINATION

Imagine a person who is both a professional judge and a professional psychologist, and who as a judge considers people to be, at least sometimes, responsible for their actions and who as a psychologist regards the actions of his human subjects as fully determined by events over which they have no control. If he judges and psychologizes on alternate days then he will, in Kant's words[1], 'today be convinced that the human will is free' whereas 'tomorrow when considering the unbreakable chain of natural events, he would consider freedom to be nothing but self-deception'. Since everybody, whatever his profession, frequently passes moral judgements on the actions of his fellow men and even his own actions, and frequently asserts that his own conduct and that of his fellows was necessary, everybody has to face this old and perplexing antinomy. One may, of course, hold that freedom, in which we all believe

[1] *Kritik der reinen Vernunft*, 2nd edition, Akademie Ausgabe, page 329. Of the English translations N. Kemp Smith's *Kant's Critique of Pure Reason* (London 1929) is the best

when acting, is merely an illusion; that science, which seems to exclude freedom, is merely a box of intellectual and mechanical tricks and must not be taken too seriously; that the antinomy rests on a verbal confusion; or that it can be resolved by subtler means. But each of these views needs to be supported by arguments which, as a glance at the history of the problem will show, are by no means easy and frequently rely on premisses drawn from a wide variety of philosophical and non-philosophical disciplines. Thus Kant's attempt at a solution of the antinomy of freedom and natural necessity presupposes his analysis of moral experience and of the structure of mathematics and the natural sciences of his day, in particular of Newtonian physics.

In looking back at the problems chosen as examples we soon realize that they are not isolated from each other. This impression is confirmed not only by a historical study of philosophy, but by independent reflection on any of them. Thus, whether we start by thinking about the problem of the anticipation of nature or of Zeno's dichotomy, we shall in either case have to inquire into the proper manner of applying mathematics to physical phenomena. Again, if we inquire more deeply into any of our sample problems we shall be confronted by some aspect of the problem of conceptual imprisonment.

Another feature of the problems which I have singled out for preliminary comments, is that we meet them in the course of trying to master difficulties which are apparently quite remote from philosophy. The problem of class-existence may arise in the course of devising a comprehensive classificatory scheme in one of the natural sciences. The problem of the relation between mental and physical phenomena may arise in the pursuit of psychology, physiology or medicine; the problem of moral disagreement, when people try to co-operate on a small or big venture; the problem of aesthetic disagreement, when an art critic in the course of meting out praise or blame suddenly becomes unsure of himself; the problem of a just society, when a politician feels that he may be in danger of losing his sense of proportion between expediency and morality, etc.

Many of the problems that a mathematician, scientist or other theorist meets in the pursuit of a particular line of inquiry fall within the scope of his or another special discipline. But some do not and, especially if they are rather general, they will usually be considered 'philosophical'.

However, philosophy is not just a refuge of problems without a home in other disciplines. It does not simply wait for their emergence, but often helps to bring it about. It is often through philosophical thought that problems have become the tractable subject-matter of a science, as is shown in the histories of most sciences, e.g. fairly recently in the history of experimental psychology and social anthropology. Again, philosophical inquiry may generate problems which are not philosophical, but belong to a non-philosophical discipline, whose results must be considered. For example, if in a philosophical inquiry into the problem of freedom and natural determination the question arises whether the impression of free choice can be created by stimulating certain nerves, the neurologist's answer is binding on the philosopher. Lastly, the pursuit of philosophy itself may give rise to philosophical problems. In choosing my examples I did not intend to prepare the ground for a definition of the notion of a philosophical problem, but to make a definition unnecessary. This should be particularly welcome if, as I am inclined to believe, an adequate definition is also impossible.

2. Philosophical Methods

In philosophy, as elsewhere, a problem is often fully understood only after its solution has been found by some particular method. But there are many problems for which we know neither a solution nor a method for obtaining one. Moreover, methods which are suitable for the solution of one family of problems may be quite unsuitable for the solution of others. A classification of problems, even if it claimed to be exhaustive, would, therefore, not necessarily correspond to a classification of methods. Often, e.g. at the time of Descartes, Locke or the rise of logical positivism in the first quarter of the twentieth century, when a characteristic method of philosophizing seemed particularly fruitful, its users were so carried away by their enthusiasm that they declared this method to be the only proper method of philosophy. They even tended to define philosophy as the use of this method.

There have always been philosophers who condemn any interest in philosophical method as philosophically harmful and self-defeating. They tend to tell the story of the centipede which, by inquiring into its method of walking, lost the ability to do so. But this attitude is also suspect. As a recommendation against a certain kind of philosophical reflection, namely philosophical reflection about philosophy, it seems to violate its very spirit. And should not the earnest squarer of a philoso-

phical circle, who refuses to examine the method which he is
in fact employing, be told for his own good why it is irremedi-
ably hopeless? A detailed examination of the scope and limits
of all hitherto employed philosophical methods is clearly out
of the question. A brief description and discussion of some of
them and of their interrelations will, however, supplement the
attempt, made in the last chapter, to convey a rough sketch of
philosophy by presenting some examples of philosophical
problems.

Every man is to some degree a scientist, devising and testing
predictions and explanations of natural phenomena, and an
artist, producing objects for aesthetic contemplation. Similarly
some types of commonsense thinking differ from philosophical
thinking only in degree. In the intellectual sphere, as in economic life, specialization leads to refined and more efficient ways
of fulfilling common tasks. The philosophical methods and
types of approach which I have singled out as examples are as
old as philosophy itself, although they have become clearer in
the course of time.

THE METHOD OF DOUBT AND THE METHOD
OF PHENOMENOLOGICAL DESCRIPTION

Until the middle of the nineteenth century Euclidean geometry
was generally regarded as a system of indubitable axioms and
of theorems, deduced from them by strict logical reasoning.
As such it seemed to thinkers of a rationalist turn of mind to
be the perfect model of all good theories and so of good philosophical theories. To construct a system of philosophy after the
fashion of geometry is the chief aim of Descartes' method to
which he ascribed, among other things, his own discovery of
'Cartesian' geometry. For Descartes there is 'only one way of
acquiring theoretical knowledge', namely to search for 'that
which we can intuitively apprehend as clear and self-evident'
or 'that which we can deduce with certainty' from clear and
self-evident truths. Theoretical thinking should thus start
with 'intuition' which Descartes defines as 'the undoubting

conception of an unclouded and attentive mind'[1]; and it should proceed by 'deduction', i.e. the recognition of 'necessary connection' between self-evident truths. He calls a connexion between two self-evident truths necessary 'when one is so implied in the concept of the other in a confused sort of way that we cannot conceive either distinctly, if we judge them to be disjoined from one another'.[2]

Descartes' conception both of intuition and of necessary connection is open to objection. In trying to reduce the doubtfulness of our assumptions as much as we can we only arrive at propositions which are indubitable to us; and not necessarily at propositions which are in principle indubitable. Propositions which seemed indubitable to many generations of thinkers have turned out to be false. The feelings of being certain and of being unable to doubt a proposition are by themselves no sufficient ground of their truth. This becomes clearer if we consider some propositions which Descartes himself singled out as indubitable and therefore as suitable foundations for his philosophical system. There are on the one hand propositions which many people nowadays would still regard as indubitable, even though they may disagree about the grounds of their truth. Examples are the propositions that $4 + 3 = 7$, that figure implies extension, that movement implies duration and, perhaps, the famous Cartesian *dictum* 'I think, therefore I am'. On the other hand there are propositions which Descartes conceived as indubitable, but which many people would nowadays regard as highly dubious. For example, Descartes tells us that he has 'learned to think of something more perfect than himself', which surely no reasonably modest person will find difficult. He then states that he 'clearly recognized' that he must have received this notion 'from some nature which in reality was more perfect'.[3] But the preceding statement, whose

---

[1] *Regulae ad directionem ingenii* (Rules for the Direction of the Mind), *ca.* 1628 Rule III

[2] See his comments to Rule XII

[3] *Discours de la Méthode* (1637), part IV

truth Descartes claims to have clearly recognized, is highly dubious.

Similar objections can be raised against Descartes' notion of deduction. The concept of a necessary connexion, on the recognition of which deduction depends, is again defined in terms of mental states, such as the feeling of a confused sort of conception and its opposite. Indeed, if we take the phrase 'implies' in our last example to stand for a necessary connexion, then it will not only discredit Descartes' account of 'intuition', but also of 'deduction'. It is, moreover, not clear how the two accounts can be reconciled with each other. On the one hand we are required to use only premisses which are by themselves clear and distinct. On the other hand a deduction involves the recognition of a necessary connexion between a premiss and a conclusion, neither of which is clear and distinct apart from the other. A deduction thus is either unnecessary, if the premiss is clear and distinct, i.e. already grasped as necessarily connected with its conclusion; or else its use is forbidden if the premiss is not clear and distinct because its connection with the conclusion is not yet grasped. For our present purpose, however, a discussion of the last difficulty, and of ways for overcoming it, is not important.

The most remarkable claims made by Descartes are, on the one hand, that there are absolutely certain propositions which do not belong to logic or mathematics and are not based on linguistic conventions; and, on the other hand, that his method enables one to discover these absolutely certain 'truths of fact'. Somewhat similar claims have in recent times been made by Brentano and Husserl, both of whom acknowledge the influence of Descartes on their thought. They reject the identification of the feeling of certainty with self-evidence, which they regard as a peculiarity of certain judgements which 'characterises them as correct'.[1] According to Brentano all judgements describing inner perceptions are self-evident and there are no other self-evident truths of fact. Examples are the judgements

[1] See e.g. Brentano's posthumous *Wahrheit und Evidenz* (Leipzig 1930), section IV

that I am perceiving, judging or desiring, provided that they are made when I am in fact perceiving, judging or desiring. The method of arriving at these self-evident truths is simply the closest possible description of my inner perceptions of my perceiving, judging, etc., without the admixture of alien elements arising from interpretation. It is for example self-evident that every act of perceiving has an object, but not that the object exists apart from, and independently of, this act.

In order to achieve complete purity of the reports on one's inner perceptions, Husserl devised what he calls the method of 'phenomenological reduction'. It demands the elimination of 'our natural attitude', i.e. the suspension – not the rejection – of all beliefs in anything apart from our inner perceptions, in particular any belief in external, extra-mental existences.[1] Husserl claims that his method, although very similar to Brentano's pure description of inner perceptions, reveals so great a wealth of absolutely certain truths of fact that the Cartesian ideal of philosophy as systematic, certain and comprehensive theoretical knowledge once again seems capable of realization.

Brentano's and Husserl's allegedly absolute separation of the description of phenomena from their interpretation is an extreme form of a very common and familiar procedure. When I meet a person in the street I may 'describe' his conduct towards me as a greeting and 'interpret' it as friendly. My interpretation is, of course, in greater danger of error than my description. If I wish to reduce the possibilities of error I can decide to 'describe' his conduct in terms of the words he utters and the gestures he makes and 'interpret' it as a greeting. And I may decide to set even stricter limits to my description, e.g. by using qualifying phrases like 'as it seems to me', 'apparently', etc. Whether or not I shall in the end ever arrive at an ultimate and incorrigible description is an undecided and, I believe, undecidable question. Yet the philosopher will often have to push the distinction between description and interpretation as far

[1] See e.g. *Ideen zur einer reinen Phänomenologie und phänomenologischen Philosophie* (Halle 1913), section II

as possible and to give as 'phenomenological' a description of the phenomena as he possibly can. Any attempt at dealing with the problem of freedom and natural necessity is likely to call for such a description of the phenomenon of choice; any attempt at dealing with the relation between mental and physical phenomena is bound to involve such a description of the former at least. Whether or not Husserl's absolute phenomenological reduction is possible, phenomenological description in our more modest and relativized sense has always been a useful philosophical method.

THE METHOD OF PHILOSOPHICAL ANALYSIS

Like the method of phenomenological description this differs only in degree from common and familiar modes of thought. Even a person who is not at all philosophically minded or given to theorizing will on occasions feel the need for analysing the concepts which he uses, the propositions which he habitually asserts and the system of beliefs which he holds. He will be compelled to do this when he finds that the intellectual tools which he employs with comparative ease in ordinary situations prove inadequate in extraordinary circumstances. He might, for example, have used his concepts of moral and political obligation to his own satisfaction in a well-regulated, peaceful society, but find himself hopelessly confused when he tries to apply them in an extraordinary situation such as a war or revolution. The files of the tribunals for conscientious objectors contain many analyses of the conceptual equipment of people in many different walks of life. Again, many theorists who have no particular interest in philosophy are at times forced to interrupt employing their concepts and examine them. The history of science and mathematics frequently describes situations in which the analysis of concepts became necessary in order to ensure their efficient use. Thus large parts of the differential and integral calculus were developed by using the rather obscure concept of 'infinitesimals', defined, e.g., as arbitrarily small or infinitely small quantities, or in even less intelligible ways. At some stage, however, the further development of the theory had for a time to yield to an analysis of its concepts and assumptions. Similarly, it was Einstein's analysis of the concept of simultaneity which prepared the way for the special and the general theories of relativity.

It seems pointless to propose a criterion by which the ordinary man's, the mathematician's or the scientist's analyses could be sharply distinguished from philosophical ones. On the whole the philosopher will be concerned with the analysis of very general concepts which, like 'cause', 'number', 'existence', pervade all thought or large regions of it, or which like the concept of an experiment are common to virtually all the sciences. True to his role as the guardian of perplexities which have no home in any special science the philosopher will also undertake the task of analysing such concepts as 'beauty' and 'moral obligation'. Last, though not least, he will assume the right to analyse concepts, like 'memory' or 'perception', if their analysis by non-philosophical specialists seems one-sided or otherwise unsatisfactory to him.

As might be expected, there are philosophers – the so-called 'analytical philosophers' – who regard philosophical analysis as the only proper method of philosophy. It is then somewhat surprising that comparatively few of them have turned their analytical acumen on the concept of analysis itself. In view of the vast claims made for analysis, especially the claim that there is no other legitimate method in philosophy, some analysis of 'analysis' seems desirable. It is, I think, particularly useful to distinguish between two types of analysis, the confusion of which has led to avoidable mistakes. I call them 'exhibition-analysis' and 'replacement-analysis'.

EXHIBITION-ANALYSIS

The aim of an exhibition-analysis is, as the word indicates, to exhibit the meanings of expressions used by a group of speakers and thinkers. It is, more precisely, the exhibition of accepted rules by reference to which the correct and incorrect uses of expressions are determined. This is by no means an easy matter. It is fairly obvious that a person may be perfectly capable of conforming to a complicated set of rules without being able to formulate them. Long before Aristotle people were able to distinguish between correct and incorrect syllogistic inferences. But it was an extremely difficult task to exhibit clearly the rules which govern the locutions 'follows from' or 'hence' in such inferences and the logical relations expressed by them. Thus, for example, in many passages of the Platonic dialogues Socrates tries but fails to bring these rules to light. The very familiarity of correct use can be an obstacle to formulating the rules which govern it, as many people have found when explaining the idioms of their native language to foreigners. The passage from regular conduct of any sort to the rules governing it is often precarious, especially as the difference between regular and rule-governed conduct is not sharp. Another difficulty is how to distinguish between merely grammatical rules and rules of thinking which are closely related to truth and falsehood.

It is, naturally, out of the question to exhibit all the rules which govern even an apparently simple concept such as the concept of being green, since every concept is part of a complex network of concepts from which it cannot be isolated. Which rules are to be exhibited depends on the context and on the purpose in hand. Sometimes the indication of a synonym or near synonym will be sufficient. Thus if I do not know the rules governing the expression 'sibling', but do know those governing 'brother', 'or' and 'sister', I have learnt a great deal about the use of 'sibling' – though perhaps not a great deal of philosophy – by being told that 'sibling' is a near-synonym for 'brother or sister'. (If, however, I wish to inquire whether any natural language contains full synonyms, I shall soon be in the deep waters of the philosophy of meaning.) Another more important short-cut is to exhibit logical implications between the analysed term and others. For example, in stating that 'x causes y' logically implies 'x is always followed by y', one asserts that the rules governing the former relation include the rules governing the

27

latter. Again, one may show that an expression which seems to belong to one class of expressions belongs in fact to another, e.g., that 'existence' is not an attribute of things, but of attributes. And there are other short-cuts.

It will be helpful to consider the last mentioned example a little more closely. When somebody asserts that lions have the properties of strength, gracefulness, and existence, whereas unicorns, although also strong and graceful, lack the property of existence, we might suspect that his way of thinking is very different from ours or that he is simply confused. Let us assume the latter and try to remove his confusion. We might, following Kant and the main stream of modern logic, point out that the assertion that lions exist is tantamount to the assertion that the concept 'lion' has instances, and that the assertion that unicorns do not exist is tantamount to the assertion that the concept 'unicorn' has no instances. In somewhat more technical language, the concept 'lion' is not empty, whereas the concept 'unicorn' is empty. 'Existence' and 'non-existence' are, if their analysis as non-emptiness and emptiness of concepts is accepted, unlike 'strength' and 'gracefulness', not attributes of things, e.g., of individual lions or unicorns, but of attributes, e.g., the attribute (or concept) of being a lion or of being a unicorn. If our interlocutor has to admit that his use of language and way of thinking are in fact no different from ours, then we have provided a successful exhibition-analysis of his use. If he makes no such admission, but explains and justifies his own use, a philosophical argument may ensue which cannot be settled by mere exhibition-analysis. It might be settled by one party reforming its use of language and way of thinking in the light of principles, criteria or purposes on which both parties agree.

To exhibit meanings, uses or rules is not to modify them. It may happen that at the conclusion of an exhibition-analysis we merely recognize that our implicitly accepted rules are incompatible with each other, ambiguous or in other ways defective. Our conscientious objector, for example, may regretfully have to admit that his thinking was confused. On the other hand the analysis may reveal that we suspected confusion where

there was none, that the confusion consisted merely in sus-
pecting that we were confused. The conscientious objector may
find that he simply disagrees with his judge or even that it is
the judge, and not he himself, who needs to put his intellectual
house in order. Some philosophers have elevated the negative
characteristic of exhibition-analysis, namely its being forbidden
to modify what it reveals, into a principle of all analysis and
even of all legitimate philosophy.

REPLACEMENT-ANALYSIS

In practice those analytical philosophers who in their methodological pronouncements condemn any attempt to tamper with
ordinary language as futile do not always confine themselves
to making rules, uses or meanings explicit, but sometimes introduce modifications. Others regard the reconstruction of
language, if it proves inadequate to certain general or specific
purposes, as the main business of analysis. The aim of such a
replacement-analysis is to replace a concept or set of concepts
which is in some ways defective, by another concept or set of
concepts, which is free from these defects, but nevertheless
preserves those features which are useful and desirable. For
example, the concept of class, which leads to Russell's antinomy, can by a successful replacement-analysis be so modified
that the new concept no longer leads to the antinomy, while
still sharing the useful features of the old one.

In explaining the strategy of replacement-analysis it will be
useful to introduce some technical terms. Let us, as is usual,
call A, the concept which is to be replaced, the 'analysandum',
and B, the concept which is to replace A, the 'analysans'.
Before we can engage in an analysis of A, we must be clear
which features of a concept we regard as defects and which
features we regard as sound. We must, in other words, be able
to formulate a criterion of defectiveness. Internal inconsistency
is likely to be accepted by everybody as a defect. Elsewhere one
man's meat may well be another man's poison. A religious
person will consider as defective any conceptual system

29

which – in the absence of all empirical evidence for or against God's existence – leaves no room for his religious faith. An atheist will find no fault with such a system. Again some people will consider any imprecise concept defective, while others might hold that in the case of some imprecise concepts there are good reasons for not making them artificially precise; that for example too precise a classification of the animal world would not do justice to the fact that some animals are hybrids and that some species imperceptibly merge into others.

Not every replacement of a defective by a sound concept will count as a replacement-analysis. It would obviously be absurd to say that in replacing the defective concept of class, which leads to Russell's antinomy, by the sound concept of an elephant, we analyse the former. The analysandum and the analysans must stand in a closer relation to each other. This replacement-relation may again, like the criteria of defectiveness, vary from one group of analytical philosophers to another. Thus one may require that a certain set of statements which contain the analysandum and are regarded as true, should be true if the analysans is substituted for the analysandum in these statements. For example, one might require that all accepted statements about 'normal' classes (which are not members of themselves) should be true if in them the defective class-concept is replaced by its analysans; or that all statements about our moral obligations to other persons which one accepted as true, before discovering an incompatibility between one's concepts of moral and political obligation, should remain, or become, true after one's defective concept of moral obligation has been replaced by a sound one. Sometimes, however, no more than a close resemblance between analysans and analysandum is required.

Exhibition-analysis and replacement-analysis are obviously very different procedures and it is worthwhile to emphasize some of the differences between them. First, if we ask what the rules are which govern a concept or term, as used by a person or a group of persons, the question admits only one correct answer. It consists in the clear formulation of the rules, what-

ever their alleged merits or defects. If a sign which has a sup-
posedly correct use should turn out to have none, then this too
will have to be stated as the result of the analysis. Thus every
successful exhibition-analysis has one, and only one, result.
We have, however, no right to assume that the results of replacement-analysis are similarly unique. Such an analysis may
have no solution, e.g., if we try to replace a self-contradictory
concept by a self-consistent one and require at the same time
that from the applicability of the analysans the applicability of
the analysandum should follow logically. Again, a successful
replacement-analysis may have more than one solution. If our
analysandum is the defective class-concept of our earlier
example and our replacement-relation requires that all statements about normal classes should remain true after substituting the analysans for the analysandum, then more than one
concept will serve as analysans. Different concepts have in fact
been proposed, all of which remove the defect of the analysandum and stand to it in the required replacement-relation.

Secondly, a successful exhibition-analysis answers an empirical question about actual linguistic behaviour and the rules
to which it conforms. It is like an anthropological inquiry which
proceeds from the observation of, say, the ritual behaviour of a
tribe to the formulation of its ritual code. A successful replacement-analysis, on the other hand, answers a logical question of
the following general form: given an analysandum A, a
criterion of defectiveness, say, D by which A is defective, and a
replacement-relation R – to find or construct an analysans X
such that (1) X is not defective by the criterion D and (2) A
stands to X in the replacement-relation. Whilst any replacement-analysis presupposes an exhibition-analysis providing a
clear formulation of the analysandum, an exhibition-analysis
proceeds independently of any replacement. Yet, as closer
study of actual exhibition-analyses would show, even the most
austere exhibition-analysts rarely avoid modifying the rules
which they purport merely to exhibit.

Thirdly, replacement-analysis almost unavoidably leads to
questions to which neither it nor exhibition-analysis can pro-

vide the answers: why *should* we adopt one replacement-relation rather than another, and why *should* we adopt one criterion of defectiveness rather than another? The reasons for the choice are often found in more or less clearly articulated convictions as to what constitutes an intellectually satisfactory apprehension of the world. The atheist, as has been said earlier, may be forced to choose other criteria than the theist, the mechanist other than the vitalist, the marxist other than the idealist, etc. The systematic formulation and defence of such convictions belong to metaphysics. Although philosophical analysis, both as exhibition and as reconstruction of rules, uses, or meanings, is by no means a recent invention, modern analysts have often employed it in a new spirit. They tend to contrast analysis with metaphysics and have sometimes even gone so far as to regard analysis as the only respectable way of philosophizing and to condemn all metaphysics as disreputable nonsense. However, replacement-analysis depends in theory and in practice on metaphysical presuppositions, and exhibition-analysis depends on them to a large extent, at least in practice. The analytical philosopher who condemns the metaphysician thus often implicitly condemns himself.

METHODS IN METAPHYSICS

Before one can discuss any method for the establishment of metaphysical propositions, something must be said about the highly controversial question concerning their nature. Consider two typical examples: (i) the thesis that man has an immortal soul and (ii) the principle of causality, namely that every event has a cause. It is almost universally agreed what metaphysical propositions are not. They are not logico-mathematical propositions and they are not empirical propositions in the sense in which the truth or falsehood of such propositions can be established by observation or experiment. The non-empirical character of the principle of causality is not perhaps immediately obvious. However, it does become obvious, once we consider that if we have so far been able to find the cause of every observed event it does not follow that every event has a cause; and that if we have not been able to find the cause of a particular event, it does not follow that it has none.

Can we go beyond this purely negative characterization of our examples and of metaphysical propositions in general? An extreme position towards them was adopted by the so-called logical positivists, who held that metaphysical propositions are nonsense and thus really not propositions at all, but pseudo-propositions. However, their argument in support of this position was surprisingly weak. It boiled down to defining 'meaningless' as 'non-logico-mathematical and non-empirical', to asserting quite rightly that metaphysical propositions are meaningless *in this sense* and lastly to identifying 'meaninglessness' in this very special and uncontroversial sense with 'nonsense' as ordinarily used. At the other extreme we find almost all the great philosophers of the past, who hold that metaphysical propositions can be true or false – even though they differ in other respects from logico-mathematical or empirical propositions.

Between these two extremes lies at least one other position. It conceives metaphysical propositions as rules of conduct or as regulative principles. Thus the thesis in the first example is interpreted as: (ia) conduct yourself *as if* man had an immortal soul, and the thesis in the second as: (iia) conduct yourself *as if* every event had a cause. It should be noted that the second regulative principle in particular is relevant not only to a person's practical but also to his theoretical interests. A theorist who accepts it will conform to it in trying to construct causal rather than non-causal theories. If a person believes that (i) or (ii) are true propositions it will be reasonable for him to accept the corresponding regulative principles. But he may accept the latter without believing the former. In a similar manner a biologist might find it useful to proceed *as if* there existed purposes in nature, even though he holds that nature is not purposive.

If metaphysical propositions are all nonsense there can be no general or specific methods for establishing their truth. There

33

can only be methods for 'debunking' metaphysics. It is certainly no more immune from nonsense than other fields of intellectual endeavour. One method for uncovering metaphysical nonsense is exhibition-analysis. It has often been successful, but its success in some cases does not imply its success in all. If metaphysical propositions are merely regulative principles, then they can only be supported by showing that the conduct which is regulated by them is more successful by its own standards than conduct regulated by other such principles. Thus to support the acceptance of the regulative principle of causality is to show, e.g., that the construction of scientific theories which conform to it is more successful from the scientific point of view than the construction of scientific theories which violate it. It is thus experience and the success of ordinary empirical methods on which the justification of merely regulative principles depends. There are then no independent specifically metaphysical methods by which merely regulative metaphysical principles are established, or by which their acceptance is enforced.

If metaphysical propositions are neither nonsensical nor merely regulative, but true or false, then there may exist special methods for establishing them. First of all, it might be held that although there are perhaps truths of different kinds, there is only one method for discovering them, e.g., the Cartesian method of doubt or Husserl's phenomenological method at its most ambitious. Second, it might be held that the proper method of metaphysics consists, as do the other philosophical methods I have so far examined, in pushing a familiar mode of thinking to the extreme. Thus it has often been said that the proper method of metaphysics is an extreme form of the argument by analogy: after a careful synopsis of all that can be known, we are to search for the common features of the universe as it is accessible to us, and then to extend them to the universe as a whole. Many metaphysicians have argued in this way. Thus Aristotle, having found purposes in human and social life, extended purposiveness to the universe as a whole. Hobbes, judging that the known physical universe had been shown to be mechanistic by Galileo and other physicists, extended this feature to social life and the universe as a whole. There are many other examples of this use of the method of analogy in metaphysics.

The method of analogy in metaphysics shares one weakness with all arguments by analogy. It lacks cogency. It is not necessary that the whole possesses the same features as a part of it. Sometimes it does and sometimes it does not. Outside metaphysics the method of analogy has often great heuristic value in that it suggests new ideas which can be tested by other methods. This is in particular so in the empirical sciences where suggestions by analogy are testable by experiment and observation – even though the tests may not be conclusive. But suggestions by metaphysical analogy are not open to any kind of test.

Indeed, the method of metaphysical analogy can be turned against itself. Every whole has features not possessed by its parts, e.g., the feature of consisting of all its parts. A human body contains all human organs, but no human organ contains all human organs. A human body lives in a sense in which none of its separate organs lives, etc. By analogy then, the universe as a whole is quite different from any of its parts. 'Therefore' our experience of the universe does at best only partial justice to its nature. 'Therefore' what we apprehend is not reality, but mere appearance. Just as the straightforward use of the method of analogy leads to what might be called a *pars-pro-toto* metaphysics, which extends features of the accessible universe to the whole of it, so the inverted use of this method leads to what might be called an appearance-versus-reality metaphysics which denies the features of the accessible universe to the universe as a whole. This style of metaphysics has found its representatives among ancient Indian, ancient Greek, and modern Western thinkers, e.g., F. H. Bradley whose work *Appearance and Reality* was published in 1893.

If metaphysical propositions are true or false we may look in yet another direction for an appropriate metaphysical method. It may be that metaphysical truths are of a peculiar

35

kind, and that the full recognition of their peculiar nature leads to the recognition of a particular method by which they are justifiable. Such, for example, are the doctrines of Kant and Hegel. Kant held that all true metaphysical propositions are what he called 'synthetic and *a priori*' and that the method for establishing them is what he called a 'transcendental deduction'. Hegel held that all true metaphysical propositions are what he called 'dialectical' and that the method for establishing them is what he called the 'dialectical method'. According to these philosophers the nature of metaphysical truth and of the proper metaphysical method are so intimately linked, that it would be useless to try to expound or examine them separately. I shall return to these topics (in Part 4), after the ground for a more searching discussion of the nature and function of metaphysics has been prepared.

Part 2

THE PHILOSOPHY OF LOGIC, MATHEMATICS AND EMPIRICAL THOUGHT

Introduction

I have chosen the general heading of this part of the book in preference to more traditional titles such as 'Logic and the Theory of Knowledge' or 'Logic and the Philosophy of Nature' in order to express my conviction that philosophy can, and should, take note of the existence and results of formal logic, mathematics and the natural sciences. Logic, as opposed to the philosophy of logic, has in the last hundred years become an independent subject and has been developed mainly in the hands of mathematicians by mathematical methods. The philosophy of mathematics cannot neglect a fairly recent branch of mathematics, called metamathematics, some of whose results are in direct conflict with ancient dogmas of philosophy. Lastly an analysis of empirical thinking cannot afford to pass over the use made in it of scientific theories.

About half of the chapter entitled 'The Philosophy of Logic' will be devoted to the bare elements of modern formal logic. The remaining half of the chapter will deal with the philosophy of logic. The next chapter, on the philosophy of mathematics, presupposes, apart from very elementary arithmetic and geometry, some metamathematical results. These will be explained, though not proved. Chapter 5, on the philosophy of science, presupposes no special scientific knowledge, but merely well-known general ideas. The last chapter of Part 2, on the philosophy of commonsense empirical thinking (and the remainder of the book), presupposes no more than what is learned at one's mother's knee and in the common pursuits and transactions of ordinary life.

If the relevance of modern logic to the modern philosophy of logic, mathematics and science can hardly be doubted, its relevance to other branches of philosophy might perhaps be called into question. Yet the philosophy of such seminal modern thinkers as Peirce, Frege, Russell and Wittgenstein has been no less profoundly affected by modern logic than had been the thought of Plato, Aristotle, Thomas Aquinas, Leibniz or Kant by the logical theories of their times. It thus seems implausible that the advent of modern logic should mark the end of the influence of logic on philosophical thinking. All this does not imply that a knowledge of modern logic is indispensable to the understanding of every philosophical problem – whether or not it belongs to the philosophy of logic, mathematics or science. Indeed as we move away from these fields of philosophical inquiry explicit references to specific principles of logic will rarely be needed.

The development of logic and mathematics is inseparable from the invention and use of symbolic, as opposed to natural, languages; and the philosophy of logic and mathematics presupposes some acquaintance with symbolism. To avoid symbols in discussing them would, therefore, be pedagogically unsound, if not downright dishonest. The symbolic expressions which occur in the next two chapters and – much less frequently – in the rest of the book are simple, even though they may be unfamiliar. It is helpful and advisable to translate them into words and to write them down, until they become as familiar as their verbal counterparts.

3. The Philosophy of Logic

Let us imagine a reflective student of theoretical physics who questions the validity of an argument which his teacher uses. The argument claims to deduce by means of mathematics a proposition of theoretical physics from other propositions of theoretical physics. The physics teacher may point out that the mathematical theory which he used in his deduction, say the differential and integral calculus, is presupposed by the physical theory; and he may advise the student to attend a course in the relevant mathematical theory. Let us assume that the student takes the advice and attends a course in the mathematical theory. There again he questions the validity of an argument in which his new teacher asserts that the axioms of the theory together with theorems already proved logically imply a further theorem. The mathematics teacher may point out that the logical theory, which he used in his deduction, is presupposed by the mathematical theory, which, as the student already knows, is in turn presupposed by the physical theory. He may even advise the student to take a course in logic or, more precisely, to take a course in that logical theory which underlies all the branches of mathematics employed, up to the present day, in theoretical physics and the other theoretical sciences using mathematics. This theory is the so-called (standard) elementary logic which includes the logic of truth-functions, quantification-theory, and the theory of equality. It is the subject of countless textbooks, from which a working knowledge of the theory can be gained.[1] Only a rough sketch of the theory will be needed here, before some philosophical questions about it, and logic generally, can be raised.

THE LOGIC OF TRUTH-FUNCTIONS

This theory is concerned only with propositions that are true or false and only in so far as they are true or false. No third or further 'truth-value', such as e.g. 'indeterminate' or 'neutral', is considered. The sense or meaning of a true or false proposition is irrelevant. Propositions are combined into compounds by means of so-called 'connectives' in such a manner that the truth-value – truth or falsehood, briefly T or F – of a compound depends only on the truth-values of its components. A compound proposition whose truth-value is a function of the truth-values of the components is called a truth-function. Some truth-functions are familiar from ordinary usage, others differ from it. In order to explain the notion of a truth-function it is convenient to start by explaining familiar uses of 'not', 'and' and the non-exclusive 'or', i.e. the 'and/or' of legal contracts. Let p, q, r, etc. be 'propositional variables' for which only T or F may be substituted (just as in school-algebra x, y, etc. are numerical variables for which only numbers may be substituted). The use of 'not', for which we write '$\neg$', is explained as follows: p is true if $\neg p$ is false, and p is false if $\neg p$ is true. The use of 'and', which we write as '$\wedge$' is explained as follows: $(p \wedge q)$ is true if both p and q are true, otherwise it is false. Writing '$\vee$' for the non-exclusive 'or', its use is explained as follows: $(p \vee q)$ is true if at least one of the members is true, otherwise false. These truth-functions are respectively called 'negation', 'conjunction', 'disjunction' (or 'alternation').

Next I define the truth-function called the 'conditional', which represents a common use of 'if . . . then' in mathematics. (*If p then q*) – or briefly $(p \rightarrow q)$ – is false if p is true and q is

[1] See e.g. W. V. Quine, *Methods of Logic* (London 1952)

false, otherwise it is true. The 'biconditional': $(p \rightarrow q) \wedge (q \rightarrow p)$ or more briefly $(p \leftrightarrow q)$ is true, if p and q are both true or both false. These definitions can be conveniently summarized by so-called truth-tables.

p	$\neg p$
T	F
F	T

p	q	$p \wedge q$	$p \vee q$	$p \rightarrow q$	$p \leftrightarrow q$
T	T	T	T	T	T
F	T	F	T	T	F
T	F	F	T	F	F
F	F	F	F	T	T

A truth-table contains on one side all the different possible truth-values for the components and on the other the corresponding truth-value for the compound. Thus a glance at the above tables shows that if p is false and q is true, $(p \wedge q)$ is false, $(p \vee q)$ is true, $(p \rightarrow q)$ is true and $(p \leftrightarrow q)$ is false.

Two truth-functions are equivalent, if their truth-value is the same whenever the truth-value of their components is the same. Thus the truth-functions $\neg\neg\neg\, p$ and $\neg p$ are equivalent, as can be seen from the following table:

p	$\neg p$	$\neg\neg\, p$	$\neg\neg\neg\, p$
T	F	T	F
F	T	F	T

The second column, characterizing $\neg p$, and the fourth column, characterizing $\neg\neg\neg\, p$, are the same. Again $(p \rightarrow q)$ and $(\neg p \vee q)$ are equivalent, as can be seen by constructing the table for the latter and comparing it with the table for the former function:

		(1)	(2)
p	q	$\neg p$	$\neg p \vee q$
T	T	F	T
F	T	T	T
T	F	F	F
F	F	T	T

The column marked (2) is indeed the same as the column of the values for $(p \rightarrow q)$. It can be shown that all possible truth-functions can be expressed by means of '$\neg$' and '$\vee$'. ($(p \wedge q)$, for example, is the same truth-function as $\neg (\neg p \vee \neg q)$). They can also be expressed by means of '$\neg$' and '$\wedge$' or by means of '$\neg$' and '$\rightarrow$'. It is even possible – though it is not worthwhile stopping to explain how – to express all truth-functions by means of one connective only.

From the point of view of logic and the philosophy of logic the most important truth-functions are those which are 'identically true' or 'valid'. A truth-function is valid if, and only if, it becomes true, whatever truth-values are substituted for its component propositional variables, provided that the same truth-value is substituted for the same variable wherever it occurs in the function. More concisely, a truth-function is valid if, and only if, all its substitution instances are true. An example is the so-called law of the excluded middle: $p \vee \neg p$. The truth-table for negation shows that only two substitution instances are possible, namely: $T \vee F$ and $F \vee T$; and the truth-table for disjunction shows that both of them are true. By means of the truth-tables we can in a purely mechanical manner decide for any truth-function whether it is valid or not. The task could be entrusted to a machine.

It is possible, and for many purposes useful, to 'axiomatize' the set of all valid truth-functions, i.e. to organize them in the form of an axiomatic or deductive system. The conception of such a system brings together ideas with which we are familiar on the one hand from learning the vocabulary and grammar of a foreign language, on the other from learning school algebra. An axiomatic system has the following features: (1) a list of primitive symbols, i.e. symbols which are neither composed of nor defined by, other symbols. (In school algebra 'x' and ' $+$ ' are primitive symbols, whilst '$x + y$' and '$x = x$' are not.) (2) A set of rules for constructing well-formed formulae. Well-formed formulae correspond to grammatically well-formed sentences. (In school algebra '$x + x = 2.x$' is well-formed and true, '$x + x = 3.x$' well-formed and false, '$x + = +$' ill-formed and thus neither true nor false.) (3) A set of axioms, i.e. of formulae which – unlike deduced formulae or theorems –

43

are accepted as true without proof (*e.g.* '$x + y = y + x$').
(4) A set of rules of inference, i.e. rules for deducing theorems
from axioms, from previously deduced theorems or from axioms
and previously deduced theorems. (E.g. from '$x + x = 2.x$'
we deduce '$2 + 2 = 2.2$' by the inference rule of substituting constants for variables.)

In setting out the following axiomatization of the set of all
valid truth-functions I merely wish to illustrate the general
idea of axiomatizations. Skill in their manipulation can come
only from using them in the solution of examples and problems.
Our axiomatic system consists of the following stipulations:
(1) *Vocabulary* or list of the separate symbols: they are the
propositional variables p, q, $r \ldots$, the connectives $\neg$, $\rightarrow$ and
brackets. Brackets are used to avoid ambiguities. Thus $(p \rightarrow q)$
$\rightarrow r$ differs from $p \rightarrow (q \rightarrow r)$. (2) *Rules for constructing well-
formed formulae*: (a) every propositional variable, by itself, is a
well-formed formula, (b) if an expression A is well-formed,
so is $\neg A$, (c) if A and B are well-formed, so is $A \rightarrow B$, (d)
only formulae formed in accordance with (a) – (c) are well-
formed. Thus $(p \rightarrow q) \rightarrow r$ is, but $p \rightarrow \rightarrow p$ is not well-formed.
The rules (a) – (d) are, as it were, rules of grammar. (3) *Axioms*:
(i) $p \rightarrow (q \rightarrow p)$ (ii) $(p \rightarrow (q \rightarrow r)) \rightarrow ((p \rightarrow q) \rightarrow (p \rightarrow r))$ (iii)
$(\neg p \rightarrow \neg q) \rightarrow (q \rightarrow p)$. They are, as can be seen by the
method of truth-tables, all valid truth-functions. (4) *Rules of
inference*: (α) Rule of detachment, also called *modus ponens*:
if A and $A \rightarrow B$ are axioms or theorems already deduced, then
B is a theorem. (β) *Rule of substitution*: if in an axiom or
theorem, say A, a propositional variable is replaced, wherever
it occurs in A, by the same well-formed formula the resulting
formula is also a theorem. It has been proved that a formula is
an axiom or theorem of the system if, and only if, it is valid.

As an example we deduce: $(p \rightarrow p) \rightarrow (p \rightarrow p)$ in our system.
The steps are numbered on the left, their justification is given
on the right.

(1) $(p \rightarrow (q \rightarrow r)) \rightarrow$
  $((p \rightarrow q) \rightarrow (p \rightarrow r))$ Axiom (ii)

(2) $(p \rightarrow (p \rightarrow p)) \rightarrow$
    $((p \rightarrow p) \rightarrow (p \rightarrow p))$ Substituting p for q and then p for r in (1)

(3) $p \rightarrow (q \rightarrow p)$ Axiom (i)

(4) $p \rightarrow (p \rightarrow p)$ Substituting p for q in (3)

(5) $(p \rightarrow p) \rightarrow (p \rightarrow p)$ From (4) and (2) by rule of detachment.

We may, or may not, have known that (5) is valid. The proof shows, however, that it can be deduced from the axioms by the rules of inference. As has been said already, the technique of deduction can only be learned by practice.

QUANTIFICATION

Let us consider a universe of discourse consisting of two individuals a (Arthur) and b (Bertha) and of two attributes $P(x)$ ('x is a philosopher') and xLy ('x loves y'). The attributes are neither true nor false. But they can be completed and made into true or false propositions in two ways, namely by substitution and by quantification. Substitution consists in substituting individual names for x and y which are called 'free individual variables' – because they are free for substitution by names of individuals. Examples of such completion are: $P(a)$, i.e. 'a is a philosopher'; 'aLb', i.e. 'a loves b'; 'bLb', i.e. 'b loves b' or 'b loves himself'. The last expression could also be derived from the attribute 'xLx', i.e. 'x loves x', which shows that xLy must be distinguished from xLx. The former contains two distinct free variables, the latter only one.

Quantification consists in 'binding' the free individual variables by the 'existential quantifier' $\exists x$, i.e. 'There exists an x, such that x . . .', or by the 'universal quantifier' $\forall x$, i.e. 'For every x, x . . . .' Examples are $\exists x \, P(x)$, i.e. 'There exists an x, such that x is a philosopher'; $\forall x \, P(x)$, i.e. 'For every x, x is a philosopher'; $\forall x \, \exists y \, (xLy)$, i.e. 'For every x, there exists a y such that x loves y' ('Everybody loves somebody'); $\exists x \forall y \, (xLy)$, i.e. 'There exists an x such that for every y, x loves y' ('Some-

45

body loves everybody'); $\exists y \, (yLy)$, i.e. 'There exists a y such that y loves y' ('Somebody loves himself'), etc.

It is not difficult to see that for our tiny universe of discourse all expressions containing quantifiers are no more than convenient abbreviations of truth-functions. For example: $\forall x P(x)$ is an abbreviation of: $P(a) \wedge P(b)$, since to state that for every x, x is a philosopher, is in our universe of discourse to assert that a is a philosopher and b is a philosopher. Again $\exists x P(x)$ is an abbreviation of: $P(a) \vee P(b)$, since to state that there exists an x such that x is a philosopher is to assert that a is a philosopher or b is a philosopher. Similarly $\forall x \exists y(xLy)$ is an abbreviation of: $((aLa) \vee (aLb)) \wedge ((bLa) \vee (bLb))$, since both expressions state that for every x in our universe there exists a y such that x loves y, i.e. that in it everybody loves somebody. Again $\exists x \forall y(xLy)$ is an abbreviation of: $((aLa) \wedge (aLb)) \vee ((bLa \wedge bLb))$, since both state that there exists an x in our universe such that for every y in it, x loves y, i.e. that in it somebody loves everybody. All these expressions are truth-functions whose truth-value depends only on the truth-value of their components.

Each quantifier is definable in terms of the other and of negation. Thus $\forall x P(x)$ is equivalent to $\neg \, \exists x \, \neg \, (P(x))$ in the sense that they abbreviate the same truth-function. Similarly, $\exists x P(x)$ is equivalent to $\neg \, \forall x \, \neg \, P(x)$. Thus $\forall x \exists y(xLy)$ can also be written as: $\neg \, \exists x \, \neg \, \neg \, \forall y \, \neg \, (xLy)$ or as $\neg \, \exists x \forall y \, \neg \, (xLy)$ as can be checked by writing the expressions as truth-functions. The rule is that $\forall x$ can be replaced by $\neg \, \exists x \, \neg$; and $\exists x$ by $\neg \, \forall x \, \neg$.

If we extend our universe of discourse by additional individuals and attributes matters become more complex, but not essentially different – provided that our universe remains finite. Once we allow it to be infinite, as we must, e.g. in arithmetic when we wish to talk of the totality of all integers, an entirely new assumption is introduced. This assumption of an infinite class of individuals must be shown not to lead to contradictions and requires further justification from the point of view of philosophy. Leaving this point aside it has been shown that allowing our individual variables to range over an infinity of individuals does not make quantification theory inconsistent. We may then regard $\forall x P(x)$ as a possibly infinite conjunction and $\exists x P(x)$ as a possibly infinite disjunction and decide not to bother about the philosophical implications of assuming such propositions to be possible.

We can extend the concept of a valid expression to quantificational formulae, defining a formula containing propositional variables, individual variables, truth-functional connectives and quantifiers as valid if all their substitution-instances are true – a substitution consisting in replacing the same individual variable by the same individual name and the same propositional variable by the same truth-value. An example is: $\forall x P(x) \vee \exists x \neg P(x)$. Here (if we assume that $P(x)$ is the specific attribute 'x is a philosopher') there are no free variables. We can rewrite this formula as: $\neg \exists x \neg P(x) \vee \exists x \neg P(x)$ or more clearly as $\neg (\exists x \neg P(x)) \vee (\exists x \neg P(x))$ which is of the form $\neg p \vee p$, and obviously valid. Another example is: $\forall x P(x) \rightarrow \exists x P(x)$ which is a possibly infinite truth-function: $(P(1) \wedge P(2) \wedge \ldots) \rightarrow (P(1) \vee P(2) \vee \ldots)$, where the numerals, like house-numbers, are used as the names of our individuals. Such a truth-function is valid for any finite number of individuals and it has been shown that in quantification-theory the assumption that it remains valid for an infinite number of individuals leads to no contradiction.

There is, however, no decision procedure which (like the method of truth-tables) would enable us mechanically to distinguish between valid and invalid quantificational formulae.[1] Our only hope of capturing all of them systematically is thus the construction of an axiomatic system of all valid quantificational expressions. There are many such systems. From among them I choose one which is an extension of the axiomatic system of truth functional logic described earlier. I shall not present it in detail, but merely try to give a general idea of its vocabulary, its well-formed formulae, its axioms and its rules

[1] A. Church, 'A Note on the *Entscheidungsproblem*' (and correction), *Journal of Symbolic Logic* I, (1936)

of inference. *Vocabulary*: We use $\rightarrow$, $\neg$, $\forall$ and brackets; propositional variables p, q, r; attributes such as $P(x)$, (xLy). ('$\exists$' is definable in terms of '$\forall$' since '$\exists x$' = '$\neg \, \forall x \, \neg$'). *Rules for constructing well-formed formulae*: they include all the rules for constructing well-formed truth-functional expressions to which further rules for the combination of individual variables, attributes and quantifiers are added. *Axioms*: they include the axioms (i) – (iii) of the truth-functional axiomatic system and in addition (iv) $(\forall x \, (p \rightarrow P(x))) \rightarrow (p \rightarrow \forall x P(x))$ and (v) $(\forall x(Px)) \rightarrow P(y)$. For any finite universe, say a universe of two individuals and one property, these axioms are abbreviations of valid truth-functions. The first becomes: $((p \rightarrow P(a)) \wedge (p \rightarrow P(b))) \rightarrow (p \rightarrow (P(a) \wedge P(b)))$, the second becomes: $((P(a) \wedge P(b)) \rightarrow P(a)) \vee ((P(a) \wedge P(b)) \rightarrow P(b))$. *Rules of inference*: they include (α) *Modus ponens*, (β) the rule of substitution of propositional variables, (γ) a rule of substitution of individual variables, (δ) a rule of substitution of attributes and (ϵ) the rule of generalization: if an expression $A(x)$, in which x is a free individual variable, is an axiom or theorem, then so is $\forall x A(x)$. It is not necessary for our purpose to explain the two new substitution rules or to mention the rule which allows us to change bound variables, e.g., $\forall x P(x)$ into $\forall y P(y)$.

THE THEORY OF EQUALITY

The ideas of truth-function and quantification, of valid truth-functional and quantificational formulae and of their axiomatization may be unfamiliar, but they are simple and one can familiarize oneself with them by applying them to a small, finite universe, such as the one we started with. In order to complete the edifice of standard elementary logic one further idea is needed, namely the familiar idea of the equality or identity of individuals. We formulate it by adding the symbol $=$ to our logical vocabulary, by stipulating that $x = x$, $y = y$, etc. are to count as *well-formed formulae*, and adding the *axioms*: (vi) $x = x$, (vii) $(x = y) \rightarrow (y = x)$, (viii) $(x = y) \rightarrow ((y = z) \rightarrow (x = z))$. In technical language the first of these shows that the relation of equality is reflexive, the second that it is symmetrical, the third that it is transitive. The third axiom can, perhaps more transparently, be written in terms of the connectives $\rightarrow$ and $\wedge$ as: $((x = y) \wedge (y = z)) \rightarrow (x = z)$.

We can extend the concept of a valid formula from the theory of truth-functions and quantification to the whole of elementary logic. It was moreover proved by Gödel in 1930 that all theorems of axiomatic elementary logic are valid formulae and all valid formulae are theorems of this theory. It will be convenient to indicate that a formula, say A, is valid by putting $\vert\!\!-$ in front of it, i.e. by writing $\vert\!\!- A$. Examples are: $\vert\!\!- p \vee \neg p, \vert\!\!- (\forall x P(x)) \rightarrow (\exists x(Px)), \vert\!\!- (x = x) \rightarrow (x = x)$. It will also be convenient to distinguish in a uniform manner between expressions containing free variables and their true substitution-instances. I shall indicate this by adding subscripts to the letters designating substitution-instances. For example if $\vert\!\!- A$ is a valid formula, then $\vert\!\!- A_0$ is a true substitution-instance of it. Such are $\vert\!\!- p_0 \vee \neg p_0, \forall x P_0(x) \rightarrow \exists x P_0(x), \vert\!\!- (x_0 = x_0) \rightarrow (x_0 = x_0)$. Often it will be clear from the context whether formulae containing variables or their substitution-instances are meant.

AN ANALYSIS OF 'LOGICAL NECESSITY' AND 'LOGICAL CONSEQUENCE'

Having given a rough sketch of standard elementary logic, I now turn to some philosophical problems to which it is relevant and to which it gives rise. As one might expect it is highly relevant to an analysis of the concept of logical necessity. Some propositions are true or false because the world is what it is, whereas the truth or falsehood of others is not so dependent. For example, the truth of the proposition that a certain person called 'Arthur' is a philosopher depends on the state of the world. It may be true or it may not. On the other hand, the truth of the propositions 'Arthur is a philosopher or Arthur is not a philosopher' and 'If Arthur loves somebody, then somebody loves somebody' does not depend on the world. Leibniz, in his *Monadology*, calls propositions of the first kind 'truths of fact' and those of the second kind 'truths of reason', 'truths of logic' or 'logically necessary'.[1] The former are, he says, true in the actual world only; the latter are true in all possible worlds.

It is easily seen that our examples of truths of reason are substitution-instances of valid expressions of elementary logic, namely of $|— p \lor \neg p$ and of $|— \forall x \exists y(xLy) \rightarrow \exists x \exists y(xLy)$ respectively. This suggests the following analysis of logically necessary propositions, which is true to the spirit of Leibniz. A proposition is logically necessary if, and only if, it is a substitution-instance of a valid expression of standard elementary logic. In other words, a proposition A_0 is logically necessary if, and only if, it is a substitution-instance of some expression A such that $|— A$; if so we can write $|—A_0$. We can define the notions of logical impossibility and contingence in terms of the notion of logical necessity. A proposition is logically impossible if, and only if, its negation is logically necessary; it is contingent if, and only if, neither it nor its negation is logically necessary. In other words A_0 is logically impossible if, and only if, $|— \neg A_0$; and it is contingent if, and only if, neither $|— A_0$ nor $|— \neg A_0$.

The following analysis of the concept of logical consequence is closely related to the analysis of logically necessary propositions as substitution-instances of valid expressions of standard elementary logic. Instead of saying that a proposition, say B_0, is a logical consequence of A_0, we can also say that B_0 is deducible from A_0, that A_0 logically necessitates B_0, that A_0 entails B_0, etc. I shall abbreviate these locutions by: $A_0/— B_0$. Now to state that $A_0 |— B_0$ is to state *at least* that if A_0 is true then B_0 is also true – and true not merely as a matter of fact, but as a matter of logical necessity. It is as a matter of fact true that if I drink sherry, then I get a headache. But it is logically true that if I drink sherry, I drink alcohol. This suggests the following analysis of logical implication: $A_0 |— B_0$, i.e. A_0 logically implies B_0 if, and only if, $|— (A_0 \rightarrow B_0)$, i.e. if $A_0 \rightarrow B_0$ is a

[1] *La Monadologie* (1714), sections 31 ff

substitution-instance of a valid conditional $(A \rightarrow B)$ in standard elementary logic. An example is: 'Arthur is a philosopher and Arthur loves Bertha' /— 'There exists a philosopher who loves somebody', since the corresponding conditional is a substitution-instance, e.g. of /— $(P(x) \wedge (xLy)) \rightarrow (\exists x \exists y (P(x) \wedge xLy))$, where $P(x)$ may be any one-variable, or one-place, and (xLy) any two-variable, or two-place, attribute. This expression can be shown to be a theorem and can easily be verified for a small universe.

In order to be able to use the valid conditional $A \rightarrow B$ for the deduction of a non-logical, or 'substantive', conclusion B_0 from a substantive premiss A_0, we must assume A_0. We must, for example, assume that Arthur is a philosopher and loves Bertha, in order to be able to deduce that there exists a philosopher who loves somebody. In general, in order to use logical implication as defined in terms of elementary logic for the deduction of substantive conclusions from substantive premisses, we must extend elementary logic by 'substantive axioms' – making suitable adjustments in its vocabulary and rules for constructing well-formed formulae. If the substantive axioms of a theory – zoology, geometry, physics, etc. – are added in this manner to standard elementary logic, we say that standard elementary logic 'underlies' the theory; or that the theory is 'embedded' in standard elementary logic. With one exception, which will be discussed in the next chapter, all theories of pure mathematics are embedded in standard elementary logic and the same holds *a fortiori* for all scientific theories in which deductive connexions are mathematically established.

THE SO-CALLED PARADOXES
OF STANDARD LOGICAL IMPLICATION

A number of objections have been raised against the foregoing analysis of logical implication. Thus it is often pointed out that it leads to paradoxical statements which are not in accord with ordinary language. Let us consider some simple, but typical, examples. In these 'p_0' will stand for 'Arthur is a philosopher' and 'q_0' for 'The English climate is temperate'. By means of the truth-tables it is easily seen that the following truth-functional conditionals are valid: $p \rightarrow (p \lor q)$; $(p \land q) \rightarrow p$; $(p \land \neg p) \rightarrow q$; $q \rightarrow (p \lor \neg p)$. It follows that their substitution-instances are all logical implications so that we have: (1) $p_0 \mid\!\!- (p_0 \lor q_0)$; (2) $(p_0 \land q_0) \mid\!\!- p_0$; (3) $(p_0 \land \neg p_0) \mid\!\!- q_0$; (4) $q_0 \mid\!\!- (p_0 \lor \neg p_0)$. The first says: 'Arthur is a philosopher' logically implies 'Arthur is a philosopher or the English climate is temperate' and the other three are equally out of tune with ordinary usage.

The reasons are not far to seek. Normally we try to avoid using logical implications containing irrelevant components, i.e. components which can be dropped without impairing the correctness of the logical implications. We have, therefore, ordinarily no occasion to use implications which, like (1) and (2), contain an obviously irrelevant component, namely q_0. Again we usually try to avoid logical implications with logically impossible antecedents or logically necessary consequents. We have ordinarily no occasion to use logical implications which, like (3), contain an obviously impossible antecedent or, like (4), an obviously necessary consequent. Should one, therefore, require that logical implications, to deserve the name, should not contain obviously irrelevant components, obviously impossible antecedents or obviously necessary consequents? In my view, certainly not. For to introduce the concept of obviousness into logic is to confuse logical with psychological considerations. What is obvious to one person may well be obscure to another. Thus, it is obvious to all logicians that the antecedent of: $\neg (p_0 \lor \neg p_0) \mid\!\!- q_0$ is impossible; but it may not be immediately obvious to a beginner. It would surely be absurd if the concept of logical implication were affected by different people's ability to grasp particular instances of it.[1]

---

[1] Although I used these points (*Conceptual Thinking*, Cambridge 1955, New York 1959, chapters VIII and XII) as objections against C. I. Lewis's account of logical implication, I now think that he must have been aware of them

STANDARD ELEMENTARY AND MODAL LOGIC

Another objection to standard logical implication is that it cannot express various logical relations between so-called 'modal propositions' containing modal terms such as 'It is (logically) possible that', 'It is (logically) impossible that', 'It is (logically) necessary that', etc. As we have seen, these notions can be defined in terms of valid expressions of standard elementary logic. We can define them also in terms of logical implication. Thus writing '*Imp p*' for 'It is impossible that *p*' we may define '*Imp p*' by '*p* /— ⊐ *p*'; '*Mp*' ('It is possible that *p*') by ' ⊐ *Imp p*' and '*Np*' ('It is necessary that *p*') by '⊐ *M* ⊐ *p*'. By reducing these expressions to their definitions in terms of standard logical implication, we can prove such intuitively obvious relations between them as: if ⊐ *M* ⊐ (*p* ∧ *q*) then (⊐ *M* ⊐ *p* ∧ ⊐ *M* ⊐ *q*) and: if *M*(*p* ∨ *q*) then *M*(*p*) ∨ *M*(*q*). But difficulties soon arise when the modal terms are iterated. Shall we say that *MM*(*p*) (it is possible that it is possible that *p*) is equivalent to *M*(*p*)? What shall we say about: *MNNNM Imp Imp M*(*p*) and about other combinations of these modal terms? Clearly some rules for reducing them to a finite number of permissible combinations are needed. But elementary logic itself provides no criteria of preference.

There exists a fairly large number of systems of modal logic. Some are extensions of elementary logic by adding axioms governing the use of modal terms to it. Examples are the systems of 'strict implication' constructed by C. I. Lewis.[1] Others are independent systems which use an implication differing from standard logical implication. In these latter systems not all standard logical implications are correct. Their aim is to keep more closely to some ordinary uses of 'logically follows from'. An example is the system of 'rigorous implication' constructed by Ackermann.[2] However, these systems are on the whole not meant to analyse or to discredit mathematical reason-

[1] C. I. Lewis and C. H. Langford, *Symbolic Logic* (New York 1932)

[2] Hilbert and Ackermann, *Grundzüge der theoretischen Logik*, 4th edition, (Berlin 1959), Chapter I, section 11

ing or reasoning by means of mathematics, but to analyse other types of reasoning and to serve other purposes. Some of them are, it seems, still waiting for a useful application.

STANDARD AND INTUITIONIST LOGIC

Let us consider the even numbers greater than 2, i.e. 4, 6, 8, 10, etc. and let us say that an individual number belonging to this class possesses Goldbach's property, briefly $G(x)$ – where x is an individual variable ranging over the even numbers greater than 2 – if, and only if, it can in at least one way be represented as the sum of two prime numbers. Thus we have $G(4)$ because $4 = 2 + 2$, $G(6)$ because $6 = 3 + 3$, $G(100)$ since $100 = 47 + 53$. We do not know whether every even number greater than 2 has Goldbach's property and we do not know any such number which does not possess Goldbach's property. Yet according to classical elementary logic $\forall x\, G\,(x) \vee \exists x \neg G\,(x)$ is logically necessary, since it is a substitution-instance of a valid expression. For as we have seen, $\forall x\, G\,(x) \vee \exists x \neg G\,(x)$ means the same as $\forall x\, G\,(x) \vee \neg \forall x\, G\,(x)$, which is a special case of $p \vee \neg p$. In classical logic one regards $\forall x\, G\,(x) \vee \neg \forall x\, G\,(x)$ as an abbreviation of $(G(4) \wedge G(6) \wedge G(8) \wedge \ldots) \vee (\neg G(4) \vee \neg G(6) \vee \neg G(8) \vee \ldots)$, where the dots express the assumption that the conjunction and the disjunction are in some sense completely given, because the totality 4, 6, 8, 10 ... is also in some sense completely given.

For reasons to be discussed in the next chapter the intuitionists admit a statement to the effect that there exists a number possessing a certain property, e.g. the property G, only if such a number has actually been constructed. Since this in the present case has not been done, $\forall x\, G\,(x) \vee \exists x \neg G\,(x)$ is from the intuitionist point of view not admissible. But this means that '$p \vee \neg p$' – the law of the excluded middle – which is classically valid, is invalid by intuitionist standards. The intuitionists' interpretation of mathematical existence-assertions and their consequent rejection of the law of excluded middle and other principles amounts to a rejection of classical elementary logic for mathematical reasoning. The intuitionist logic which is proposed in place of classical logic will be discussed in the context of the philosophy of mathematics.

STANDARD ELEMENTARY LOGIC AND INEXACTNESS

Standard elementary logic is strictly two-valued. It assumes that every proposition is either true or false and that given any object and any property, the property either applies to the object or does not apply to it. It recognizes no border-line or neutral cases and consequently no neutral propositions. Yet most empirical attributes, especially perceptual characteristics, such as colour-properties, and observable characteristics occurring in the description of experiments and observations, such as pointer-readings, are not exact but inexact. They admit of neutral cases. This makes it desirable for many purposes to distinguish clearly between exact and inexact attributes and to exhibit the rules governing the use of the latter. Such a distinction and analysis is, I believe, particularly needed in the philosophy of science, where the relation between the exact concepts of a theory embedded in standard elementary logic and inexact observational concepts must be understood.

It is possible to generalize the elementary theory of propositions and of quantification by taking inexact attributes and propositions into account. Such a theory will distinguish not only the truth-values T and F but also a third value 'neutral', which, under certain circumstances, can be turned into either T or F. The discussion of this possibility is best postponed to the chapter on the philosophy of science.

THE PROBLEM OF ALTERNATIVE LOGICS

Systems of modal logic whose concept of logical implication diverges from the standard concept, intuitionist logic, and the logic which accommodates not only exact, but also inexact, propositions and attributes are genuine competitors of standard elementary logic. This is perhaps most obviously so in the case of intuitionist logic with its rejection of the law of excluded middle and consequently of other principles of standard elementary logic. There are other competitors, e.g., some many-valued logics and systems which, as it were, are even more intuitionist than the standard intuitionist logic which underlies almost all intuitionist mathematics. This apparent multiplicity of logics raises the philosophical problem whether, and in what sense, any one of these systems is indispensable to thinking.

Let us examine some arguments to the effect that, e.g., standard elementary logic is indispensable to all thinking. First, the point is often made that a person may believe that he employs certain principles in his thinking which he does not in fact employ, or that he does not employ principles which in fact he does employ. A careful analysis – of the kind I have called 'exhibition-analysis' – will, it is argued, show that everybody does in fact reason by the principles of standard elementary logic. Even if a person says that he rejects the general validity of the principle of excluded middle, he nevertheless uses it surreptitiously. The point at issue is one of fact. But it is a fact that the intuitionist mathematicians reject mathematical existence-assertions which are not backed up by an actual example of the entity which is asserted to exist. It is thus a fact that they do not use the unrestricted principle of excluded middle.

Second, assume that a thinker has correctly come to the conclusion that he is using standard elementary logic in his thinking and that it is inconceivable to him how he or anybody else could use a different set of principles. So far, so good. But if he then argues that since thinking without the use of standard elementary logic, in particular without the principle of excluded middle, is inconceivable to him, it is, and will remain, inconceivable and impossible to everybody, then he is clearly committing a fallacy. It does not follow (even in his logic) that what is inconceivable to one person is inconceivable and impossible to everybody.

Lastly, a person may 'argue' that the very nature of thinking involves the employment of standard elementary logic, in particular the unrestricted principle of excluded middle. But this argument boils down to an arbitrary definition of 'thinking', which would commit one to the statement that, e.g., the intuitionists do not think. A person who decides to reserve the term 'horse' only for white horses will not thereby remove black and brown horses from the world.

Even if the multiplicity of logical systems is admitted one might still be tempted to argue that there is a hard core common to them all. More specifically one might hold that it is impossible to think without accepting the principle of non-contradiction, i.e. that no proposition is both true and false. Now, it must be admitted that each of the systems which have been mentioned, and every other now in use, contains a principle of non-contradiction. But the principles differ in meaning. Thus the principle of non-contradiction of standard elementary logic (in this logic) logically implies, and is logically implied by, the principle of excluded middle. We have for an arbitrary p_0: $\neg (p_0 \wedge \neg p_0) \, / \!\!-\!\!- (p_0 \vee \neg p_0)$ and also: $(p_0 \vee \neg p_0) \, / \!\!-\!\!- \neg (p_0 \wedge \neg p_0)$. The first of these logical implications does not hold in intuitionist logic, in which, as we have seen, the principle of excluded middle is not valid (compare p. 54 above and pp. 64 ff below).

From this discussion one important moral can be drawn. Since the concepts of logical implication and logical consequence, etc. vary with the logic underlying the reasoning in which they are used, the locution 'A logically implies B' is strictly speaking incomplete or elliptical. It requires, where it is not clear from the context, supplementation by referring to the logic in terms of which 'logically implies' is understood. Thus if any doubt could arise as to whether we refer, e.g., to the logical implication of standard logic, say L, or of intuitionist logic say I, it will be desirable to make the reference explicit. This might conveniently be done by writing '$A \, /_{\overline{L}} \, B$' in the first, and '$A \, /_{\overline{I}} \, B$' in the second case. Many philosophers use the term 'entails' for 'logical implication' without referring to its underlying logic. They do this on the assumption that ordinary language leaves no doubt about the principles governing its use. In many cases no harm comes from this practice. But when an argument turns precisely on the use of 'entails' it is advisable to be more specific. In such cases the assertion that *A* entails *B*, without mentioning the principles governing the use of 'entails', reminds one of advertisements which 'assert' that a certain brand of detergent washes whiter, or that a certain brand of tobacco gives more satisfaction.

By emphasizing the relevance of modern symbolic logic to problems which are clearly philosophical the preceding remarks may have helped to counteract the aversion from formal reasoning and from the use of symbols which is sometimes felt by those whose education was mainly literary. This attitude is the mirror image of the equally unreasonable distaste which many scientifically trained people feel for metaphysical, moral or religious thinking, in so far as it is not, and cannot be, formalized. Philosophers should not, I believe, take sides in any spurious conflict between the humanities and the sciences. To do so is to betray their traditional function of exhibiting the interrelation between all aspects of human thought. The next two chapters are devoted to problems which still require the use of formal methods. But I shall no more apologize for discussing these problems than I shall for dealing later with so non-logical a subject as mystical experience.

4. The Philosophy of Mathematics

Mathematical truth and mathematical reasoning are, leaving logic aside, generally considered to be more securely founded than truth and reasoning in other fields. The apparent security of mathematics and the desire to achieve a similar security in other disciplines is one of the main reasons why the analysis of mathematical thinking, and thereby the nature of mathematical truth and mathematical reasoning, is one of the oldest philosophical tasks. In the present chapter I intend to explain and to examine some philosophical theories about the nature of 'pure' mathematics, and to confront their tenets with recent mathematical or, more precisely, 'metamathematical' discoveries. The nature of 'applied' mathematics will be discussed in the chapter on the philosophy of science.

LOGICISM

A clear formulation of the logicist doctrine is found in the writings of Leibniz. Its central idea is as attractive as it is simple: mathematics is logic. In order to demonstrate its truth we would have to show: (i) that all mathematical propositions can be expressed wholly in logical terminology; (ii) that all true mathematical propositions are valid expressions of logic. The first part of the programme implies that the language of logic is rich enough for all mathematical expressions to be defined in terms of it. The second part of the programme would, for example, be fulfilled by proving that every true mathematical proposition is by purely logical reasoning deducible from the axioms of an axiomatized theory of logic. I shall presently argue that the second part of the programme, and thus the programme as a whole, cannot be fulfilled. But the attempts by Frege, and later by Russell and Whitehead and their followers, to carry it out have led to many important discoveries and insights.

The scope and limits of logicism can be illustrated by explaining and examining Frege's analysis of the concept of number. When we say that Arthur and Bertha are two philosophers we ascribe the attribute of being a philosopher, but not the attribute of being two, to each of them individually. So much will be generally admitted. The first step in Frege's analysis of the concept of number is the thesis that a number is an attribute of a class, e.g., that the class consisting of Arthur and Bertha as members – briefly: {Arthur, Bertha} – has the attribute of being two. The second step is the definition of the concept of 'equinumerous classes': two classes α and β are equinumerous if, and only if, there can be brought about a one-to-one correspondence between them. That is to say we can match each member of class α with a unique member of class β in such a way that each member of β is associated with one and only one member of α. For example the class {Arthur, Bertha} is equinumerous with the class {Bertha, Cyril} or the class defined by the property of being a parent of Queen Victoria; but not with the class {Arthur}, the class {Arthur, Bertha, Cyril} or the class defined by the property of being a descendant of Queen Victoria. We may be able to show that two classes are equinumerous without being able to determine their number. We may know that all football teams have the same number without being able to determine what that number is.

In order to do this a third step is needed, namely the purely logical construction of a sequence by reference to which the number of any class can be determined as being equinumerous with a member of the sequence. This can be done in a number of ways of which the following, due to von Neumann,[1] is particularly simple. One begins by defining the so-called 'null-class', briefly the class Λ, as the class of all individuals x, such that $\neg(x = x)$. Since all individuals are self-identical, Λ is empty or memberless. Next we define the successor of Λ as the class which has only Λ as its member, i.e. the class $\{\Lambda\}$. (This class has a member, namely Λ, whereas Λ itself has no member.) Next we form the class which has the previously formed classes as members, i.e. the class: $\{\Lambda, \{\Lambda\}\}$; next the class: $\{\Lambda, \{\Lambda\}, \{\Lambda, \{\Lambda\}\}\}$ and so on. The operation by which we form the successor of Λ and successively the successor of every already formed class is called the 'successor operation'. Let us write the sequence consisting of Λ and its successors as: $\Lambda, \{, \{\{, \{\{\{, \{\{\{\{, \ldots$ by collecting the left brackets used in each expression when written out fully. We then can define the sequence of attributes of classes 0, 1, 2, 3, ..., i.e. the non-negative integers, as follows: a class has 0, 1, 2, 3, ... members if, and only if, it is respectively equinumerous with $\Lambda, \{, \{\{, \{\{\{, \ldots$. We might call this 'von Neumann's sequence'.

Having defined the sequence of natural numbers as attributes of classes in terms of equinumerousness with von Neumann's sequence we could go on to define the arithmetical concepts of non-negative integers, negative integers, rational numbers (fractions) and irrational numbers (that is numbers such as π or $\sqrt{2}$ which cannot be expressed as fractions) and the familiar operations with them. The process is extremely illuminating since it exhibits the structure of the number system. However, what interests us here is whether by proceeding in this manner one really fulfils the logicist programme by avoiding any resort to non-logical concepts and non-logical assumptions. I shall divide this question into two parts, namely: (a) can the reduction of mathematics to standard elementary logic be achieved? and (b) would this reduction, if

[1] 'Eine Axiomatisierung der Mengenlehre', *Journal für reine und angewandte Mathematik*, vol. 27 (1928)

possible, demonstrate that mathematics is logic? The answer to both parts of the question is negative.

Standard elementary logic contains rules for the quantification of individuals, but no rules for the quantification of attributes. It does not allow for the construction of well-formed expressions containing the locution 'For all attributes P, P has the attribute . . .' or 'There exists an attribute P such that P has the attribute . . .'. Consequently it also does not contain any axioms in which attributes, as opposed to individuals, are quantified. Frege held that the 'extension' of any attribute, i.e. the class of entities to which it is applicable, can without further ado be treated as a new individual. This means that e.g. the attribute of being a man not only defines the class or plurality of all men, but also an individual, namely the individual totality of all men. If every plurality defined by an attribute were also an individual, then standard elementary logic could be applied to all classes *qua* individuals of this sort. We could then go on by treating not only a class of individuals but also a class of classes, *qua* individuals, as a new individual, a class of classes of classes, as a further individual, and so on *ad libitum*. But, as e.g. Russell's antinomy[1] shows, we cannot treat every plurality determined by an attribute as an individual totality, since to do so leads to contradictions.

In order to avoid Russell's and other antinomies, the standard elementary logic must be supplemented by additional axioms. There is no need here to discuss the various possibilities. Instead I shall make some rather dogmatic-sounding assertions, which will be borne out by a study of the relevant literature.[2] There are a number of possible extensions of standard elementary logic, none of which is philosophically preferable to all the others. In particular, none of them can be regarded as being more genuinely a part of 'logic' than any other. Up to a point the notions of, and the operations with, numbers (natural, positive and negative, rational) can be ex-

[1] See chapter I
[2] See e.g. W. V. Quine, *Set Theory and its Logic* (Harvard University Press 1963)

pressed within the framework of standard elementary logic. But when we come to introduce the irrational numbers, e.g. $\sqrt{2}$ or π, in any mathematical theory embedded in this logic, additional axioms must come into play.

Among the axioms which Russell and other logicists have added to standard elementary logic the following two are especially noteworthy: (1) there exists a class N, which contains 0 and which, if it contains any natural number n, also contains its successor; (2) if a class C exists, then there also exists the class $Sub(C)$ which has all the subclasses of C as its members. (The null-class Λ and the class C itself count as subclasses of C, so that if e.g. $C = \{a, \ b\}$ then $Sub(C) = \{\Lambda, \{a\}, \{b\}, \{a, b\}\}$). Axiom (1) guarantees the existence of the class $\{0, 1, 2, 3 \ldots\}$, i.e. of the infinite class of all natural numbers as an infinite, individual totality. Axiom (2) in conjunction with axiom (1) guarantees the existence in the same manner of the infinite class $Sub(N)$ which has all the subclasses of $N = \{0, 1, 2, 3 \ldots\}$ as its members. In a logicist system of the Russellian kind it can, moreover, be proved that N is a 'less numerous' infinite class than $Sub(N)$ in the sense that N is equinumerous with a subclass of $Sub(N)$ whilst $Sub(N)$ is not equinumerous with any subclass of N. Since the principles (1) and (2) are neither axioms nor theorems of standard elementary logic a mathematical theory which employs these principles is not reducible to standard elementary logic.

We now consider our second question. Logicism, in asserting the reducibility of mathematics to logic, should be able to provide a clear criterion for distinguishing logical from non-logical principles – a criterion based on a clear conception and definition of logic. Since, for example, their definition of irrational numbers presupposes the existence of infinite totalities such as the classes N and $Sub(N)$, the logicists would not only have to show that the assumption is true, but also explain in what sense of the term it is a principle of logic. Neither of these tasks seems capable of fulfilment. The assumption is as controversial now as it was at the time of Plato or Aristotle. If it were true, it would be a metaphysical truth about the actual world. Few logicists, it seems, would be prepared to make logic, which following Leibniz they regard 'as true in all possible worlds', dependent on a metaphysical assumption about the actual world. In any case, not even the assumption of infinite totalities would obviate the need for supplementing standard elementary logic by principles which are essentially no more than technical expedients for avoiding contradictions.

INTUITIONISM

According to the intuitionist philosophy of mathematics, whose founder is L. E. J. Brouwer, any attempt to reduce mathematics to logic is based on a fundamental misconception. Mathematics for him is not true in all possible worlds, but has a specific subject-matter, namely mathematical constructions performed in the mind or intuition of the mathematician. The construction of mathematical entities (e.g. the step-by-step construction of a natural number by starting with 1 and iterating the operation of forming the successor of an already constructed number) is contrasted on the one hand with the postulation of mathematical entities (e.g. the postulation of a class $Sub(C)$ for every class C), on the other with arguments to the effect that mathematical entities of a certain unexemplified kind exist (e.g. a proof of the existence of irrational numbers which – unlike the proof that $\sqrt{2}$ is irrational – contains no exemplification of such a number). We have seen that the logicist needs for the development of mathematics, among other things, the non-logical or 'synthetic' assumption that actual infinities of objects exist. The intuitionists not only insist that the assumption is synthetic, but regard it as false or even meaningless. The existence of mathematical entities can, according to them, be asserted only if we can actually construct them. Mathematical existence is not mind-independent; it is constructibility in the mathematician's mind.

To assert that all integers have a certain property P, briefly $\forall x P(x)$, is to assert that we possess a construction by which we can show for each integer that it possesses P; to assert that there exists an integer which possesses not–P, briefly $\exists x \neg P(x)$, is to assert that we possess a construction by which we can show that the assumption that a specific integer possesses P would lead to a contradiction. As we have seen earlier, we possess in some cases, e.g. with respect to Goldbach's property for even numbers greater than two, neither kind of construction. We are, therefore, not entitled to assert: $\forall x P(x) \lor \exists x \neg P(x)$ and consequently also not: $p \lor \neg p$, i.e. the principle of excluded middle. The denial of the existence of infinite totalities, the thesis that mathematical existence is constructibility, and the consequent denial of the principle of excluded middle imply that the logic in which (intuitionist) mathematics is embedded is *not* standard elementary logic.

Intuitionist logic is not truth-functional. Negation is not truth-functional, since an expression $\neg A$ is assertable if, and only if, the assumption that a construction proving A has been carried out leads to a contradiction. The other propositional connectives are also defined quite differently from the truth-functional ones. Thus an expression $A \land B$ is assertable if, and only if, A and B are assertable in the strong sense of being backed by a construction; an expression $A \lor B$ is assertable if, and only if, at least one of them is *separately* assertable; and an expression $A \to B$ is assertable if, and only if, a construction proving C is assertable which joined to any construction proving A would *ipso facto* amount to a construction proving B.[1] With this interpretation of the propositional connectives it is clear that many expressions which are valid in standard logic are not assertable in the intuitionist system. Examples, apart from $p \lor \neg p$, are $\neg \neg p \to p$, $(\neg p \to \neg q) \to (q \to p)$. It is possible to axiomatize the intuitionist logic of propositions, quantification-theory and theory of identity. Although we cannot pursue these matters further, it may be of some interest to mention that we arrive at an axiomatic system of intuitionist propositional logic by a single change in the axiomatic system of truth-functional logic, described earlier. It consists in replacing the third axiom of that system, i.e. $(\neg p \to \neg q) \to (q \to p)$ by the weaker axiom: $(p \to q) \to (\neg q \to \neg p)$.

[1] For details see A. Heyting, *Intuitionism* (Amsterdam 1956)

Philosophically intuitionism is, in my view, superior to logicism on at least two counts. Firstly, it fulfils the programme which it sets itself. It makes no use of assumptions which the programme excludes; and the principles of intuitionist logic describe in fact the principles of reasoning used in intuitionist mathematics. Logicism, on the other hand, bans all non-logical or synthetic assumptions from mathematics and yet uses such principles in the theory of real numbers and, in some cases, even in the theory of natural numbers. Secondly, intuitionism implies that mathematical axioms and theorems are logical neither in Leibniz's sense of being true in all possible worlds nor in any other sense which can be regarded as a successful reconstruction (replacement-analysis) of it.

The weakness of the intuitionist philosophy of mathematics is its conception of mathematical intuition, which at once raises all the difficulties raised by the Cartesian conception of intuitive knowledge. How, in particular, are we to safeguard against apparent intuitions which later turn out to be false? And how do we adjudicate between conflicting intuitions? Neither of these questions is philosophically or historically pointless; and neither admits of a satisfactory answer. There is no other criterion of self-evident truth than the feeling of self-evidence which is notoriously unreliable. As some antinomies show, a conjunction of apparently self-evident propositions may lead to contradictions, and many statements which are at one time supported by feelings of self-evidence may later lose this merely psychological support. The inter-subjective foundation of self-evidence is equally shaky. The intuitionists themselves are divided about the acceptability of the concept of intuitionist negation due to Brouwer which was explained above. A radical wing of intuitionists rejects as counterintuitive, or at least as non-intuitive, the idea of a construction which cannot be carried out but which, if assumed to have been carried out, would lead to a contradiction.

It is sometimes said that intuitionism, whatever its philosophical merits, must, if compared with logicism, be rejected on pragmatic grounds. It is accused of using unfamiliar methods and of sacrificing large parts of classical mathematics. But surely what is unfamiliar may in the course of time become familiar. The second objection is usually elaborated by statements to the effect that physics, as we know it, is embedded in a mathematics which in turn is embedded in standard elementary logic. This is certainly so. But it may well be that an intuitionist reconstruction of classical mathematics could be found, which, though fundamentally different from it, was technically not more difficult to handle. Some recent attempts in this direction seem to bear out this conjecture. The feature of intuitionism which probably makes it most unpalatable to working mathematicians and others is the rejection of the principle of excluded middle. But the intuitionists would reply that since the application of this principle constitutes the nerve of most non-constructive proofs, its elimination from mathematical reasoning is not a weakness but one of the strong points in favour of the intuitionist mathematics and philosophy of mathematics.

HILBERTIAN FORMALISM

The formalist philosophers of mathematics agree with the intuitionists in holding that mathematics cannot be reduced to logic because mathematics comprises synthetic propositions which are true descriptions of very simple perceptual situations, e.g. sequences of distinct objects such as strokes. Like the intuitionists, the formalists divide classical mathematics into two parts, namely 'finitist' and 'infinitist' mathematics. The former is to a large extent, though not completely, identical with that part of mathematics which is regarded by intuitionists as meaningful. It excludes in particular the assumption of infinite totalities, of the law of excluded middle and of other principles dependent upon these. Only such propositions are admitted as describe finite aggregates of distinct concrete objects, e.g. sequences of strokes, and operations performed on such aggregates. However – and here formalism differs radically from intuitionism – the infinitist mathematics is not rejected

67

but preserved in so far as its adjunction to the finitist mathematics does not lead to contradictions.

According to Hilbert, the founder of modern formalism,[1] this aim was to be achieved in two stages, namely (i) the 'complete formalization' of mathematics, and (ii) the demonstration that the resulting formal system is 'formally consistent'. To formalize a theory is to make all its assertions and rules of inference explicit and to consider only their form abstracted from any content. As an example we might consider the system of propositional logic, described on page 44. Its vocabulary, i.e. $p, q, r, \ldots \to, \neg$, becomes on formalization what might be called a formal vocabulary – a set of mere symbols, i.e. of symbols symbolizing nothing, though capable of doing so if interpreted. Its rules for the construction of well-formed formulae become rules of formal construction, i.e. for stringing together formal symbols to produce well-formed formulae which are so called simply to signify that the formal symbols they contain are strung together in accordance with these rules. Its axioms become formal axioms, i.e. well-formed strings of formal symbols upon which formal transformations may be performed in accordance with rules of formal inference. For example, the formal axiom: $p \to (q \to p)$ is a meaningless, uninterpreted pattern, which differs from, e.g., the pattern: $p \to (q \to r)$ only by its function in formal inferences. The rules of inference become formal rules of inference, i.e. rules for transforming certain patterns into others. For example, *modus ponens*, as a formal rule, allows us to write down a formula B, if $A \to B$ and A are formal axioms or formal theorems, i.e. derivable from the formal axioms in accordance with the formal rules of inference. A theory is completely formalized if, and only if, every axiom or theorem of the theory corresponds in an unambiguous manner to a formal axiom or theorem of its formalized counterpart and vice versa.

A meaningful theory is consistent if, and only if, it contains no two theorems such that one is the negation of the other. The

[1] See especially Hilbert and Bernays, *Die Grundlagen der Mathematik* (Berlin 1934 and 1939)

consistency of a formal system cannot be so defined since such a system does not contain propositions, nor therefore negations of propositions. But it may contain formal theorems and their formal negations. For example, viewed as a formal system the logic of propositions contains: $p \vee \neg p$ as a formal theorem; but not its formal negation: $\neg (p \vee \neg p)$. In fact, it can be shown that the formal theory of propositions is formally consistent, i.e. that it contains no two theorems of which one is the formal negation of the other.

Hilbert thought that classical mathematics – finitist and infinitist – could, like the standard logic of propositions, be completely formalized and shown to be formally consistent by purely finitist reasoning. Formalization would reduce the whole of classical mathematics to finite strings of symbols and operations upon them; and the proof of formal consistency would use *no infinitist assumptions* since it would refer only to strings of symbols and operations on them. A pure mathematician who, apart from formal consistency, made no further logical demands could then with a clear conscience let his mathematical imagination roam over the whole field of classical mathematics – leaving any worry about infinitist assumptions to the philosophers. Whether such philosophical self-denial can be expected from all mathematicians is, at least, doubtful. However this may be, Hilbert's original programme cannot be executed; classical mathematics can be neither completely formalized nor shown to be formally consistent by purely finitist methods.

This was proved in a famous paper by Gödel who showed that if standard elementary logic is so extended that it contains the arithmetic of natural numbers the resulting theory is not completely formalizable, since there will always be theorems of the theory to which no formal theorems of the formal system correspond.[1] Gödel's proof even provides a method for exhibiting actual examples. In the same paper Gödel also proved that the formal consistency of such a formal system cannot be

[1] Über formal unentscheidbare Sätze der *Principia Mathematica* und verwandter Systeme' I, *Monatshefte für Mathematik und Physik*, vol. 38 (1931)

proved by finitist means. These results dealt a very severe blow to the formalist programme. The first reaction of its protagonists was not to abandon but to liberalize it. Instead of demanding proofs of formal consistency by purely finitist means they allowed some infinitist methods to be used so long as they fell short of the unbridled infinitism of classical mathematics.

There can be no doubt that the attempts to analyse, or reconstruct, classical mathematics in a logicist, intuitionist or Hilbertian manner have been attended by rich mathematical and philosophical insights. Yet it would seem that, in spite of its philosophically dubious doctrine of mathematical intuition, intuitionism has been least affected by the discoveries made in the course of attempts to found mathematics on the secure basis of logic, of intuition or the manipulation of uninterpreted symbols. If I were forced to guess the direction of future progress in the general field of the 'foundations of mathematics' I should expect it to follow a path which combined the intuitionist scepticism about infinite totalities, and in particular of infinite totalities of infinite totalities, with the formalist requirement that mathematical assertions should be checkable in accordance with rules governing performable operations on finite aggregates of distinct public objects. This does not mean that these objects themselves – the symbols or strings of symbols written on paper – should be regarded as the subject matter of mathematics. Their use could, for example, be conceived after the fashion of geometrical diagrams which, as perishable and imperfect representatives of non-perceptual mathematical objects, help us to fix our ideas on what they represent.

THE ALLEGED UNIQUENESS OF MATHEMATICS

All major philosophers from Plato to Kant have held the doctrine that arithmetic, geometry or any other mathematical theory which existed in their day was true. Their reasons differed. Some held that its truth was grounded in empirical reality, others that it described some super-empirical reality or intersubjective intuition and still others that it rested on logic. That mathematics describes some very general features of the empirical world was held by, e.g., the ancient Egyptian geometers and by John Stuart Mill. That it describes some non-empirical, mind-independent reality was held by, e.g., Plato and many mathematicians of all epochs. That it describes an intersubjective intuition was held by, e.g., Kant and by Brouwer. And that it rests on logic – that it is logic – was held by, e.g., Leibniz, Frege and Russell. But the doctrine of the uniqueness of mathematics is by no means universally held at the present time. The main reason for doubting it lies in the actual existence of apparently alternative mathematical theories. Such apparent alternatives first attracted the attention of philosophers when non-Euclidean geometries were discovered, proved to be consistent, and shown to be no less useful in theoretical physics than Euclidean geometry. The essential difference between Euclidean and non-Euclidean geometry can be roughly explained as follows: Euclidean geometry can be formulated as an axiomatic system one of whose axioms is the statement that the sum of the angles of any triangle equals the sum of two right angles, i.e. 180°. In a non-Euclidean geometry this axiom is replaced by its negation, more specifically either by an axiom to the effect that the sum of the angles is less than, or by an axiom to the effect that the sum of the angles is greater than, 180°.

At first sight it might seem feasible to test the truth of Euclidean geometry or its alternatives by actual measurements. Such a test would not be conclusive for at least two reasons. First, it would at best establish the Euclidean or non-Euclidean character of physical space within the limits dictated by the sensitivity of the available instruments for measuring distances and angles. Since no measuring instrument is infinitely sensitive it is always possible that small deviations from 180° could remain undiscovered. Second, since measurement is a physical process subject to the physical laws of nature our measurements do not only test our geometrical but also our physical assumptions, so that it might always be argued that a Euclidean or non-Euclidean outcome can be secured by a suitable change in the physical laws – a point which was forcefully argued by Poincaré.[1]

If neither Euclidean nor non-Euclidean geometry describe the physical world or sense-experience, one or both of them may yet describe some other 'reality'. The problem might be stated thus: if they describe the same subject-matter they are wholly incompatible with each other, since the space they would then describe cannot be both Euclidean and non-Euclidean; and if they each describe a different subject-matter they are wholly compatible with each other, since each of them would describe a different space. Yet neither their incompatibility on the former interpretation, nor their compatibility on the latter, would seem to do justice to the respects in which they agree and to the respects in which they differ. The first exaggerates their conflict, the second their common features.

These alternatives are not the only possibilities. It is more in line with the use of geometry in the transactions of ordinary life and in the sciences to compare Euclidean and non-Euclidean geometry with each other in terms of the relation which each of them bears to sense-experience – even if neither of them describes it. A triangle drawn on a blackboard, a triangle formed by three light rays, or any other empirical triangle, is neither Euclidean nor non-Euclidean for the simple reason that neither a Euclidean nor a non-Euclidean triangle could be perceived in the physical world. A triangle drawn on a blackboard is an irregular three-dimensional object, which is a very different thing from any two-dimensional figure bounded by (one-dimensional) lines. For a start such lines would be invisible. And any other alleged physical realization of an Euclidean or non-Euclidean triangle would have similar shortcomings. Yet, although no geometrical triangle is identical with any physical triangle it may, for certain purposes and

[1] See e.g. *La Science et l'Hypothèse* (Paris 1912), especially chapter V. 'L'Expérience et la géométrie'

within certain more or less precisely specified limits, be identifiable with a physical triangle.

For the purposes of a civil engineer the physical triangles which he meets, designs or constructs in the course of his work are all identifiable with Euclidean triangles. For many of his purposes the triangles which a relativity-physicist observes in nature and uses in his calculations are identifiable with non-Euclidean triangles, whose precise geometrical structure need not concern us here. Lastly, for many purposes physical triangles are identifiable with both Euclidean and non-Euclidean triangles. It is this co-identifiability for certain purposes of different geometries with observed aspects of nature, which expresses what they have in common; and it is their non-co-identifiability for certain other purposes which expresses their conflicts. The merit of this comparison of different geometries by reference to the physical world is that it does justice to their multiplicity, without either demanding the assumption of a super-empirical reality or forcing us to confuse descriptions of the empirical world with various geometrical idealizations of it.

It might be, and it has been argued, that the discovery of non-Euclidean geometries does not amount to a refutation, but only to a restriction, of the doctrine of the uniqueness of mathematics; that the doctrine, although no longer tenable for Euclidean geometry, is nevertheless true for arithmetic and some other branches of mathematics. This line of defence is adopted in particular by Brouwer and other intuitionists. It often takes the form of a critical revision of Kant's philosophy of mathematics. According to Kant the axioms and theorems of Euclidean geometry describe the intersubjective intuition of the structure of space; and the axioms and theorems of arithmetic describe the intersubjective intuition of the structure of time. Brouwer rejects the former, but accepts the latter thesis. For him the fundamental intuition is 'the perception of *a move of time*, i.e. of the falling apart of a life moment into two distinct things, one of which gives way to the other, but is retained by memory'. If 'the two-ity thus born is divested of all quality, there remains the *empty form of the common substratum of all two-ities*' which is 'the basic intuition of all mathematics'.[1]

Yet there is a multiplicity even of arithmetics. 'Being a natural number' in the intuitionist sense means being a member of a potentially infinite sequence, whereas 'being a natural number' in the logicist sense means being a member of an actually infinite sequence. Again if one conceives a natural number in Fregean fashion to be an attribute of a class or set, then the meaning of 'natural number' will depend on the meaning of 'set' and will vary with the sort of set-theory one adopts. Moreover the differences between these set theories have increased in recent years. A recent discovery has led to a bifurcation of set-theory which is widely, and in my view correctly, regarded as perfectly analogous to the bifurcation of geometry into Euclidean and non-Euclidean geometry.[2]

A strong case can thus be made against the doctrine of the uniqueness, not only of geometry, but also of arithmetic and mathematics generally. On the other hand a strong case can be made also for the view that every (extant) mathematical theory – and not only Euclidean or non-Euclidean geometry – is an idealization of empirical discourse; that mathematical concepts describe neither a super-empirical reality, an inter-subjective intuition, nor, indeed, sense-experience; and that the connexion of a mathematical theory with sense-experience consists in the identifiability, within certain contexts and for certain purposes, of mathematical with empirical concepts. This view derives additional support from the account, given in the preceding chapter, of the multiplicity of logical systems and from the analysis to be given in the next chapter, of empirical discourse and scientific theories. It also harmonizes well with the critique to be given in Chapter 13 of a large and in-

[1] See e.g. 'Historical Background, Principles and Methods of Intuitionism', *South African Journal of Science* (October–November 1952)

[2] See P. J. Cohen, 'The Independence of the Continuum Hypothesis', *Proceedings of the National Academy of Sciences* vol. 50 51 (1963, 1964)

fluential family of arguments, which – in various fields of inquiry ranging from logic to metaphysics – purport to establish the uniqueness and indispensability of some actually adopted conceptual framework.

5. The Philosophy of Science

An important aim of science is to predict and to explain the course of nature. Of the many answers to the philosophical question as to how this aim can best be achieved two have exerted a particularly strong influence on the development of science. They might be called the Platonic and the Baconian answers, after the philosophers often regarded as their original proponents. According to Plato the only way of understanding the infinitely complex, perceptually indefinite, and ever changing physical world is to apprehend its structure by means of simple, conceptually definite, invariant principles, especially mathematical principles. According to Bacon it is to observe the course of nature and to make the correct inductive generalizations from observation and experiment. Although the Platonic and the Baconian conceptions of scientific inquiry are one-sided and in many details obsolete, scientists have in varying degrees followed both methodological prescriptions. Science is recognizably both Platonic and Baconian: it is neither empirical discourse without theoretical, including mathematical, organization, nor theorizing, divorced from observation and experiment. An analysis even of the most general features of scientific thinking involves, therefore, some account of (i) the logical structure of empirical discourse before it is subjected to more or less rigid theoretical organization, (ii) the manner in which it is organized, and modified, by being incorporated into scientific theories and (iii) the nature of the harmony or disharmony between a scientific theory and the empirical evidence for it.

SOME FEATURES OF ORDINARY EMPIRICAL DISCOURSE

Many attributes of ordinary language – including those which refer to the results of measurements such as 'having such-and-such a length', 'having such-and-such a weight', 'lasting for such-and-such a time' – depend for their meaning either directly or indirectly on exemplification. That is to say that these attributes themselves, or others in terms of which they are defined, require for an understanding of their correct use that standard examples and counter-examples of their applicability be available. For example, the judgement that an object is green presupposes its comparison with objects which it sufficiently resembles and others from which it is sufficiently dissimilar in colour. Such comparisons are also the ground for judgements that a certain type of measurement has yielded a certain result.

That empirical attributes are introduced into language (partly) by examples and counter-examples of their applicability accounts for two closely related features of empirical discourse, which it does not share with standard elementary logic, classical mathematics or any theory embedded in standard elementary logic. These are (a) the inexactness of many empirical attributes and (b) the non-transitive character of perceptual equality (in judgements that empirical objects are indistinguishable with respect to certain attributes). Of these features the first has been emphasized by Wittgenstein and his successors, the second by Poincaré and other philosophers of science.

I shall say that an attribute $P(x)$, such as 'x is green', is inexact if, and only if, the following three relations are possible between any object b and the class of things characterized by $P(x)$: (1) b is a member of the class, i.e. $P(b)$; (ii) b is a non-member of the class, i.e. $\neg P(b)$ and (iii) b is a 'neutral' or borderline case of the class, in which case I shall write $*P(b)$. The third possibility is not acknowledged by standard elementary logic. It represents the frequent situation in which the rules governing the use of an attribute are violated neither by assigning it nor by refusing it to an object. The rules governing the use of an inexact attribute may be likened to the rules for admission to many clubs, universities and other institutions. Some applicants are qualified and must be admitted, some are not qualified and must be rejected; and some – the borderline cases – may, without violating the rules for admission, be treated as qualified and be accepted or treated as not qualified and be rejected. In the absence of any further conventions for dealing with borderline cases, e.g. by tossing a coin, by admitting every second one, etc., the decision is perfectly free. In a similar fashion some things must – by the rules governing the attribute 'green' — be judged to be green, others judged to be not-green, whereas the borderline cases may, after being recognized as such, be judged green or not green.

If we acknowledge inexact attributes and their neutral cases we must admit, besides the truth-values T (truth) and F (falsehood), a third truth-value $*$(neutrality) which unlike the others is provisional in the sense that it may, by a free decision, be turned into truth or falsehood. It is fairly easy to extend standard elementary logic so as to accommodate neutral propositions. All that is needed is to show how, if at all, the neutrality of a component affects the neutrality of the compound. For example, if in: $p \wedge q$, p is true and q is neutral, then the conjunction is also neutral, since it can be made true by making the neutral q true and false by making the neutral q false. On the other hand, if in: $p \vee q$, p is true and q is neutral, then the disjunction is true, since whether we make q true or false the disjunction remains true because one of its members is true.

The combination by means of the truth-functional connectives of true, false and neutral propositions can be presented by truth-tables. It will be convenient to use a method which is somewhat different from that used earlier (page 42). In the table for $\neg$ (not), the values for p and $\neg p$ are found, as before, in the first and second column. In the other tables the values for p are found in the first column, the values for q in the first row and the values of the compound (conjunction, disjunction, conditional) in the intersection of the column containing the value of the p-component with the row containing the value of the q-component. If we ignore the third rows and the third columns, the truth-tables become those of standard elementary logic.

$\neg p$

p	$\neg p$
T	F
F	T
*	*

$p \wedge q$

$p \backslash q$	T	F	*
T	T	F	*
F	F	F	F
*	*	F	*

$p \vee q$

$p \backslash q$	T	F	*
T	T	T	T
F	T	F	*
*	T	*	*

$p \rightarrow q$

$p \backslash q$	T	F	*
T	T	F	*
F	T	T	T
*	*	T	*

Quantification-theory can be developed as before (page 45) by first considering universally quantified propositions as possibly infinite conjunctions and existentially quantified propositions as possibly infinite disjunctions; and then showing that no inconsistency arises when truth-functional compounds with an infinite number of components are introduced.[1]

I now turn to the non-transitive character of perceptual equality or indistinguishability. We have seen that equality as defined in standard elementary logic is transitive, i.e. that for all individuals x, y, $z : ((x = y) \wedge (y = z)) \rightarrow (x = z)$. Let us now consider a specific example of perceptual equality, namely equality in weight as determined by a pair of scales, so that two objects are equal in weight if they balance each other on them. Assume that the scales are insensitive to weight differences smaller than $1/1000$ gram. It is then obviously possible to find three objects, say a, b, c, such that a balances b, b balances c, but a does *not* balance c. This will be so if the weight-differences between a and b and between b and c are

---

[1] For details see *Experience and Theory* (London 1966) chapter 3

smaller, but that between a and c greater than $1/1000$ gram. We could, of course, use a more sensitive pair of scales, but since no infinitely sensitive pair of scales exists, the assertion that equality in weight as ascertained by balancing objects on pairs of scales is transitive can always be refuted by a suitable triplet of objects. Since the argument applies also to the determination of equality in weight by other means and to determining equality in respect of other empirical attributes by actually performed measurements, we must conclude that operationally ascertainable, empirical (unlike mathematical) equality is non-transitive.

THE THEORETICAL ORGANIZATION
OF EMPIRICAL DISCOURSE

Scientific theories, especially quantitative theories, are embedded in a more or less extended mathematical framework, which in turn is embedded in standard elementary logic. The extent to which mathematics is used is smallest in the merely classificatory sciences which can get by with a minimum of arithmetical reasoning, and greatest in theoretical physics which uses almost all branches of mathematics at one point or another. The logico-mathematical framework of any scientific theory imposes certain constraints and modifications on the propositions incorporated into it.

Since the standard elementary logic which underlies theoretical reasoning has no room for inexact attributes and neutral propositions, it follows immediately that such attributes and propositions have to be replaced by exact ones. This elimination of inexactness is the most fundamental and common modification of empirical discourse enforced by its theoretical organization. Again, insofar as a theory employs the transitive relation of mathematical equality it enforces the modification of the non-transitive relation of perceptual equality. If the theory in question involves quantitative reasoning, further, even more radical, modifications of empirical discourse become necessary.

Quantitative reasoning in the full sense of the term involves a great deal more than judgements of equality or inequality. It presupposes first of all that numbers are assigned to things and that classes of quantities are formed – a quantity being a pair consisting of an object (a piece of iron, a gas, etc.) and a number assigned to the object as the result of some measurement (of weight, of pressure, etc.) If quantities belonging to the same class (e.g. pieces of iron with their numbers assigned by weighing) are to be added, multiplied by a number or otherwise quantitatively manipulated, these operations must conform to certain theoretical postulates, which were first exhibited by Helmholtz and later more clearly formulated by others, in particular Karl Menger.[1] These postulates – like the postulates governing the relation of mathematical equality – do not describe, but idealize the operations of physical addition, subtraction, etc.

Still more radical idealizations are involved in reasoning about assumed laws of nature expressed as functional relations between classes of quantities, e.g. between the quantities called 'mass', 'velocity', 'force', etc., in classical mechanics. When the theory of real numbers, especially those branches dealing with the differential and integral calculus, are employed the idealization of empirical discourse is even more striking. Without going into further detail we may thus say that the 'deductive unification' of empirical discourse, namely the systematic incorporation of empirical attributes and propositions into standard elementary logic and the mathematical extensions of this logic, is *ipso facto* an idealization. The modified theoretical propositions no longer describe what the unmodified empirical propositions describe. However, the transition from description to idealization is a small price to pay for the enormous advantages thereby gained, namely conceptual simplicity and definiteness and the consequent efficiency of inference and calculation.

[1] See e.g. 'Mensuration and Other Mathematical Connections of Observable Materials', *Measurement: Definitions and Theories* ed. C. W. Churchman and P. Ratoosh (New York 1959)

Apart from idealization by deductive unification, i.e. the modification imposed on all substantive theories by their logico-mathematical framework, most theorizing involves another kind of idealization which varies from theory to theory and is not enforced by the logico-mathematical framework. The nature of this idealization, which might be called 'deductive abstraction', can be briefly explained by an example. Assume that an experiment or observation involving a material object is carried out with a view to using classical mechanics for predicting its future on the basis of its present behaviour. In such a context and for such a purpose not all the perceptual characteristics of the material object are relevant, but only its empirically ascertainable mass and relative position at a certain time. The other perceptual characteristics, which are irrelevant in the context, are not only ignored in classical mechanics, but are not allowed for by its postulates: whereas a material body necessarily has, as well as perceptual mass (determined, e.g., by weighing) and spatio-temporal position, characteristics such as colour or temperature, its theoretical counterpart in classical mechanics, namely a particle, has *only* mass and relative position. In other words, whereas in empirical discourse 'having mass and position' implies 'having other characteristics apart from mass and position', the idealized 'mechanical' concepts of mass and position are so determined that a particle's possession of these characteristics logically implies that it possesses no others – except, of course, such as are definable in terms of mass and position. By thus eliminating deductive relations which the theoretically relevant characteristics may bear to theoretically irrelevant ones, deductive abstraction adds to the simplifying modifications which deductive unification imposes upon empirical discourse.

THE HARMONY BETWEEN THEORY AND EXPERIENCE

Thus there exists a gap between, on the one hand, a scientific theory, i.e. a deductively more or less strictly organized system of concepts and propositions, resulting from the modification of empirical discourse by deductive unification and deductive abstraction, and, on the other hand, empirical discourse itself. It is ignored by the so-called 'deductivist' account of the relation between theory and experience. This account is frequently embodied in a schema and best explained, and criticized, by commenting on it in this form:

$$b_1 \wedge A_0 \,/\!\!\underline{L}\, b_2 \qquad\qquad \text{(i)}$$

Here A_0 is the conjunction of the substantive axioms of a theory T_0; b_1 and b_2 are two so-called 'state-descriptions', which allegedly describe two different states of the universe in the vocabulary of T_0; $/\!\!\underline{L}$ expresses the relation of logical deducibility within the logical framework of the theory T_0. For example, if T_0 is classical mechanics, then b_1 and b_2 describe two distinct states of a mechanical system in terms of the momenta and relative positions of particles, whilst A_0 is the conjunction of Newton's laws of motion. The whole schematic proposition may be read as: the state-description b_2 is (by means of standard elementary logic and its mathematical extensions, which together constitute the formal framework of the theory) deducible from the state-description b_1 in conjunction with A_0, the axioms of the theory; or more briefly as: the state-description b_1 in conjunction with the axioms A_0 logically implies b_2.

The mistake of this attractively simple, and, within limits, useful account lies in regarding b_1 and b_2 as empirical propositions describing the physical world, and, at the same time, as being formulated in terms of a theory which, as we have seen, does not accommodate empirical concepts, but only more or less radically idealized substitutes for them. In other words, the deductivist account conflates two very different kinds of state-descriptions, namely *theoretical* state-descriptions, which are not empirical propositions, and *empirical* state-descriptions which are. By distinguishing them, as we must, from each other, i.e., by exhibiting the gap between them, we face the problem of explaining how the gap is bridged, i.e. how empirical and theoretical statements are linked in scientific reasoning.

Clearly no two empirical propositions, say e_1 and e_2, can be identical with their respective theoretical idealizations b_1 and b_2. But e_1 and e_2 may nevertheless be under certain conditions identifiable, i.e. capable of being treated *as if* they were identical with b_1 and b_2. The conditions which any suitable identification has to fulfil will depend on the theory in question, as well as on the context in which the theory is employed. I call the former the 'theory-dependent' and the latter the 'context-dependent' conditions of the identification.

The theory-dependent conditions for identifying the theoretical propositions b_1 and b_2 with the corresponding empirical propositions determine the kind of empirical information which the latter must contain if they are to be relevant to the purposes, in particular to the predictive use, of the theory. For example, if b_1 and b_2 are two theoretical state-descriptions of classical mechanics, then the relevant empirical information required of e_1 and e_2 is the empirically ascertained masses and spatio-temporal positions of material objects, which are then identified with the (theoretical) masses and spatio-temporal positions of particle-configurations. In other words, the theory-dependent conditions are satisfied when the information needed by the theoretician for his deductions has been ascertained, expressed in empirical propositions, and transposed into the logically more regimented and conceptually more austere language of the theory.

However, the successful use of the theory for predictions and retrodictions depends not only on identifying empirical with theoretical propositions by such transpositions. The context in which the identifications are made is, at least, equally important. For it may happen that some features of a situation which from the point of view of the theory are irrelevant, and which have therefore been neglected (especially by deductive abstraction), turn out not to be negligible. Thus, from the point of view of classical mechanics the electric charges of the bodies involved in a mechanical experiment are irrelevant. But this does not mean that they will have no effect on the behaviour of these bodies. Indeed, there may always be theoretically neglected factors which are as yet unknown but are none the less effective in influencing the course of events. The existence and effectiveness of such factors depend quite obviously not on the theory which is being employed, but on the context in which it is employed, i.e. on nature. The context-dependent conditions for identifying theoretical with empirical state-descriptions (e.g. b_1 and b_2 with e_1 and e_2 respectively) are thus satisfied when the empirical features which in the context of the identification have been neglected as ineffective, are in fact ineffective.

The upshot of these remarks can again be compressed into a schema which is more complex, but also more adequate than the deductivist schema, namely:

If the theory- and context-dependent conditions for identifying e_1 with b_1 and e_2 with b_2 are satisfied, then (ii) $b_1 \wedge A_0 \mathrel{/_{\overline{L}}} b_2$ justifies the inference from e_1 to e_2.

The schema relates empirical to theoretical propositions. Because of the neutrality of some empirical propositions and the inexactness of some empirical predicates, the schema cannot be formalized in standard elementary logic. It is, however, possible to formalize it in the logical system outlined above on pages 77 ff. (Let us write 'c_0' in order to indicate that the context-dependent conditions of identification are satisfied; '$e_1 \approx b_1$' and '$e_2 \approx b_2$' in order to indicate that the theory-dependent conditions of identification are satisfied; and let us stipulate that the connectives '$\wedge$' and '$\rightarrow$' are those defined by the truth-tables on page 79. Schema (ii) can then be written as

$$[e_1 \wedge c_0 \wedge (e_1 \approx b_1) \wedge (b_1 \wedge A_0 \mathrel{/_{\overline{L}}} b_2) \wedge (b_2 \approx e_2)] \rightarrow e_2 \qquad \text{(ii)}$$

Which of the two formulations is preferred is for our purpose here not important.)

That schema (ii) corresponds to a more realistic account of testable scientific reasoning than schema (i) can be seen for instance in a situation where the theory T_0 is employed to predict that e_2 will happen on the ground that e_1 has happened. If e_2 does not happen, then the deductivist schema implies that the theory T_0 has been falsified. Schema (ii) on the other hand leaves us with two possibilities, namely (a) to abandon the theory as falsified or (b) to ascribe the non-occurrence of e_2 to a failure in satisfying the conditions of identification, in particular to having neglected features of the situation described by e_1 which, in the context of employing T_0, were not in fact negligible. That *both* possibilities have to be considered is amply borne out by the history of science.

Some further comments on schema (ii) may be useful. As it stands it might give the impression of presupposing that every scientific theory is a full-fledged axiomatic system. However, the schema applies also to very much less organized theories, insofar as they contain stretches of deductive reasoning in accordance with classical logic and its extensions. The symbol $\overline{L}$ then refers to these stretches. Again the schema contains no reference to statistical methods, e.g. to the so-called theory of experimental error, which are often alleged to bridge the gap between experience and theory. In fact statistical theories are themselves highly idealized theories of mass-phenomena; and the relation between a statistical theory and the observed phenomena is of the same kind as that between any other theory and the subject matter which it idealizes. Finally, the stress which has been placed on the need to modify empirical concepts before admitting them into theories must not be taken to imply that all concepts which occur in a theory are modified empirical concepts with easily recognizable empirical counterparts. The concepts of a theory may have other origins. They may, for example, be suggested by metaphysical speculation; they may have their roots in mathematical imagination; or last but not least, they may originate in the course of scientific inquiry itself.

It lies outside our scope to consider the lively conceptual interchange between scientific and extra-scientific thinking. But it may be of interest to show, by means of an example, how empirical discourse may in turn be enriched by theoretical thinking. Consider, then, the empirical generalization: 'All magnetized pieces of iron attract iron filings' as formulated, e.g., by a shrewd observer of nature in Greek times, who knows nothing of the later theories of electro-magnetism, and for whom 'magnetization' means no more than a simple, observable, physical process involving suitable pieces of magnetic and non-magnetic iron. The empirical generalization has the form: $\forall x(P(x) \rightarrow Q(x))$ (and is embedded in the three-valued logic admitting not only exact, but also inexact attributes). After the discovery of a *theory* of magnetism we learn that the empirical attributes $P(x)$ and $Q(x)$ can, with great advantage, be identified in certain contexts with the attributes of the theory, say $P'(x)$ and $Q'(x)$. We learn in particular that, through this identification, a theory becomes available which leads (in accordance with schema (ii)) from instances of the empirical attribute $P(x)$ to instances of the empirical attribute $Q(x)$. What we have learned can be expressed in at least two different ways: either by saying that we have recognized a new feature of these empirical attributes, namely their identifiability in important contexts with attributes of the theory; or by saying that the empirical attributes have been replaced by different ones. By being identified – or being seen to be identifiable – with theoretical attributes, they do not cease to be empirical, and they remain free from the restrictions to which their theoretical counterparts are subject. The same holds for attributes which, like 'energy', 'entropy', 'molecule', have seeped from theoretical into empirical discourse.

INDUCTION

So far nothing has been said about the role of inductive thinking in the sciences. What can be said about it is either obvious or highly controversial. It is obvious that the scientist, like everybody else, makes non-deductive transitions from premises of the form: 'All (a certain proportion of) *observed* P's are Q's' to conclusions of the form: 'All (a certain proportion of) P's are Q's'. It is also obvious that the scientist, unlike everybody else, in making such non-deductive transitions often makes use of various statistical theories based on various notions of probability. And it is obvious that the scientist, again unlike everybody else, makes non-deductive transitions from observations and experiments to theories. In short, there can be no doubt that scientific thinking involves (a) naïve inductions, (b) statistical inductions and (c) theory-construction, which some philosophers also regard as a kind of induction. The results of these activities must, of course, stand the test of observation and experiment.

But is there any well-regulated method of inductive *reasoning* by which one would be enabled to distinguish between correct and incorrect inductions independently of subsequent observations and experiments? Is there, in particular, a method of validating the inductive transition, as Hume puts it, from 'I have found that such an object has always been attended with such an effect' to 'I foresee, that other objects, which are, in appearance, similar, will be attended with similar effects'? Hume's answer is a decided 'No', and whoever disagrees with it will have to consider very seriously the challenge expressed in the passage from the *Enquiry Concerning Human Understanding*, quoted in Chapter I.[1]

Some thinkers – e.g. Bacon before Hume; Mill, Keynes and many others after him – have suggested that an additional suppressed premiss is indeed involved in all correct inductions. Examples are various principles of the uniformity of nature, such as the principle that the various attributes of individuals occur in nature only in a finite number of clusters, so that the co-existence of attributes in a subclass of individuals of a certain kind is a good reason for assuming its co-existence in the whole class. But even if this or a similar principle were true its truth, as Hume pointed out, could only be discovered by induction; and we are back where we started, still faced with the challenge to produce 'the medium' for this new induction.

If, as Hume thought, any inductive justification of induction is viciously circular, then the outlook for discovering a justification seems indeed poor. Only two ways for arriving at it are *prima facie* open. One is to look for *a priori* principles the truth

[1] See page 11

of which is independent of experience. Various attempts in this direction have been made, e.g. by regarding the relation between inductive premisses and inductive conclusions as a relation, which though weaker than logical implication, is yet 'true in all possible worlds'. It is at present by no means clear whether these attempts will, or could, have the desired result. The other is to revise and liberalize the concept of a justification of induction. Indeed, the only justification which would satisfy Hume would, it seems, consist in showing that induction is really deduction – a contradiction in terms. In that case Hume's challenge could be met only by showing that induction is what it is not. It would be like the challenge to justify the assertion that $2 + 2 = 4$ by showing that $2 + 2 = 5$; and such a challenge is no cause for philosophical uneasiness.

It is often said with, I think, good reason that the problem of the justification of induction is largely the problem of defining a suitable notion of justification which would be neither internally inconsistent nor trivial. In any case, without first explaining the conditions which a justification of induction in general or any particular kind of induction, such as statistical induction, would have to fulfil, the problem of the justification of induction is not clearly enough stated. It might even turn out that the disagreement between those philosophers who consider a justification of induction impossible and those who consider it feasible can be resolved by showing that it has its root in different conceptions of what a justification of induction would have to be. Indeed, it might turn out that induction is both justifiable, in the sense used by some philosophers who are searching for a justification; and at the same time unjustifiable, in the sense used by other philosophers who claim that it is unjustifiable.

The philosophy of science does not confine itself to the analysis of the general structure of scientific theories. It also analyzes specific theories, the concepts of which demand clarification because of their novelty, or for other reasons. In recent years a major topic of the philosophy of science has been the analysis of new conceptions in quantum-mechanics, in particular the so-called principle of complementarity first enunciated by Bohr and of the concept of probability used in his theory. It has occasionally been argued that the theoretical organization of the empirical facts which gave rise to quantum-theory requires a radical revision even of the logical framework in which the theory is to be embedded. Various philosophers, mathematicians and physicists have suggested replacing standard elementary logic by an exact three-valued logic. If this were to come about our schema (ii) would as regards quantum-mechanics have to be modified by replacing '$/\overline{L}$', which denotes deducibility in the usual exact two-valued logic, by '$/\overline{L_3}$' denoting deducibility in the new exact three-valued logic. I mention this possibility in order to emphasize that not even the logical framework of theories is immune from conceptual change.

In concluding this chapter a brief word must be said about the nature of *scientific explanation*. Part of what we want from such explanation is that it should enable us, by means of a theory, to proceed from the description of a certain state of affairs to the testable conclusion that another spatio-temporally distinct state of affairs is also part of nature. However, scientific explanation is not just prediction. This becomes obvious when we consider disputes between groups of scientists about two alternative theories, neither of which from the point of view of logical propriety and predictability is superior to the other. In such disputes it is often the case that one group regards one of the competing theories as being the 'real explanation', while rejecting the other as 'intellectually unsatisfactory'. What is required for a 'real explanation' depends on the scientist's conception of what constitutes a 'good' theory – e.g. that such a theory must be mechanistic, statistical, teleological, etc. These conceptions or attitudes are articulated by normative, regulative or programmatic principles for the construction of theories and are not captured by any analysis of the formal structure of theories and their relations to experience. They are rooted not only in logic and observation, but also in the scientist's view of the world as a whole, i.e. in his metaphysics.

6. The Philosophy of Mind

Because of the great success of the physical sciences in answering many of the questions about nature which had originally been asked by philosophy, the philosophy of nature has to a large extent become the philosophy of the physical sciences. That the philosophy of mind has not to an equal extent become the philosophy of psychology can be explained on two main counts. First, psychology has so far had nothing like the success of the other natural sciences. Second, although scientific psychologists regard psychology as a branch of the biological sciences, they have not yet reached the high degree of consensus about their subject which is characteristic of the physical and the other biological sciences. There does not yet exist a sufficiently large body of *common* theory, which philosophers could make the starting point and subject matter of their reflections.

The task of the philosophy of mind is, broadly speaking, the phenomenological description of mental phenomena and the philosophical analysis of the propositions describing or, in some cases, misdescribing them. The phenomena include: perception, belief and knowledge, which involve claims to an apprehension of factual truth; prudential, moral, and aesthetic evaluation, which involve claims to an apprehension of values; desire and emotion, which may or may not involve claims to an apprehension of factual truth, value, or both. The philosophical inquiry which examines the truth-claims involved in mental phenomena is often called 'the theory of knowledge' in a wide sense of the term. The philosophical inquiry which examines claims to the apprehension of value is called 'the theory of value' of which the main branches are ethics and aesthetics. However, such classifications may be very misleading, since philosophical problems are not as neatly separable as the titles and chapter-headings of books on philosophy seem to suggest. In the present chapter I shall consider two of the most important general problems of the philosophy of mind: namely, (i) whether and, if so, how the class of mental phenomena can be demarcated and distinguished from the class of physical phenomena, and (ii) whether and in what sense mental phenomena are 'reducible to' or 'analysable in terms of' physical phenomena. I shall conclude the chapter by considering some so-called theories of truth, i.e. some answers to the question whether and, if so, in what sense the truth of a proposition depends on a relation between it and a non-propositional reality.

THE CHARACTERIZATION OF MENTAL PHENOMENA

One of the starting points of most recent philosophical discussions of mental phenomena is to be found in the philosophy of Franz Brentano.[1] But the following account of mental phenomena, though greatly indebted to Brentano, would probably not be acceptable to him, even if it were elaborated beyond its rough outlines.

All mental phenomena consist in a person's awareness of something – 'awareness' not being further analysable. The objects of his awareness may be either propositions, as in the case of knowledge or doubt, or else non-propositional, as in the case of desire. I shall say that a relation between a person and the object of his awareness is an 'intentional relation' and the

[1] *Psychologie vom empirischen Standpunkt* vol I, book II (1st edition, Leipzig 1874)

object an 'intentional object' if, and only if, one of the two following conditions is satisfied: (i) if the object is a proposition, then the relationship between the person and the proposition does *not* logically imply that the proposition is true or that the proposition is false; (ii) if the object is non-propositional, then the relationship between the person and the (non-propositional) object does *not* logically imply that the object exists in the physical world.

Examples of intentional relations of the first kind – whose intentional objects are propositions – are a person's belief that Brutus killed Caesar or, for that matter, that Caesar killed Brutus, since the fact that someone believes a proposition does not imply the truth or falsity of the believed proposition. Examples of intentional relations of the second kind – whose intentional objects are non-propositional – are a man's desire to possess the Crown Jewels or his desire to possess Sherlock Holmes' pipe, since the fact that someone desires an object does not imply the existence of the desired object.

If we accept the original definition of intentional relations – in terms of 'awareness' – we must, I think, agree that all intentional relationships are mental phenomena. But the converse is not true, as can be shown by means of counter-examples. Thus, my *knowing* that Brutus murdered Caesar logically implies that the known proposition is true – at least if the term 'knowing' is used in the usual way according to which 'knowing a false proposition' is a contradiction in terms. Again, my *perceiving* a dog logically implies that the perceived object exists in the physical world – at least if the term 'perceiving' is used in the usual way according to which 'perceiving a physically non-existent dog' is a contradiction in terms. However, each of these non-intentional relationships includes an intentional relationship: knowing that Brutus murdered Caesar includes being under the impression of knowing that Brutus murdered Caesar as a constituent relation and this latter relation is intentional. Similarly perceiving a dog includes being under the impression of perceiving a dog and this latter relation is intentional. We might thus characterize mental phenomena as being either (a) intentional relationships (such as a person's believing a proposition or desiring an object) or else (b) intentional relationships existing in conjunction with non-intentional situations which guarantee the truth or falsehood of the intentional object, if it is a proposition (such as a person's knowledge that Brutus murdered Caesar), or the existence or non-existence of the intentional object, if it is non-propositional (such as a person's perceiving a material object).

It should, incidentally, be noted that the distinction between terms describing purely intentional and those describing mixed phenomena is not always clear in the natural languages and depends on the context. Thus when we say that somebody loves the goddess Minerva, we normally use 'love' as a purely intentional term, whereas when we say that a man loves his wife, we imply that the object of his love does not exist only 'in his mind'.

Having provided a general characterization of mental phenomena, the next task of the philosophy of mind is a classification of them and a description of the interrelations between mental phenomena of different types. One of many such classifications is Brentano's division of all mental phenomena into presentations, e.g. of having a red flower before my mind or being conscious of it; judgements, e.g. that the red flower exists; emotional phenomena, e.g. that the red flower presented to my mind and judged to be existent is liked by me.[1] According to Brentano any emotional phenomenon presupposes a judgement and any judgement presupposes a presentation.

A further task of the philosophy of mind is to describe particular mental phenomena with the greatest possible detail. At this level of concreteness the descriptions of a Marcel Proust may well be preferable to those of many a minute philosopher. Yet the detailed descriptions of particular mental phenomena by Brentano, Husserl, Wittgenstein and some of their followers are highly illuminating. (They are indispensable in the case of Wittgenstein, whose *Philosophical Investigations* mark the beginning of a new era in the philosophy of mind.

[1] *op. cit.* chapter VI

Indeed we cannot rule out the possibility that his approach, perhaps in conjunction with as yet unforeseeable scientific developments, may lead to so drastic a conceptual change that the concept of intentionality will be as little used or needed as that of sorcery.[1])

To the phenomenological distinction between physical and intentional phenomena there corresponds a logical distinction between the propositions describing these phenomena. Propositions describing physical phenomena are *truth-functional*, i.e. the truth-value of a compound proposition depends for its truth-value on the truth-value of the component propositions. Both standard elementary logic which acknowledges the truth-values T and F and the logical theory sketched in the preceding chapter which acknowledges in addition the truth-value $*$ (neutrality) are truth-functional. Propositions describing intentional relations between a person and a proposition are, as we have seen, not truth-functional. The truth-value of, for example, 'Arthur believes that p' does not depend on the truth-value of p. Propositions describing an intentional relation between a person and a proposition cannot without modification be incorporated into a truth-functional logical framework.

Again, propositions describing physical relations are *existentially quantifiable* with respect to the related terms. Thus $L(a, b)$ (e.g. a is to the left of b) logically implies $\exists x (x L b)$, $\exists y (a L y)$ and $\exists x \exists y (x L y)$. (There exists an object x such that x is to the left of b, there exists an object y such that a is to the left of y, there exists an x and a y such that x is to the left of y.) Both standard elementary logic and our three-valued logic permit such existential quantifications. Propositions describing intentional relations between a person and a non-propositional object are, as we have seen, not existentially quantifiable with respect to this object. For example 'Arthur desires the possession of the pipe smoked by Sherlock Holmes' does not logically imply that there exists a pipe which had been smoked by Sherlock Holmes and whose possession Arthur

---

[1] An adequate account of Wittgenstein's philosophy of mind cannot be given here. For the problem of conceptual change, see part 4

desires. Again, 'Arthur dreamt of Helen of Troy' does not logically imply that there exists (outside Arthur's dreams) an object of which he dreamt. Propositions describing an intentional relation between a person and an object cannot be incorporated *without modification* into a logical framework which contains the principle of existential quantification with respect to both the person and the object.

It is now clear that propositions about intentional relations or, briefly, intentional propositions must be modified if they are to be incorporated into standard elementary logic or our three-valued extension of it and, more particularly, if they are to be 'analysed' in terms of non-intentional propositions about physical phenomena. There are, however, very great differences of opinion as to the nature of the modification. Some philosophers hold that intentional relations are wholly spurious (or at least empty) and should be eliminated from discourse. Nothing would be lost by their elimination except confusion. Others hold that intentional propositions are 'equivalent' or 'reducible' to propositions about physical phenomena. Whether anything is lost by such an analysis depends of course on the notion of equivalence or reducibility, employed in the analysis. Lastly, some philosophers hold that intentional propositions constitute an important and independent class of propositions whose attempted 'reduction' to propositions about physical phenomena is based on the confusion of two entirely different types of propositions with each other. Let us consider some arguments which are put forward in support of each of these positions.

THE ALLEGED SPURIOUSNESS
OF INTENTIONAL PHENOMENA

It is sometimes argued that the concept of awareness (and therefore of intentionality) is inapplicable since its alleged application would lead to an infinite regress: I can truly assert that I am aware of something only if I am aware of my awareness of it; and I can truly assert that I am aware of my awareness of it, only if I am aware of my awareness of my awareness of it – and so forth *ad infinitum*, so that I can never truly assert that I am aware of something. But the correct application of 'I am aware of *x*' does not depend on a step by step traversal of an infinite sequence. It depends on learning to demarcate a class of situations by means of, among other things, examples and counter-examples. One of the countless examples is described by the true proposition that I am now aware of using my pen, one of the countless counter-examples by the false proposition that I am now aware of using my lawn-mower. That the demarcation of the class, and thus the correct application of 'I am aware of *x*', can be learned follows from the fact that it has been learned.

Another argument against the assumption that there are intentional phenomena is to point out that one day machines to which nobody would ascribe consciousness might be constructed, which imitate human behaviour so perfectly that it would be impossible to provide criteria for effectively distinguishing between a machine and a man. But to assert that the behaviour of an unconscious machine might be indistinguishable from that of a conscious person (or indeed a conscious machine) is not to imply that the person has no consciousness, nor, for that matter, that the machine has consciousness. A philosopher who distinguishes between conscious human beings including himself on the one hand, and unconscious beings, e.g. stones on the other, solely in terms of their external behaviour, must of course be impressed by the argument from the possibility of perfectly imitated human conduct. A person who – like myself – is aware of his awareness as distinct from his behaviour will admit that unconscious objects might perfectly simulate the external behaviour of conscious beings. But the possibility, or the fact, that an entity of one kind is in certain respects indistinguishable from an entity of another kind does not affect their difference in kind.

It may be a useful working assumption to take only the outward behaviour of people into account and to construct theories in which the concept of consciousness or awareness is not employed at all. Such is the procedure of methodological behaviourism. However, from the (very likely) true proposition that the concept of consciousness is not needed for the purposes of the psychological behaviourist it does not follow that the concept is empty. The doctrine that it *is* empty might, in order to distinguish it from methodological behaviourism, be called 'philosophical' or 'dogmatic' behaviourism.

THE PROBLEM OF REDUCIBILITY

Among the oldest philosophical problems is the so-called mind-body problem, i.e. the problem of the relation between mental and physical phenomena. One answer to the problem, the answer which we have just rejected, is simply to assert that the concept of an intentional or mental phenomenon is empty. Another is to admit that there are mental phenomena, but hold that they can be 'analyzed in terms of' physical phenomena. The reasonableness of this claim and the feasibility of its realization depend, of course, on what is meant by such an analysis. It will be useful to consider two kinds of such analyses, namely 'correlation' and 'reductive' analyses of mental in terms of physical phenomena.

By a 'correlation-analysis' of mental in terms of physical phenomena I understand any analysis which implies that there is a perfect correlation between mental and physical phenomena. That is to say that to every particular mental phenomenon there corresponds exactly one particular physical phenomenon such that neither can occur without the other. For example to my feeling of toothache at a certain time there corresponds on this account a certain neurophysiological process occurring at the same time in a certain region of my body. Such a correlation is compatible with most metaphysical theories about the relation between mind and body. It is, for example, compatible with a doctrine of complete psychophysical parallelism according to which bodies do not influence minds nor minds bodies. It is compatible with the doctrine of mental epiphenomenalism according to which only bodies exist as independent substances, while mental phenomena are dependent features of them. It is compatible with material epiphenomenalism according to which only minds exist as independent substances, while physical phenomena are dependent features of them. And it is compatible with a dualism which implies the existence of two kinds of independent and interacting substances.

A correlation analysis presupposes *two* kinds of phenomena which it correlates and thus cannot be used to reduce the two kinds to one kind. It is of course always possible to hold that neither mental nor physical phenomena have any independent existence, but are merely two different aspects of a reality which is strictly speaking neither mental nor physical. And it is possible to give this 'double-aspect theory' a linguistic form by saying that the language in terms of which we speak about the mental and that in which we speak about the physical are simply different languages devised to describe the same subject matter. Philosophers who hold such a theory are wont to appeal to an analogy based on the possibility of using attributes which have different sense (meaning, connotation), but the same reference (application, denotation). They say that just as 'evening star' and 'morning star' differ in sense, but refer to one and the same object, namely the planet Venus, so the 'mental' and the 'physical' languages only differ in sense and refer to the same subject matter. This, though perhaps far fetched, is not inconceivable. But, whilst we have good empirical evidence for the statement that 'morning star' and 'evening star' refer to one and the same object, we have no empirical evidence which would support the double-aspect theory rather than the correlation theory. Yet, the future may nevertheless lie with some form of a double-aspect theory.

A 'reduction analysis' of mental in terms of physical phenomena would have to show that mental phenomena are, contrary to first impressions, physical phenomena. It would have to show that propositions about mental phenomena are 'synonymous' with propositions about physical phenomena in the sense of which propositions about fathers are synonymous with propositions about male parents. Since the propositions about physical phenomena are embedded in a logical framework which is truth-functional and includes the principle of existential quantifiability for all individuals, whereas propositions about mental phenomena are embedded in a non-truth-functional logic which does not contain the principle of existential quantifiability, the reduction presupposes a reduction of the latter framework to the former. Such a reduction, however, is not possible though the proof of this apparently obvious fact involves technical considerations which are out of place here.

The practice of medicine depends to a large extent on correlations between physical and mental phenomena. A patient's report on a pain in a certain part of his body, or a feeling of pain in this region of his own body, will help a doctor to diagnose a state of the body, e.g. appendicitis. A certain physical state in a person's body, e.g. after some operations, will lead a doctor to expect reports on a mental depression, or if the doctor is also the patient, to expect the mental depression itself. Such correlations between two classes of phenomena imply their distinctness, and thus the incorrectness of dogmatic behaviourism.

However, the assumption of such correlations is no argument against methodological behaviourism, i.e. the thesis that for certain purposes a psychologist should proceed *as if* there were no mental phenomena. Behaviourist psychology – like physics, which also cannot do without simplifying assumptions – must be judged by its scientific and, in particular, its predictive successes and failures. To attack any simplification merely because it is a simplification is almost as naïve as to defend it on the ground that it describes what it simplifies. The first of these errors is often found in the writings of philosophers of mind, the second in the philosophical *obiter dicta* of scientific psychologists.

THEORIES OF TRUTH

Although the notion of a true proposition was essential to our characterization of mental phenomena and to much else that has been said, no analysis of the notion of a true proposition has so far been given. The following remarks are intended to remedy this defect, if it is a defect, to some extent. First of all a few words on the notion of a proposition. Not every string of words embodies a proposition. For a string of words to embody a proposition it must be used in a certain manner, which I shall not try to characterize, as a proposition. A parrot's utterance 'Brutus murdered Caesar' does not embody a proposition. Are there propositions apart from strings of words embodying them – are there, as it were, disembodied propositions which are not clothed in language? I am inclined to think that there are, but shall leave the question open. Are there propositions which exist independently of being apprehended by a person? I am inclined to think that the answer depends on linguistic conventions only, but shall leave this question too an open one.

The oldest, and, it would seem, the most natural analysis of truth is the so-called 'correspondence-theory' of truth which is due to Aristotle.[1] Every proposition expresses something as being the case. A proposition is true if, and only if, what it expresses as being the case is the case; and it is false if, and only if, what it expresses as being the case is not the case. The theory may be supplemented by Leibniz's distinction between what is the case in the actual world and what is the case in a merely possible world, e.g. an imagined world. We then can distinguish between (a) contingently true propositions which express what is the case only in the actual world; (b) logically true propositions which express what is the case in all possible worlds; and (c) 'ideally true' or ideal propositions which express what is the case only in a possible world. A correspondence theory of this kind has been constructed by A. Tarski[2] in great detail. In the light of what has been said earlier about alternative logics,[3] we would have to relativize this theory by admitting that what is to count as a possible world may depend

[1] *Metaphysics* book IV, 1011b
[2] 'Der Wahrheitsbegriff in den formalisierten Sprachen', *Studia Philosophica*, vol. 1 (1936), original in Polish (1930–31)
[3] See pages 55 ff

on which of the available (or yet to be constructed) logical theories one decides to adopt. Instead, however, of discussing these and other versions of Aristotle's correspondence theory I shall examine some arguments, which objectors to it regard as fatal to all its versions.

According to the correspondence theory of truth, the notion of truth is an attribute, more particularly a relation between a proposition and something non-propositional. This is denied by some philosophers who hold that truth is not an attribute at all. The latter view was, as far as I know, first propounded by F. P. Ramsey who described the locutions 'is true' and 'is false' as used merely 'for emphasis or stylistic reasons, or to indicate the position occupied by the statement in our argument'.[1] The merit of Ramsey's point must be judged in the light of his philosophical concerns. He wanted to show that for certain purposes of logic – in particular his own reconstruction of Russell's and Whitehead's *Principia Mathematica* – the attribute of truth was not needed. And this redundancy might be admitted without concluding that truth is not an attribute. Again, it can be admitted that in many contexts the locutions 'is true' and 'is false' are used in the manner to which Ramsey draws attention.

Yet they are not always used in this way. When somebody says that all propositions can be divided into two jointly exhaustive and mutually exclusive classes, namely those that are true and those that are false, he is using 'true' and 'false' as attributes of propositions. He is similarly using 'true' as an attribute of propositions when he says that even the most inveterate liar occasionally asserts a true proposition. These statements are comparable with the following two statements, in which we use 'mathematical' as an attribute of propositions: the statement that all propositions can be divided into two jointly exhaustive and mutually exclusive classes, i.e. those that are and those that are not mathematical; and the statement that even the most inveterate hater of mathematics occasionally asserts a mathematical proposition. It is difficult to conceive of

[1] *The Foundations of Mathematics* (London 1931), page 142

any general philosophical account of the relation between language and what it expresses which would dispense with the attribute 'true'. But even if such an account were possible, it would not show that 'truth' is never actually used as an attribute. It is, of course, an attribute of a special kind – an attribute of propositions, statements, or perhaps even sentences, and not of, e.g., things or words. Indeed, if those philosophers who hold that 'truth' is not an attribute would explain more clearly what they mean by 'attribute', the disagreement might turn out to be merely verbal.

Another objection to all versions of the correspondence theory of truth is that it involves a vicious infinite regress. To assert that the truth of a proposition consists in its correspondence with a non-propositional something is presumably to assert a true proposition. The proposition asserting the correspondence must itself correspond to a non-propositional something; and the proposition expressing this second-order correspondence must, if true, again correspond to a non-propositional something. In this manner we are driven to propositions expressing correspondences of increasingly higher order, without ever coming to an end. But this objection is just as groundless as the objection, considered earlier, that the concept of awareness leads to an infinite regress. It is not the case that in order to understand a correspondence–statement of the first order we must go through an infinite sequence of correspondence statements.

In order to appreciate the correspondence theory of truth it is important to see how small its claims are. It merely explains *non-logical* truth as a relation between propositions and something non-propositional which they express as being the case. It does not imply that what a proposition expresses as being the case can, or cannot, be grasped apart from being so expressed. It does not imply a one-to-one correspondence between propositions and their subject-matter but is compatible with different ways of apprehending the world through propositions. It does not imply that propositions can, or cannot, express their subject matter completely. Lastly it only claims to provide an analysis of the notion of truth, and not a general criterion of truth. The correspondence-theory does not claim to help us to decide whether an empirical generalization or other contingent proposition is true, but only tells us that if it is true, then it corresponds to a non-propositional something. It does not even help us to decide whether propositions which we regard as having a truth-value do or do not have it. Thus it does not help us to decide whether propositions expressing moral convictions are, or are not, merely disguised rules of conduct; or whether they are, or are not, merely disguised expressions of likes or dislikes. The correspondence theory of truth, then, says very little; and it is mainly this paucity of content which renders it immune to most objections which have been raised against it.

Those who, like Ramsey, object to the correspondence theory of truth on the ground that truth is not an attribute of propositions have to show that, and how, one can get by without employing such an attribute. The other objectors have to propose alternative analyses of the attribute. To this group belong the proponents of the so-called 'self-evidence' and 'coherence' theories of truth, both of which go back at least as far as Descartes' conception of the proper method in philosophy and science.[1] The former lean heavily on notions of self-evidence which remind one of Descartes' 'clear and distinct' indubitabilities, the latter on notions of necessary connection which remind one of Descartes' peculiar concept of a 'necessary connection'. Both descendants have inherited some of the shortcomings of their common ancestor.

According to the self-evidence theory of truth a proposition is true if, and only if, it is self-evident or, though not self-evident, logically implied by self-evident premises. The theory is open to two serious objections. First, as has been pointed out earlier, it regards a feeling or conviction of self-evidence as a sufficient condition of truth, although such feelings or convictions may – and do – change both in the same person and from person to person. Experience shows that feelings or convic-

[1] See pages 21 f

tions of self-evidence may be deceptive, and the theory provides no criteria for distinguishing between those which are and those which are not deceptive. Second, even if one were to agree that there are absolutely self-evident propositions – e.g. some reports about inner experiences or mathematical constructions – it has not been shown that these propositions *logically imply* all other true propositions; nor is it at all clear how this could be shown. As Descartes knew, the set of the *logical* consequences of any set of premisses is never richer in content than the premisses themselves. Yet only if the logical consequences were richer in content than the premisses could all truths be logically implied by self-evident truths. For this reason Descartes rejects *logical* deduction as a means of expanding knowledge and introduces his own notion of 'deduction' by means of non-logical, necessary connexions between propositions.

All coherence theories of truth employ such an obscure, non-logical, yet necessary connexion between propositions. Let us, for the moment, call this unanalysed notion 'involvement' and speak of propositions 'involving' other propositions in the same manner in which we speak of propositions 'logically implying' other propositions. In terms of the notion of involvement we can define the concept of a 'coherent set of propositions' and of a 'true proposition' and state the fundamental thesis of the coherence-theory of truth. A set of propositions is coherent if, and only if, (*a*) every proposition of the set involves every other proposition of the set, (*b*) every proposition which is involved by a proposition belonging to the set belongs itself to the set. A proposition is true – in the sense of the coherence theory – if, and only if, it belongs to a coherent set. The fundamental thesis of the coherence theory is: there is one and only one coherent set of propositions. The famous archetype of such a coherence theory of truth is the philosophy of Hegel who, however, talks of involvement not between propositions, but between attributes. He sets out to show that starting with the attribute of pure Being one can find out how it involves all the other attributes of reality and how all these attributes involve each other.[1] The Hegelian archetype is still recognizable in many of Hegel's idealist and materialist followers.

Before criticizing this theory one may well ask whence it might have derived its plausibility. The answer lies, I think, in the fact that many types of reasoning seem to fit it. Imagine, for example, a palaeontologist who finds the petrified imprint of a little toe. From it he reconstructs first the foot, then the leg, then the skeleton, then the organs, then the whole animal, then its narrower environment, its wider environment, etc. Again, remember your favourite detective, provided that he is a thinker rather than a doer, who from the tiniest clue will reconstruct a whole complex crime. However, if such reasonings are examined more closely, especially by making the reasoner's implicit premisses explicit, it will soon become clear that it proceeds by ordinary logical deductions, ordinary inductions and, very likely, lucky guesses. The appearance of an unanalysed 'involvement' between propositions is thus explained by familiar relations.

The difficulties to which the coherence theory of truth in every version (known to me) gives rise all stem from the notion of 'involvement'. Some writers use this relation between propositions as if it were a 'very strong' logical implication which they could easily explain if they were not prevented from doing so by pressure of more important work. But there is no known notion of logical implication – understood as the converse of logical deducibility – such that any true proposition logically implies any other. There is no known notion of logical implication such that e.g. the proposition that Brutus murdered Caesar 'logically implies' that all magnetized pieces of iron attract iron filings in their vicinity. How one would have to strengthen any of the available logical implications to achieve this, is not at all clear. Indeed it is not even clear what is meant by such 'strengthening'.

Ironically, there is one 'if – then' relation which, if taken for the relation of involvement, would have the consequence that

[1] See pages 220 f

every true proposition 'involves' every other true proposition, and which would make true the thesis that there exists one and only one 'coherent' set of propositions. This relation is none other than the truth-functional conditional '$p \rightarrow q$'. For according to the truth-table defining it every true proposition implies every other true proposition.[1] However, to define involvement by the truth-functional implication would be abhorrent to any coherence theorist, since he regards involvement as a relation between meanings and not truth-values. More seriously, the truth-functional conditional is itself defined in terms of truth and one could thus not without circularity define truth in terms of coherence, coherence in terms of involvement and involvement as the truth-functional conditional.

[1] See page 42

Part 3

THE PHILOSOPHY
OF ACTION
AND VALUE

Introduction

The topics of the preceding part of this book stem mainly from reflection about matters of fact. The topics of this part arise mainly from reflection about practical possibilities and their evaluation. This division, which corresponds to the traditional division of philosophy into theoretical and practical philosophy, is not the only possible one. Thus one might quite reasonably consider most of the topics of this part of the book, at least in so far as they concern mental phenomena, as being part of the philosophy of mind. The usual divisions of philosophy into branches are, as has already been emphasized, a matter of pedagogical convenience rather than of substance.

Chapter 7 contains the bare bones of an analysis of the concept of action, which is fundamental to practical philosophy, and some brief remarks on the structure of practical and evaluative thinking. In chapter 8 I shall discuss some topics of moral philosophy and aesthetics which belong to the pure theory of value. The next chapter will be devoted to political philosophy, which is to some extent applied moral theory, and to the philosophy of history, since history is largely an attempt at recording, explaining and – at least for some historians – evaluating human actions. Chapter 10, the last chapter of this part, deals with some topics in the philosophy of religion and might have been included under the general heading of metaphysics. Its inclusion under the heading of the philosophy of action and value is justified by the historical fact that the problem of the relation between religion and morality has been regarded as fundamental by many philosophers of religion and by many moral philosophers.

The range of the problems which fall under the heading of this part of the book is vast and there is much disagreement not only about the proper strategy in tackling them, but also about their relative philosophical importance. Thus any selection of topics which seems natural to some will seem perversely idiosyncratic to others.

7. The Concept of Action and the Formal Structure of Practical Reasoning

An action is a deliberate intervention or non-intervention by a human being in the course of nature. A person engaged on practical deliberations which are to result in an action or course of action will normally try to ascertain first of all which courses of nature are empirically possible successors to the situation in which he finds himself. He will next try to ascertain which of these empirical possibilities he can bring about. Finally, he will evaluate these practical options in accordance with his explicit or implicit prudential or moral convictions. Before examining the nature and content of these convictions it is necessary to analyse *the concept of action* and to exhibit the formal structure of practical reasoning, at least in outline.

A few preliminary definitions will make these tasks easier. We shall need a term for the conjunctions of features which are changing or capable of changing and which may characterize a particular region of space during a particular interval of time. I shall use the term 'Event' (with a capital E) for this purpose. The term thus covers not only events in the narrow sense, e.g. a clap of thunder, in which one or more features of a region of space change relatively quickly, but also states of affairs, whose features are relatively stable, processes in which changes occur in regular patterns, etc. A kind of Event which is of particular interest in analysing the notion of an action is bodily behaviour or bodily conduct, i.e. the occurrence or non-occurrence of a bodily movement or sequence of such movements. Whatever is incapable of characterizing a particular region of space during a particular interval of time is not an Event. Thus timeless mathematical truths, laws of nature, moral principles, do not describe Events. While using 'Event' as a generic term, I shall continue to use more specific terms, such as 'situation', 'event', etc.

I shall say that an Event E 'predetermines' a later Event F if, and only if, the occurrence of F depends *exclusively* on the occurrence of E – and not, for example, if it depends also on the occurrence of some other Event or on something other than an Event. In a similar manner I shall speak of a sequence of Events, say $E_1 \ldots E_n$, predetermining another sequence of Events, say $F_1 \ldots F_m$. I have chosen the term '*pre*-determination', as opposed to 'determination', in order to indicate that the dependence in question holds between temporally antecedent Events and their temporal successors. The nature of this predetermination may be left open. It has been variously conceived, e.g. as magical causation, as teleological causation, as causation after the fashion of classical mechanics or as 'probabilification' in the sense that the occurrence of an Event has a definite probability which depends exclusively on some or all of the temporally antecedent Events.

An action involves bodily behaviour, i.e. involves an Event consisting in the occurrence or non-occurrence of a bodily movement or a sequence of such movements. Suppose the bodily behaviour B is preceded by an Event E or by a sequence of Events $E_1 \ldots E_n$ and succeeded by an Event F or a sequence of Events $F_1 \ldots F_m$. This may be indicated schematically by the sequences $E\,B\,F$, $E_1 \ldots E_n\,B\,F$, $E\,B\,F_1 \ldots F_m$ and $E_1 \ldots E_n\,B\,F_1 \ldots F_m$. By itself bodily behaviour does not constitute an action. To do this it must fulfil three groups of conditions which, partly following legal terminology, might be called 'objective', 'subjective' and 'concordance' conditions. *Objectively* B together with the Event or sequence of Events preceding it must predetermine the succeeding Event or sequence of Events. This might be put schematically as $E B$ *predetermines* F or $E_1 \ldots E_n B$ *predetermines* F or $E B$ *predetermines* $F_1 \ldots F_m$ or $E_1 \ldots E_n B$ *predetermines* $F_1 \ldots F_m$. For example, E might be an Event described as a car, with a man at the driving wheel, approaching a left-hand turning, B a movement of the driver's hands to the left, F the car's continuing its journey to the left.

Subjectively the person 'to whom the body belongs' must (*a*) choose the bodily conduct in the sense that his bodily conduct must be accompanied by the impression of being chosen; (*b*) he must believe that his chosen bodily conduct together with its antecedent Event or sequence of Events predetermines a more or less clearly specified succeeding Event or sequence of Events; (*c*) he must intend the so expected Event or a member of the expected sequence of Events to happen. There must, lastly, be a certain *concordance* between the actual sequence of Events and the sequence which is expected and intended, i.e. between the objective and the subjective aspects of the action. In a weaker sense of the word an action need not satisfy the conditions (*b*) and (*c*). But we shall be concerned only with actions in the stronger sense, in which every action is deliberate. (If this is regarded as a solecism, the term 'action' as subsequently used should everywhere be replaced by 'deliberate action'.)

An action may be more or less deliberate, the degree of its deliberateness depending on the strength of the acting person's beliefs and desires. One may, for example, 'half-believe' that something will happen and 'half-intend' it to happen. Again an action may be more or less successful, the degree of success depending on the extent of the concordance between what the person believed and intended and what actually happened. Most legal systems distinguish in various ways between more or less deliberate, and between more or less successful, actions.

My explanation of the meaning of 'action' covers both positive actions in which the chosen bodily conduct consists in bodily movements, and negative actions in which it consists in the absence of such movements. A negative action must be distinguished from a mere non-action where neither the occurrence nor the non-occurrence of bodily movements is chosen. It must also be distinguished from an omission, which implies that an action was not done, though for some reason it *should* have been done. The notion of an omission, unlike that of a (positive or negative) action, presupposes some moral, legal or other obligation. The subjective aspects of an action – defined in terms of choosing, believing and desiring – are clearly intentional in the sense of the term given to it in the preceding chapter.

To the subjective and objective aspects of an action there correspond two characteristic points of view. We may look at it from the point of view of an external observer, in particular a natural scientist, to whom an action is nothing but an Event in the physical world involving a human body, conceived as a very complex physical object which is in no way exempt from the laws which govern the course of physical nature. On the other hand, we may look at an action from the point of view of the agent. This we always do, as far as our own body is concerned, when we are engaged in acting and practical deliberations, and sometimes when, even though we are not the agents, we wish to understand another person's actions and deliberations 'from the inside'. From the inside the bodily behaviour, which constitutes the physical aspect of an action, *appears* very often, if not always, as not only chosen, but 'freely' chosen.

Let us consider the following brief monologue in which a person, engaged in practical deliberation, talks about his impression of choosing freely: 'My body is now in a certain situation (Event) E; more particularly, I am sitting at the driving wheel of my car which is approaching a left turning. I am under the impression of being free to choose between, at least, two different kinds of bodily behaviour (Events) B and B', more particularly between my hands moving or not moving the driving wheel to the left. If B is chosen and occurs, then another Event F will follow, more particularly, the car will turn to the left; whereas if B' is chosen and occurs, a different Event F' will follow, more particularly, the car will continue in the original direction. Schematically speaking, I am under the impression of being free to choose between the sequence of Events $E\,B\,F$ and $E\,B'\,F'$.'

This total impression comprises three separate impressions which the practical thinker cannot avoid, even if in view of his philosophical opinions or for other reasons he regards them as illusory. They are (i) the impression that neither B nor B' are predetermined and that *a fortiori* they are not predetermined by E, (ii) the impression that the sequence $E\,B$ predetermines F and that the sequence $E\,B'$ predetermines F'; (iii) that the choice between $E\,B\,F$ and $E\,B'\,F'$ originates *somehow* in the agent, his mind or will, in a manner which is not wholly determined by his past.

Our description of the impression of choosing freely, and of actions performed or planned under this impression, gives rise to a number of metaphysical problems or, as some would have it, pseudoproblems. First, is our impression that we have freedom of choice ever correct; and if so how, if at all, can we distinguish between occasions on which we are free and occasions on which we merely seem to be free? Second, how can we make sense of a statement describing the impression that the choice between two sequences of Events originates within us, in a sense which implies that our chosen bodily behaviour is not wholly dependent on antecedent Events? If, in particular, our conduct is not predetermined by Events is it wholly undetermined or is it partly determined by non-Events? What could a determination which is not a predetermination be like? Third, if there is a determination of chosen bodily behaviour by non-Events, how is this determination related to the predetermination of behaviour by Events? Is there, in particular, a conflict between the external, especially the scientific, and the internal, especially the agent's, view of his freedom of choice? These questions will be considered in the fourth part of this book (chapter 14). In the meantime I shall try to exhibit some features of practical reasoning, without worrying whether actions or bodily behaviour are ever grounded in a freedom of choice which is more than an impression.

ON THE FORMAL STRUCTURE OF REASONING ABOUT REALIZABLE AND UNREALIZABLE COURSES OF ACTION

A person's practical deliberations concern not only isolated actions, but courses of action. He may, for example, ask himself which courses of action, if any, are open to him if he wishes to be in time for a meeting, to avoid an unpleasant encounter or to become president of the United States. Considering a course of action involves imagining a sequence of Events, one or more subsequences of which are actions. Schematically, an imagined course of action might be represented by: $A \ldots E_1 B_1 F_1 \ldots E_2 B_2 F_2 \ldots Z$. For example, A could be a situation in which a person starts worrying about being late at a meeting, $E_1 B_1 F_1$ his action of calling a taxi, $E_2 B_2 F_2$ the action of sitting down in the taxi, and Z the Event of arriving at the meeting-place.

Anybody engaged in practical deliberations is vitally interested in establishing as best he can which of his imaginable courses of action are realizable and which unrealizable, and in making correct inferences from established statements of realizability and unrealizability to other such statements. Among the tools which help us to exhibit *some* structural features of this kind of thinking is intuitionist logic, the elements of which have been explained earlier in an altogether different context.[1] But the relevance of this logic to an analysis of thinking about actions should not really come as a surprise. After all, intuitionist logic has been conceived as the logic of thinking about mathematical constructions and a mathematical construction is, whatever else it may be, also a course of action.

Our task is simply to interpret the symbols, expressions and operations of intuitionist logic as referring not to mathematical thinking, but to thinking about courses of action. Let us, then, use small Roman letters, a, b, c, etc. for variables ranging over propositions describing courses of actions (not mathematical constructions) and the same letters with subscripts, a_0, b_0, c_0,

[1] See chapter 4

etc. for constant propositions, describing specified courses of action. Thus a_0 might stand for the proposition describing the course of action mentioned in our example, where a person is worried about missing his meeting.

We remember that in intuitionist logic a proposition is assertable if, and only if, it can be proved by a mathematical construction. In practical thinking the role of a mathematical construction is played by what may be called a 'practical construction'. A practical construction of a course of action shows (a) that it is *compatible* with the best available empirical knowledge to assume that the apparently freely chosen bodily behaviour is one of at least two alternatives which – together with their predecessors – predetermine different succeeding sequences of Events, e.g., phoning and not phoning for a taxi, and (b) that, with the exception of the bodily behaviour which is assumed to be freely chosen, every Event in the course of action is in accordance with the best available empirical knowledge predetermined by all or some of its predecessors. Since what is considered the best available empirical knowledge changes from one group of persons to another and also changes in the course of time, the notion of a practical construction of the courses of action open to an agent cannot be clearly demarcated once and for all. This ambiguity does not, however, affect the following formal considerations.

Having explained what we mean by a proposition describing a course of action, as well as by a practical construction of a course of action, we can now apply the definitions, axioms and theorems of intuitionist logic, with obvious modifications, to reasoning about courses of action.[1] A proposition a_0, describing a course of action, is assertable if, and only if, we possess a practical construction of the course of action. If a_0 is assertable, then the corresponding course of action is established as realizable or is demonstrably realizable. A proposition $\neg a_0$ is assertable if, and only if, the assumption that a practical construction proving a_0 has been carried out leads to a contradiction. If $\neg a_0$ is assertable, then the course of action described

[1] See page 64 ff

by a_0 is demonstrably unrealizable. Similarly $\neg\,\neg\,a_0$ is assertable if, and only if, the assumption that a practical construction proving $\neg\,a_0$ has been carried out leads to a contradiction. If $\neg\,\neg\,a_0$ is assertable, then the course of action described by a_0 is demonstrably not demonstrably unrealizable. (This does *not* mean that it is realizable.) The definitions of conjunction, e.g., $a_0 \wedge b_0$, of disjunction, e.g., $a_0 \vee b_0$, and of implication, e.g., $a_0 \to b_0$, are the intuitionist definitions given earlier.[1] If we adopt the above interpretation of the formal system of intuitionist logic it becomes applicable to a fairly large area of thinking about realizable and unrealizable courses of action.

Instead of going into further details I shall set down some theorems and non-theorems. We remember that $a \vee \neg\,a$ and $\neg\,\neg\,a \to a$ are not valid in intuitionist logic. This is as it should be; it is indeed not true that any course of action is either demonstrably realizable or demonstrably unrealizable. And it is not true that if a course of action is demonstrably not demonstrably unrealizable it is, therefore, demonstrably realizable. On the other hand, $a \to \neg\,\neg\,a$ is valid, which is again as it should be, since if a course of action is demonstrably realizable, it is demonstrably not demonstrably unrealizable. In the case of more complex intuitionist theorems and non-theorems we find a similar agreement with our unformalized reasoning about realizable and unrealizable courses of action. Our analysis is, at best, incomplete. It would among other things have to be supplemented by distinguishing between different kinds of predetermination, in particular causal necessitation and probabilification, and by taking account of the inexactness of empirical predicates. (Last, but not least, it could be much improved in the light of recent work by logicians on the interpretation of intuitionist logic.[2])

[1] See page 65
[2] See e.g. S. A. Kripke, 'Semantical Interpretation of Intuitionist Logic I', *Formal Systems and Recursive Functions*, eds. J. N. Crossley and M. A. E. Dummett (Amsterdam 1965)

ON THE FORMAL STRUCTURE OF EVALUATIVE THINKING

Some of the courses of action which he judges to be realizable the practical thinker also regards as optional in the sense that he regards himself as capable of choosing between either realizing or not realizing them. These optional courses of action he evaluates either from the point of his own interest only, or from his moral point of view. Moral points of view, e.g. that of an early Christian or of a medieval Samurai, may differ in substance; what is fitting from one point of view may be unfitting from another. The existence of different moral points of view or, to speak more cautiously, of apparently different moral points of view, raises some of the most difficult and controversial problems of ethics. For the moment, however, I shall be concerned with questions of a formal rather than of a substantive character.

In morally evaluating an action or course of action one associates its non-moral attributes with its moral attributes. The evaluation may consist in the explicit application of criteria. A criterion is a finite conjunction of non-moral attributes with which a moral attribute is judged to be invariably associated. For example, deliberately telling another person an untruth might be judged to be unfitting in all circumstances, and fulfilling a promise given to another person might be judged to be fitting in all circumstances. The criteria can be more complex, for example when formulated by a person who believes that in certain well-defined circumstances telling a lie is morally preferable to telling the truth, or breaking a promise to keeping it. The important feature of evaluation by criteria is that there should be available a (finite) number of finite conjunctions of non-evaluative attributes by the application of which any action or course of action is judged fitting or unfitting. If this is the case, I shall call the evaluative notions 'exhaustible (by criteria)'.

A person's moral evaluation of actions and courses of action may be 'inexhaustible (by criteria)'. He may find that whenever he attempts to list moral criteria which are applicable in all circumstances, the criteria prove inadequate because he can always imagine circumstances which are not covered by the list. Even if his imagination is not vivid enough, unforeseen experiences may force him to admit that his criteria are insufficient and that his moral judgements and reactions defy exhaustion by criteria. This is often expressed by saying that in the last resort every case must be judged on its merits or in the light of all its individual circumstances. It seems plausible to assume that some persons and some groups of persons employ exhaustible notions of fittingness while others employ inexhaustible ones. Most moral philosophers have argued that there is only *one* notion of fittingness, but some take it to be exhaustible, others inexhaustible.

The application of inexhaustible notions of fittingness cannot be summarized by rules for inferring their applicability from the applicability of non-evaluative attributes. It is a matter of tact, instinct, and a sense of proportion. And it is not susceptible of generally recognized and easily manageable public checks, even where such checks are highly desirable in ensuring social co-operation. Because of these difficulties evaluative reasoning in terms of inexhaustible evaluative notions – or of evaluative notions which are exhaustible only by unmanageably complex criteria – calls for simplifications bearing a limited analogy to the simplifications by which empirical thinking overcomes the inexactness of empirical concepts and other features, where these prove an obstacle rather than an advantage.

Whereas in empirical thinking the simplifications consist mainly in the construction and employment of scientific theories (see chapter 5), in evaluative thinking they mostly take the form of the construction and employment of sets of maxims. Both kinds of simplification pay the price of some misrepresentation of their original subject matter, in exchange for great gains in clarity, inferential efficiency and the degree to which checks by other people become available. Both achieve these aims by restricting, or otherwise modifying, a prior vocabulary and prior methods of reasoning. Both, by focussing attention on some features of their prior subject matter while neglecting others, lead to the replacement of one complex and comparatively difficult conceptual schema by a plurality of more easily manageable ones: the one physical world is replaced by a plurality of simplified systems as conceived by different physical theories; and the one world of fitting and unfitting courses of action is replaced by a plurality of simplified systems as conceived by different sets of maxims.

A maxim is a conditional proposition of the following form: 'If a person is involved in an Event describable as . . . then he is to conduct himself in a manner describable as . . . .' A maxim thus consists of a descriptive antecedent and a prescriptive or regulative consequent. The descriptive antecedent might, for example, be 'if a young man finds himself sitting in a crowded bus in which an old lady is standing'. The regulative consequent might be (*a*) 'he is to leave his seat' or (*b*) 'he is to leave his seat, persuade the old lady to sit down in it and protect her from being unseated by any of the other passengers'. In the first example the regulative consequent merely requires the occurrence of bodily behaviour, in the second example it requires that the bodily behaviour be followed by a sequence of Events interspersed by more than one instance of bodily behaviour. The distinction between these two kinds of regulative consequent is not sharp and is not important for our present purpose.

Let us call a statement 'the descriptive counterpart of a maxim', if it describes in sequence what the descriptive antecedent of the maxim describes and what its regulative consequent requires. For example, the maxim 'If in E, to perform B' has for its descriptive counterpart a proposition which simply describes the sequence $E\,B$. To every set of maxims there corresponds thus the set of their descriptive counterparts.

In the analysis of the structure of thinking about optional courses of action which are fitting or unfitting *with respect to* a set of accepted maxims the intuitionist logic is again of some use. A suitable interpretation of its symbols, expressions and operations is the following. Let us use small Greek letters

α, β, γ, etc. for variables ranging over propositions describing optional actions or courses of action, and the same letters with subscripts α_0, β_0, γ_0, etc. for constant propositions describing specified optional actions or courses of action. Thus α_0 might stand for the proposition describing the optional course of action of a polite and determined young man who, as in our example, finds himself sitting in a crowded bus in which an old lady is standing, leaves his seat and protects the lady from being unseated by the other passengers.

We remember, once again, that in intuitionist logic a proposition is assertable if, and only if, it can be backed by a mathematical construction. In the evaluation of optional courses of action with respect to a set of maxims the role of a mathematical construction is played by an 'evaluative construction' with respect to the given set of maxims. An evaluative construction of an optional course of action shows that the course of action is described by the descriptive counterpart of a maxim belonging to the set of maxims. We now proceed as we did in exhibiting the structure of reasoning about realizable and unrealizable courses of action.

A statement α_0 describing an optional course of action is assertable if, and only if, we possess an evaluative construction of the course of action. If α_0 is assertable then the corresponding optional course of action is established as fitting or is demonstrably fitting. A proposition $\neg \alpha_0$ is assertable if, and only if, the assumption that an evaluative construction proving α_0 has been carried out leads to a contradiction. If $\neg \alpha_0$ is assertable then the optional course of action described by α_0 is demonstrably unfitting. Similarly $\neg \neg \alpha_0$ is assertable if, and only if, the assumption that an evaluative construction proving $\neg \alpha_0$ has been carried out leads to a contradiction. If $\neg \neg \alpha_0$ is assertable, then the optional course of action described by α_0 is demonstrably not demonstrably unfitting. Conjunction, e.g. $\alpha_0 \wedge \beta_0$, disjunction, e.g. $\alpha_0 \vee \beta_0$, and implication, e.g. $\alpha_0 \rightarrow \beta_0$ are defined in the usual intuitionist manner.

Instead of going into further details I shall, as before, set down some theorems and non-theorems. Thus $\alpha \vee \neg\, \alpha$ and $\neg\, \neg\, \alpha \rightarrow \alpha$ are not theorems. It is indeed not true that any optional course of action is either demonstrably fitting or demonstrably unfitting, since it may be indifferent. On the other hand $\alpha \rightarrow \neg\, \neg\, \alpha$ is a theorem which corresponds to the obvious inference that if an optional course of action is demonstrably fitting it is demonstrably not demonstrably unfitting. In the case of more complex intuitionist theorems and non-theorems we find a similar agreement with our unformalized reasoning about fitting and unfitting optional courses of action. The analysis of evaluation by maxims and of normative thinking in general can be taken very much further by designing formal systems expressly for the purpose of such an analysis.[1]

The multiplicity of sets of maxims replacing an original moral evaluation by means of inexhaustible, or unmanageably complex exhaustible, notions of fittingness may, as in the analogous case of scientific theories, lead to conflicts between different sets of maxims. It may be, for example, that an action of mine which is fitting when judged by the code of my profession is unfitting when judged by the code of polite behaviour. A common and effective way of resolving such conflicts between sets of maxims is to arrange the sets in a hierarchical order. The superiority, e.g. of my professional code over the code of polite behaviour is expressed by the restrictive rule that no optional course of action which is unfitting with respect to my professional code is to count as fitting with respect to my code of polite behaviour. In this way we may correct some of the crudeness which results from replacing the one method of direct evaluation by a plurality of specialized sets of maxims.

What has been said about the formal structure of evaluative reasoning from a particular moral point of view applies with obvious modifications also to the formal structure of evaluative reasoning from a particular prudential point of view. I have so far said nothing about the moral or prudential evaluation of

[1] Compare in particular G. H. von Wright, *Norm and Action – A Logical Enquiry* (London 1963)

courses of action in terms of the relations 'equal in value' and 'greater in value'. Such ranking seems to play a greater role in economics than it does in ethics, where the classification of courses of action into fitting, unfitting and not unfitting ones is usually considered sufficient.

The relation between theoretical economics and common-sense thinking about economic transactions can be expected to be in some ways analogous to the relation between theoretical physics and commonsense thinking about the physical world. I must be content to mention one rather obvious analogy. We saw (chapter 5) that whereas perceptual equality or indistinguishability is non-transitive, mathematical equality as used in theoretical physics is transitive. The mathematical framework of physics enforces the replacement of non-transitive perceptual by transitive mathematical equality. It is not difficult to convince oneself that our evaluative discrimination is no sharper than our perceptual discrimination, especially as the former depends to a large extent on the latter. The assumption of transitive evaluative equality, which is made in most economic theories, is thus an idealization of a non-transitive relation.

Even the most thorough analysis of the structure of evaluative reasoning could not determine our conduct in concrete situations, since the ability to reason correctly from premisses to conclusions neither requires nor implies the truth of the premisses used. If it is to serve as a guide to conduct, the philosophy of value must proceed beyond merely formal considerations.

8. Philosophy as a Guide to Moral and Aesthetic Evaluation

From the mainly formal preliminaries of the preceding chapter I now turn to the consideration of specific moral views which are to enable us to judge concrete actions or courses of action as morally fitting, unfitting or not unfitting. In doing so I shall not attempt to enumerate and classify all the moral theories which have so far been proposed. Instead I shall, after some remarks on ethical method, briefly examine the moral content of three important and influential ethical systems, namely those of Kant, Aristotle and the Utilitarians.

Among the most striking features of moral experience are the occurrence of inner moral conflicts and of moral disagreements. Moral philosophy must attempt their clarification and resolution, a task which unavoidably raises the question whether morality is relative or absolute. More particularly, do moral conflicts and disagreements concern propositions, whose truth or falsehood is independent of differences between persons and societies, or, at least, moral rules or attitudes whose adoption is inseparable from human nature; or do they concern conventions and attitudes which are changeable, and which in fact change in the course of social development? Not so long ago any mention of relative morality was taken by most thoughtful and well-intentioned people as a sure sign of general moral decay. Today, by contrast, one finds, even amongst theologians, those who defend the thesis of relative morality as a condition of moral health. However, both verdicts are largely based on a confusion between an academic question about the logical status of moral judgements and the question of a person's or society's moral fibre. One may believe that one's moral convictions are relative and yet be ready to die for them. And one may write tomes in defence of absolute morality without making the slightest concessions to its demands when they clash with one's self-interest. Again, a conversion from belief in absolute to belief in relative morality, or vice versa, may leave a person's moral convictions quite untouched. Our convictions about racial integration, capital punishment, abortion and other large and small moral issues are – whether absolute or relative – moral convictions and not simply dependent on what we regard as convenient to ourselves.

The content of moral convictions can be expressed in terms of (allegedly) eternal truths or of changeable or unchangeable conventions or attitudes. But how can philosophers discover and critically examine this content? The answer is that the methods of moral philosophy are the methods of all philosophizing; phenomenological description of the modest kind, exhibition and replacement-analysis and metaphysical speculation. There is no need to repeat in detail what has been said earlier about these matters.[1] Yet it may be worthwhile to say once more that not all inner moral conflicts and not all moral disagreements rest on linguistic confusions. It may turn out that our ordinary moral thinking is inadequate to extraordinary situations, that it contains unsuspected gaps, ambiguities, internal inconsistencies, or that it is incompatible with assumptions considered fundamental in other spheres of thought. Aristotle's views on slavery[2] are a good example of the way in which the results of an inquiry into ordinary moral thinking is modified by general metaphysical assumptions. He agrees with his contemporaries that the institution of slavery is not immoral – but only because some men are 'slaves by

---

[1] See chapter 2
[2] *Nicomachean Ethics*, book VIII, 1161a 35 ff

nature'. Even so he defines the concept of a natural slave in such a manner that nowadays most people would reject the definition as wholly inadequate to both their ordinary moral thinking and their conception of the nature of man.

KANT'S MORAL PHILOSOPHY

Kant's moral philosophy falls roughly into two parts, namely the exhibition and systematization of the principles of morality which he finds implicit in everyday moral thought and the justification of these principles in the light of his philosophical system as a whole. The latter, more difficult and complex undertaking will to some extent be considered later.[1] Before trying to sketch Kant's account of the content of moral thinking, I must say that in my view Kant's own exposition of it in the *Groundwork of the Metaphysics of Morals* has never been, and is unlikely to be, surpassed in clarity, simplicity and what may be called philosophical, as opposed to journalistic, elegance.[2]

The key-notions of Kant's moral philosophy are the concepts of duty and of man's freedom to do his duty. Kant's analysis of duty can be separated, at least when dealing with the descriptive part of his inquiry, from his analysis of freedom, which draws heavily on most other parts of his philosophy. A person becomes aware of his duties, and, at least dimly, of the nature of duty, when in a concrete situation his duty conflicts with his desires or interest. A duty is altogether different from a desire. A man may perform an action which it is his duty to perform *because* it is his duty, i.e. *for the sake of* doing his duty. He may, on the other hand, just happen to perform this action for reasons which have nothing to do with any intention of doing his duty; indeed he may perform it for the most disreputable reasons. To be morally right an action must

[1] See chapter 14

[2] *Grundlegung zur Metaphysik der Sitten* (1785) vol. IV (division 1) of the collected works edited by the Prussian Academy of Sciences (Ac. ed.) 1910 ff

not only objectively but also subjectively conform to one's duty. Kant is not greatly concerned with the degree of concordance between the objective and subjective aspects of an action, both of which he explains by reference to the duty of the person performing it. One is still doing one's duty for the sake of doing it if one does it grudgingly. And one can still be doing one's duty for the sake of it if one always, or on some occasions, rejoices in doing it. Kant does *not* imply that the desire to do what duty demands nullifies the moral rightness of the action.

He holds that in order to be able to judge whether an action is morally right we must know 'the maxim according to which it has been decided upon'.[1] A maxim is 'the subjective principle of action', i.e. 'the principle according to which the subject is acting'. I have explained earlier the notion of a maxim and pointed out that it consists of a descriptive antecedent, describing in general terms a situation in which a person may find himself, and a regulative consequent, requiring a certain kind of conduct from him. The maxim may be morally right, wrong or indifferent; and a person acting on it may find it hard to formulate it. Nevertheless, Kant holds that every action has one and only one maxim. A person's outward behaviour may conform to many rules; but a maxim is that rule which the person accepted and deliberately conformed to in his action.

Since, according to Kant, every action has one and only one maxim, his next problem is to distinguish the maxims of morally fitting (or at least not unfitting) actions from the other maxims. Prima facie this might be attempted by compiling and justifying a list of moral maxims and principles after the fashion of some codified system of law. Such maxims or principles are 'material' in the sense that they refer to specific circumstances or consequences of a required action. For reasons which cannot be appreciated without entering more deeply into his thought Kant holds that the morality of a maxim and, therefore, of an action of which it is the maxim can be judged by applying a 'formal' principle to it. Just as there are formal principles of

[1] *ibid.* page 399

logic, which are not arguments, but can be used to test the validity or logical rightness of arguments, so there exists, according to Kant, a formal principle of morality, which is not itself a maxim, but can be used to test the moral rightness of maxims.

Kant gives a number of formulations of this formal principle of which the following is perhaps the best known: 'Act only on that maxim through which you can at the same time will that it should become a universal law.[1]' Each of the other versions of this supreme moral principle or categorical imperative can, with the same results, be used as a test of moral rightness. The most forceful of these, which has also historically and politically been the most influential, is 'Act in such a way that you treat humanity, both in your own person and in the person of all others, never as a means only, but always equally as an end.'[2]

Let us now consider an example of applying the categorical imperative (in its first formulation) to concrete actions. In the *Groundwork of the Metaphysics of Morals*[3] Kant examines the case of a person who considers committing suicide in accordance with the maxim 'from self-love to shorten life if . . . it threatens more evil than it promises pleasantness'. He rejects this as immoral because it is impossible to will such a maxim to become a universal law. By the 'impossibility of willing a maxim to become a universal law' Kant seems to mean not a logical impossibility (i.e. that such a law would be internally inconsistent, or inconsistent with the laws of nature), but an impossibility grounded in the very nature of the human will. This last type of impossibility, though rather obscure, seems to be necessary in order to avoid moral relativism which is abhorrent to Kant. For he does not admit that one person may be able to will a maxim to become a general law which another person is unable to universalize in this manner.

Kant assumes (a) that every action is associated with a maxim, (b) that the categorical imperative, by being applied to the maxims of actions, enables us to divide all maxims in a unique way into the set of maxims which are moral and the set

---

[1] *op. cit.* page 421   [2] *op. cit.* page 429   [3] *op. cit.* page 422

of all other maxims, and (*c*) that the morality or otherwise of all actions can be evaluated by reference to the set of all possible maxims. Against each of these points strong objections can be raised. To start with the last point (*c*), it is by no means clear that everybody's – or perhaps anybody's – concept of moral fittingness is exhaustible by maxims. Thus Kant's maxim not to commit suicide from self-love if life threatens more evil than pleasantness may be accepted as applicable in most ordinary situations of life. But I cannot find the suicide of an inmate of a Nazi concentration camp morally unfitting. And I am confident that many others after a careful examination of their heart and mind will come to the same conclusion. Nor could the 'quantity' of suffering which would induce one to relinquish the application of Kant's maxim, conceived as a mere rule of thumb, be sharply demarcated and made a part of an improved maxim without exceptions.

Again, even if one were to admit for the sake of argument that everybody evaluates his and other people's actions by reference to a set of maxims, one might reasonably object to the second point (*b*) of Kant's doctrine. There would then still be maxims, which some people could, consistently with their empirical information, will to become universal laws, while others could not do so, even if their empirical information were the same. Even if we believe that Nietzsche could consistently will some of his superman's maxims to become universal laws, we may yet regard these maxims as immoral. In order to save the thesis that the categorical imperative can be used to determine the set of moral maxims in a unique way, one would have to adopt some rather desperate lines of reasoning. One would have to argue that those who in spite of having the same empirical information disagree with one's own moral evaluations are either knaves or fools. Or one would have to reduce the content of one's own and their moral maxims to a common moral principle so broad that it would be incapable of determining concrete duties in concrete situations. And it is just this capacity which Kant claims for his moral theory.

Lastly, a phenomenological description of inner moral conflicts would, I believe, reveal situations in which more than one maxim appears to be universalizable, situations in which no maxim appears to be universalizable, and situations in which the weighing of conflicting interests defies formulation in terms of any maxim. It is, of course, always possible to accept the maxim of universal justice, of universal benevolence, or both. To accept such principles is like accepting the principle to act morally. But the person who experiences an inner moral conflict wants to act morally and wonders which of the actions open to him is moral.

Kant's moral theory contains, at the very least, one important insight. A person who considers an action to be moral sincerely believes that every other person who finds himself in the same situation should act in the same way. A moral law is a law which one imposes on everybody including oneself; and it is felt to be immoral to require everybody to obey it except oneself. However, even if this or a similar claim to universality is characteristic of the moral life of every human being, it cannot bear the burden which Kant's moral theory lays upon it.

ARISTOTLE'S MORAL PHILOSOPHY

Aristotle's moral philosophy is, like Kant's, not merely conceived as a guide to concrete action. It is also a metaphysics and psychology of morals and, since according to Aristotle man's social and moral life are inseparable from each other, a political theory. For Kant the main metaphysical problem of morality is the relation between human freedom and natural necessity. For Aristotle it is the relation between a universe which is conceived as purposive and the purpose of man. His moral theory is teleological in the sense that the morality of actions is evaluated by reference to the purposes or ends which they serve or are believed to serve. Since the end of a man's actions is an ideal state of affairs which cannot fully be realized, but to which one may only more or less closely approximate, it is not possible to formulate precise maxims of moral fittingness. Aristotle's concept of the moral fittingness of actions is therefore, unlike Kant's, inexhaustible by empirical criteria. This is one of the reasons why he insists that ethics is an inexact discipline, which deals with what 'tends to be the case on the whole, rather than always, of necessity or without exception'.[1] In the following brief remarks I shall concentrate on the moral content of Aristotle's ethics.

According to Aristotle the morally relevant feature of an action is not its maxim, but its purpose. This does not mean that the purpose of an action cannot be part of its maxim; only that a maxim which does not refer to a purpose is no help in assessing the moral fittingness of an action. The immediate end of an action is often only a means to a more remote end, which in turn may not be the ultimate end. It does not follow that every action has an ultimate end or that all actions have the same ultimate end. But it may be that man is so constituted that all his actions have only one proper, legitimate or moral end. Aristotle holds that an analysis of moral experience in the light of the best available knowledge of man and nature reveals such an end. Very generally and, therefore, rather vacuously, this ultimate end is man's 'well-being', which for Aristotle and many other Greek thinkers is 'well-functioning', i.e. man's functioning in accordance with his nature or purpose.

Aristotle's own words convey this characteristic approach better than any paraphrase:

.. if we declare that the function of man is a certain form of life, and define that form of life as the exercise of the soul's faculties and activities in association with rational principle, and say that the function of a good man is to perform these activities well and rightly, and if a function is well performed when it is performed in accordance with its own proper excellence – from these premises it follows that the Good of man is the active exercise of his soul's faculties in conformity with excellence or virtue, or if there be several human excellences or virtues, in conformity with the best and most perfect among them. Moreover this activity must occupy a complete life-time. . . .[2]

[1] *Nicomachean Ethics*, book I, 1094 b 10 ff
[2] *Nicomachean Ethics*, book I, 1098 a 10 ff

Moral virtue must be distinguished from the separate moral virtues. Man's moral virtue consists in his well-functioning as a whole man, i.e. as a thinking, desiring and acting being and, we must always remember, a 'social animal'. His separate moral virtues consist in the well-functioning of parts or aspects of his nature. The well-functioning of one such part or aspect lies in achieving a 'mean' between the extremes of excessive and defective functioning. A courageous, that is to say a virtuous, reaction to dangerous situations lies between mere rashness on the one hand, and fear on the other. Determining the mean function is not an arithmetical operation. It presupposes a knowledge of the other functions, whose harmonious and balanced interaction constitutes the proper function of the whole man. Thus when Aristotle in the passage quoted above says that the Good of man is the active exercise of the most perfect of the several human excellences, one must remember the principle of the mean as the demand for a balance between the several functions of man. Even if there is a most perfect human virtue one must not disregard the claims of the other virtues and their organic connexions with each other and with the supreme virtue, if any.

Just as the moral virtues consist in the well-functioning of man as a desiring and acting being, so the intellectual virtues consist in the well-functioning of his rational nature. Aristotle distinguishes between two rational faculties, 'one whereby we contemplate those things whose first principles are invariable, and one whereby we contemplate those things which admit of variation . . .'. The former he calls the 'scientific', the latter the 'deliberative' faculty.[1] There is no need here for us to try to understand Aristotle's account of the scientific faculty and the nature of scientific knowledge. It will be sufficient to note that the highest human virtue or excellence consists in the exercise of theoretical wisdom, which, as Ross[2] points out embraces the proper pursuit of metaphysics, mathematics and

[1] *op. cit.*, book VI, 1138 b 35 ff
[2] *Aristotle*, 2nd edition (London 1930), page 218

natural science. Aristotle's concept of intellectual virtue or excellence shows very clearly how different his (and the ordinary Greek) concept of virtue as well-functioning is from our own. In contemporary use 'virtue' is almost synonymous with 'moral virtue', although traces of the older use are still evident in locutions such as 'the virtue of a drug'.

The preceding outline fails to do justice to many subtle observations and arguments contained in Aristotle's *Ethics*. They all converge towards his general conclusion about the nature of the good life: 'The life of the intellect is the best and pleasantest life for man, inasmuch as the intellect more than anything else *is* man; therefore this life will be the happiest.'[1] The life of the intellect is more precisely characterized as consisting in the contemplation of discovered eternal truths and as presupposing moderate wealth, health, moral virtue and the proper organization of the community.

The picture of the good life, as sketched by Aristotle, will meet with the approval of many a competent university professor, who loves his subject, is in good health and free from financial worries. It will meet with the approval of some young people who have a similar career in mind and perhaps of others too. But it will not appeal to a faithful follower of Christ, Buddha or Mohammed, to convinced Epicureans or Marxists or followers of other religious or metaphysical systems. Yet these dissenters, whose conception of the good life is very different from Aristotle's, will also be able to support their own ideal by an analysis of their moral experience, undertaken in the light of their metaphysical beliefs and with due regard to the best empirical knowledge available to them.

The specific content of Aristotle's conception of the good life, by reference to which the moral fittingness of actions is to be judged, is, I believe, much less important than the following two insights implied by it. These are, first, his recognition that a moral ideal is a rather complex system of relations between the natural needs and abilities of individual human beings and between human beings of very similar needs and abilities;

[1] *Nicomachean Ethics*, book X, 1178 a 5 ff

and second, his recognition that man's nature as a social animal implies the desirability of social and political institutions which tend to facilitate the achievement of the moral ideal for every human being. Aristotle's second insight is, however, vitiated by his views on the institution of slavery where the complacency of the well-to-do Greek gentleman obscured the mind of the great philosopher.

In spite of the objections which can be raised against the ethical doctrines of Kant and Aristotle, we do not come away empty-handed when we go to them for moral guidance in concrete situations. True, the application of the categorical imperative to the maxim (if any) of an action does not yield the same result for everybody; and many a person's honestly and sincerely held moral convictions can only be expressed imperfectly and approximately by moral maxims. But the formal demand that what I regard as right for myself I must be able to regard as right for everybody in the same situation, and that what I regard as right for everybody in this situation is right for me, must enter into everybody's moral deliberations. Only if my action, whatever its specific content, conforms to this demand can it be moral: conformity to this demand is part of what is meant by moral conduct. Again, the Aristotelian ideal of the good life is not the only one implicit in a person's form of life. But some such ideal must more or less explicitly enter into his moral deliberations. 'Which of the actions in my power will bring nearest that ideal state of affairs or that good life which I desire for all human beings including myself?' is, I submit, a helpful question in any attempt at solving a moral problem or inner conflict. A well considered answer to it will, as it were, combine vestigial Kantian form and Aristotelian content to yield sound moral sense.

UTILITARIANISM

Like Aristotle's moral theory, Utilitarianism is teleological in that it evaluates the moral fittingness or otherwise of optional actions and courses of action in terms of an ideal state of affairs which can be more or less closely approximated. It differs from Aristotle's theory in substituting for the concept of the good life, seen as a complex system of relations within and between individuals, a quantitative concept of utility derivable from a quantitative comparison between personal and interpersonal utilities. I shall again consider utilitarianism mainly as a guide to moral action, although it may, like the two other ethical theories, be considered also as a psychology and metaphysics of morals and as a political theory.

Its central doctrine, which was later modified in various ways, is forcefully expressed by Jeremy Bentham in the first paragraph of his *Introduction to the Principles of Morals and Legislation.*[1]

Nature has placed mankind under the governance of two sovereign masters, *pain* and *pleasure*. It is for them alone to point out what we ought to do, as well as to determine what we shall do. On the one hand the standard of right and wrong, on the other the chain of causes and effects are fastened to their throne. . . . *The principle of utility* recognizes this subjection, and assumes it for the foundation of that system, the object of which it is to rear the fabric of felicity by the hands of reason and of law.

Let us for the moment grant the tacit assumption that our sovereign masters so govern our lives that they allow for real choices in our apparent attempts to rear the fabric of felicity by the hands of reason; and let us try to understand the principle of utility as a guide to action. It is 'that principle which approves or disapproves of every action whatsoever, according to the tendency which it appears to have to augment the happiness (= benefit = advantage = pleasure = good) of the party whose interest is in question. . . .'.[2] If the party whose interest is considered is an individual the happiness is that of the individual, if the community that of the

[1] London 1789 etc., also Oxford 1948
[2] *op. cit.*, chapter 1, section 25

community, i.e. 'the sum of the interests of the several members who compose it'.[1]

Bentham provided detailed rules for personal and interpersonal comparison of pleasures and pains, for their arrangement in an order of increasing magnitude, for their addition, etc. Later utilitarians introduced some further distinctions, especially between higher and lower pleasures, so that a certain amount of a higher pleasure could never be outweighed by any amount of a lower pleasure. The possibility of such quantitative comparisons raises interesting psychological and logical problems, to whose solutions psychologists, economists and logicians have been making important contributions. Yet even on the unrealistic assumption that we could measure Benthamian happiness as we can measure weight, the principle of utility is easily seen to be only a very rough guide to moral action.

Let us assume that we have determined a unit of happiness and that – following a practice in the physical sciences – we have named it a 'bentham'. Two, rather hoary, illustrations will show that the unqualified application of the principle of utility does not correspond to most people's moral experience. First, imagine a situation in which the execution of an innocent person, whose innocence is known only to his judges, causes a loss of 100 benthams to him and his judges, but a gain of 1,000,000 benthams to the community at large. Surely, most people will (I hope) agree that the execution is immoral. This is the problem which the judges face in Bernard Shaw's *St. Joan*. In view of these and similar situations in which the principle of utility breaks down as a principle of adequate moral guidance, it has been argued that it must be supplemented by some other principle.

Secondly, imagine the choice between imposing or not imposing birth-control on an island community under the following conditions: if birth-control is imposed, 1,000 benthams will weekly be distributed among 1,000 inhabitants so that each person's ration will be one bentham. If birth-control is not

[1] *loc. cit.*

imposed then 2,000 benthams will weekly be distributed among 4,000 inhabitants so that each person's ration will be half a bentham. The principle of utility alone provides no guidance since it does not help us to choose between the greater happiness of a smaller number and the smaller happiness of a greater number of people.

Bentham's utilitarian followers soon noticed these defects and proposed various improvements. One of them is to supplement the principle of utility by an overriding principle of justice, according to which a fair distribution of utility must take precedence over its maximization. Another is to acknowledge a hierarchy of pleasures so that the value of any amount of a lower pleasure (e.g. of playing snooker) cannot exceed the value of any amount of a higher pleasure (e.g. of reading poetry). Later utilitarians have on the whole abandoned the requirement of comparing amounts of happiness by means of a 'felicific calculus'. Lastly Bentham's psychological thesis that pain and pleasure 'alone . . . determine what we shall do' has ceased to be a part of most modern versions of utilitarianism.

There is, I submit, little doubt that in spite of their shortcomings the Kantian, the Aristotelian and the utilitarian approaches to the moral evaluation of actions are all illuminating and helpful. If they lead to the same result and if we find that the result corresponds to our sincere convictions, we may with some assurance decide to act accordingly. Even so it is possible that we shall still feel guilty and mistaken after acting on our decision.

PHILOSOPHICAL GUIDANCE IN AESTHETIC EVALUATION

Some works of art express in their own peculiar – and quite untheoretical – way a whole view of life and even a recognizable metaphysics. Many critics and artists feel drawn to philosophical reflection about the nature of art and find such activity not only helpful, but illuminating. Yet they will rarely turn to philosophy for guidance in their aesthetic evaluation of individual works of art. Their instinctive refusal to do so is,

I think, justifiable on sound philosophical grounds and I shall conclude this chapter by briefly indicating some of them.

A comparison of aesthetic with moral evaluation will help. In examining the latter it was first of all necessary to characterize its subject matter, i.e. primarily optional actions. These were characterized as Events exhibiting certain subjective and objective aspects, together with a certain concordance between them. A work of art, or other aesthetic object, also combines an objective substratum with subjective aspects with which its creator, if it is man-made, or the person contemplating it, endows it. Moreover, there is also some kind of fusion between the objective and the subjective aspects. Yet the analogy soon breaks down. One reason for this is that not only an Event but anything whatsoever can become an object of aesthetic evaluation and be contemplated as if it were a work of art. This point is clear enough and is made even clearer by the occasional exhibition in art galleries of steam hammers, car radiators, brick walls and other objects which do not usually invite aesthetic contemplation. Another reason is that the fusion of the various features of an individual aesthetic object defies any general rule for separating them into more or less sharply demarcated groups which together make up the object. There are no critical codes which, after the fashion of legal codes, provide lists of specific questions the answers to which determine the final evaluation. There are, we sometimes tend to think, artistic crimes, but they are not as clearly defined or graded as are murder, theft, or treason. Although we may characterize both a poem and a criminal killing by external criteria, the distinction between accidental killing, manslaughter and murder proceeds on different lines from the distinction between a harmless versification, a bad poem and an aesthetic outrage.

The impossibility of decomposing an aesthetic object, i.e. an object *qua* object of aesthetic contemplation and evaluation, into separate and separately classifiable aesthetically relevant components, makes aesthetic evaluation by means of finite conjunctions of non-aesthetic attributes impossible. To say that a poem, a novel, a symphony, a play, etc. is aesthetically valuable if it possesses the non-aesthetic properties P_1 and P_2 ... and P_n (whatever they may be) is as absurd as it sounds. There are no maxims for the production of sublime works of art – although there are maxims, or at least rules of thumb, for the exercise of the various types of craftsmanship which underlie artistic creation in the various arts. There are, moreover, no general aesthetic ideals which can be formulated in a manner approaching the clarity and precision of, say, Aristotle's conception of the good life.

Aesthetic experience and creation defy conceptualization, more precisely, they defy the identification, classification and evaluation of aesthetic objects by means of non-aesthetic attributes. Since any adequate aesthetic theory will have to recognize this fact, it will not be able to provide aesthetic guidance even to the modest extent to which moral theory can give moral guidance. This is instinctively acknowledged by most artists. Yet aesthetic experience not only defies, but also invites conceptualization. Art critics accept this invitation as a challenge. The best of them know that they can never fully meet it.

9. The Philosophy of Society and of History

If a discipline is easy, there is little difference between laymen and those who are expert in it. Almost everybody is an expert or can become one by choosing the experts' writings as bedside or vacation reading. However, it does not follow that where the distance between experts and laymen is small the problems are easy. For it may be that the problems are almost equally intractable for everybody. This is so with the central problems arising from reflection on the laws, if any, which govern social life and historical development, on the part, if any, which human choices play in social and historical change, and on the moral implications, if any, of these choices. Economics – both as theoretical and welfare economics – is an established science which has no doubt increased our understanding of economic life within relatively stable frameworks of social, and especially technical, institutions; but it is not so far backed up by a general science of social change. Anthropology and sociology, on the other hand, describe wider areas of social life in all their aspects, but, unlike economics, do not claim to have reached the status of predictive theories.

In this situation philosophers have a contribution to make. Thus philosophers of economics can lay bare the logical structure of economic theories and their relation to experience, and can exhibit the features which distinguish these theories from those of the natural sciences. Apart from this philosophers can analyse the assumptions made by others, and make proposals of their own. In the present chapter I shall give examples of the analysis of concepts applied to social and historical phenomena, of the application of moral principles to apparent social choices and of speculations about the course of history.

ON THE CONCEPT OF THE STATE

Many of the more exciting questions of social philosophy presuppose a clear conception of the social institution of the state. It is, like any other social institution, a more or less permanent system of relations between individuals considered abstractly, i.e. only in so far as they stand in these relations. Thus the institution of marriage is the relation between a man and a woman in their 'social roles' as husband and wife, as defined by law and custom in the period under consideration. A trade union is another social institution, although it is more frequently called an association. The difference between a 'social institution' and a '(more or less permanent) association' in our rather narrow technical sense of these terms is one of emphasis – the former emphasizing the relationship, the latter the persons related by it. It is usual to distinguish a social community as the totality of all social institutions or associations from the institutions or associations which it embraces. The state is one of these associations or institutions.

Let us – following the uncontroversial and somewhat drearier parts of the text-books – set down a workable definition of the concept of a state: an association within a community is a state if, and only if, (i) its members (with some obvious exceptions) are born in its territory and (again with obvious exceptions) reside in it; (ii) the association has a 'government' which has, to a high degree, the power of regulating the life of its 'citizens' and 'residents'; and (iii) the rules of the association, or the 'legal order' have 'precedence' (on the whole) over the rules of the other associations within the community. The definition can be improved, by explaining the quoted terms. But it is not defective in allowing for exceptions and in avoiding definitional sharpness which would misrepresent the fuzziness of social reality.

The definition is, so to speak, anatomical. It describes a certain transient social structure and distinguishes it from others. A state must in particular be distinguished from organized tribal communities which do not exhibit the relationship between government and citizens found in the modern states, from the Greek *polis* or 'city-state' which was not an association within a community, but rather the community itself, and from medieval territorial associations in which the political powers of the pope put too great a limitation on the powers of the secular princes. The anatomy of states is a descriptive empirical discipline which is pursued in university departments of 'politics', 'government', 'administration' and, by itself, raises few philosophical questions.

A host of philosophical questions arises, however, when we turn from the rather pedestrian and uncontroversial question of the anatomy of states to the 'physiological' questions of their function and of the historical explanations of their evolution. If social theory and zoology are analogous in their anatomical aspects, the analogy becomes rather tenuous when we speak of the physiology and evolutionary theory of states and other social phenomena. In zoology the physiology and evolutionary theory of animals are thriving scientific concerns, whilst the social sciences have still not passed the programmatic state of discussing what a 'physiological' or 'evolutionary' explanation would have to be like.

Thanks to the empirical researches of social anthropologists and sociologists certain philosophical theories – or rather theories devised by philosophers acting as place-holders for others who had not yet come forward – have been recognized as much too crude. For example, theories which explain the origin and function of a state as based on a 'social contract' between individuals can no longer be defended. Indeed it might be argued that even Hobbes and Locke regarded a social contract assigning duties to government and citizens as little more than a useful fiction. This would mean that in their view the actual behaviour, the rights and duties of the members of a state, can best be made intelligible by considering them *as if* they were based on a contract (the content of which was conceived very differently by Hobbes and Locke). Even so the conception of a state after the fashion of an association based on a contract is still, as has often been pointed out, a crude over-simplification, which fits some states better than others and none very closely.

A similar onesidedness is found in theories which explain the functioning of any state as resulting from the government's coercive power exercised in its own interest. Thus in Plato's *Republic* the sophist Thrasymachus argues that 'justice', in the sense of the enforced, or enforceable, moral and legal order, 'is the interest of the stronger'. This aphorism would have to be much refined, if it were to fit not only Hitler's Germany, but also the United Kingdom, the United States of America, and the Soviet Union in our time. As it stands, it does not even fit Hitler's Germany because Hitler and many of his followers were often guided by confused, mystical goals which they did not identify with their selfish interests and which in fact were not identical with them. The marxist doctrine that the ancient and feudal 'states' were, as Friedrich Engels put it, 'organs for the exploitation of slaves and serfs', while 'the modern representative state is an instrument of exploitation of wage labour by capital'[1] must not be identified with the crude slogan of Thrasymachus. It must be interpreted against the background of the marxist philosophy of history. A few remarks on marxism in the latter half of this chapter will outline this background very briefly.

A third type of theory explaining the functioning and function of states and other associations is almost literally physiological. It conceives them as organisms analogous to the higher

[1] *Vom Ursprung der Familie, des Privateigentums und des Staates* (Hottingen-Zürich 1844) Marx-Engels, *Werke* (Berlin 1960–66), vol. 21, page 167. For an English translation see e.g. Karl Marx and Friedrich Engels, *Selected Works*, 2 vols. (Moscow and London 1950)

animals, especially man. The main point of the organic theories is to emphasize that the individual members of a state are not just members of a class standing in various relations to each other, but parts of a whole which is as much an organism as the individual members. This super-organism is understood in various ways, some of which imply rather bizarre correspondences between human organs and organs of government, e.g. between the nose and the secret police. Rousseau's most influential theory is expressed in essence in the following sentence from his *Discourse on Political Economy*: 'The body politic is also a moral being, possessed of a will, and this general will tends always to the preservation and welfare of the whole and every part . . . and constitutes for all the members of the state the rule of what is just and unjust.'[1] We find echoes of this doctrine not only in the writings of philosophers, but in documents as different in intention as the French revolutionary constitutions and Mussolini's Fascist Charter of Labour.

The doctrine is ambitious, ambiguous and dangerous. It is ambitious because it claims to solve with one stroke the problem of the structure and function of the state and the problem of moral and political obligation. It is ambiguous because it asserts a necessary connexion between 'the general will' and morality without providing any satisfactory method for discovering the content of the general will. Rousseau himself distinguishes sharply between the 'will of all', as emerging from a majority or even a unanimous decision of all the members of the state or a representative assembly, and the 'general will'. The 'will of all' may lead to an immoral decision, whereas the 'general will' can never have this result. However, he does not tell us how to distinguish between manifestations of the general will and the will of all – unless we already know independently what a moral decision would be. The generality of the will which determines morality is in turn determined by morality.

In practice this circle has been straightened out in a number of ways which would have been unacceptable to Rousseau as

[1] *Discours sur L'Économie Politique* (1758) *Oeuvres Complètes* (Paris 1964) vol. III, page 245

citizen of Geneva. Thus the French constitution of 1795 identifies the general will with the will of all in stating that 'law is the general will expressed by the majority'. Anyone who prefers democratic government to other forms of government will accept the practical consequences of this principle, even if he rejects the doctrine of the general will. But he – and not only he – will recoil from other methods of discovering its content, for example from the following, expressed in a book on Constitutional Law published in Germany in 1937. In it its author, a Herr Huber, tells us that the Führer's authority 'is not limited by checks and controls, by special autonomous bodies or individual rights . . . it is free of all outward ties because it is in its innermost nature firmly bound up with the fate, the welfare, the mission and the honour of the people'.[1] The doctrine of the general will is indeed ambiguous and, because of its ambiguity, dangerous.

There is no need to enlarge any further on the contract-, the force- and the organic theories of the state, or to follow their more detailed applications in order to show their onesidedness. Neither is there any need to argue that each of them contains a certain amount of truth. Let us, therefore, turn to an example of a moral problem to which social and political life gives rise, namely the problem of the best form of government. As before, we can approach it only with crude analytical tools because we have no better ones at our disposal.

THE PROBLEM OF THE BEST FORM OF GOVERNMENT

This problem cannot be avoided by simply repeating the gist of Pope's often-quoted heroic couplet: 'For forms of government let fools contest/Whate'er is best administered is best.' The problem is, at least partly, which of two more or less equally well administered forms of government is the better, and not, for example, whether one would prefer the ideal aristocracy described in Plato's *Republic* to the corrupt demo-

[1] Quoted in H. Finer, *The Future of Government* (London 1946), page 19

cracy held up to contempt and ridicule in the same work. The solution will obviously depend on the type of community which one has in mind. For example, representative government would be unworkable in most primitive tribes. Again, one should recognize that a form of government which is prima facie workable might turn out to be in fact unrealizable, so that another form of government which on purely moral grounds seems less attractive is preferable because realizable. We wish to choose between realizable options and know too little about what is politically realizable and what is not. In spite of these severe limitations of our knowledge it is nevertheless possible to set down some general guiding principles.

First of all, we must agree upon a standard for measuring the goodness of forms of government. John Stuart Mill suggests that the degree to which they 'promote the general mental advancement of the community' and the degree to which they 'organize the worth already existing in the community' provides such a measure.[1] Since he also admits that the achievement of these purposes presupposes freedom from hunger, fear and disease, we may accept his standard in the confident belief that most political thinkers have also accepted it. Plato and Marx, for example, would not have found it objectionable, even though they might have added some qualifications.

Next, we must agree on some classification of forms of government. Let us call a form of government a 'complete democracy' if each member of the community has an equal share in the deliberations and decisions of government, a 'complete oligarchy' if a minority, and a 'complete dictatorship' if one person only exercises political power. Actual forms of government approach these complete types more or less closely, and we shall – without further refinements – call a form of government a 'democracy', 'oligarchy' or 'dictatorship' according to the complete type to which it approximates most closely.

Mill has no doubt that, if we accept his standard of goodness,

[1] *Considerations on Representative Government* (London 1861). Quoted from *On Liberty* and *Considerations etc.* (Oxford 1946)

democracy is best *in so far as it is practicable*. 'It is not', he says 'sufficiently considered, how little there is in most men's ordinary life to give any largeness either to their conceptions or sentiments.'[1] In a despotism – even an ideal one – 'all the collective interests of the people are managed for them, all the thinking that has relation to collective interests done for them' and 'their minds are formed by, and consenting to, this abdication of their own energies'.[2] Democracy, more than any other form of government, forces people to transcend the morally and intellectually narrow sphere of their daily lives. This transcendence, as Mill points out, is likely to occur in any democratic assembly be it a legislative assembly or a parish council. Nevertheless, the defence of democracy as a powerful educator of people's minds and character is perhaps less obvious than its defence on other grounds. Among these are, for instance, the claim that the democratic process of arriving at decisions is more likely than any alternative to take all interests into account and the view that the duties which it imposes are more nearly self-imposed than the duties imposed by an oligarchy or a dictator.

Since Mill's main argument in favour of democracy – as well as most other such arguments – is subject to the limitation of practicability we may again expect many political philosophers to agree with him. Sharp disagreement arises when it comes to demarcating the limits. Mill concedes, and indeed insists on, the need for experts in government – experts in economics, technology and even administration. In a representative democracy 'it is essential that the political supremacy should reside with the representative' but it is 'an open question what precise part in the machinery of government shall be directly and personally discharged by the representative body'.[3] There is, he holds, in all civilized communities a large area of political problems which all members of the community are more or less equally competent (or incompetent) to decide. These are,

[1] *op. cit.* page 149
[2] *op. cit.* page 139
[3] *op. cit.* page 163

roughly speaking, questions of ends rather than means. The citizens of a country may have different conceptions of social justice and of their country's legitimate political aspirations. But there are no experts on social justice and political aspirations.

Mill profoundly disagrees with the Platonic doctrine of the philosopher-king, i.e. the doctrine that there are experts in the craft of government (both as regards ends and means) just as there are experts in the crafts of shoe-making or medicine. Plato considers the wish for democratic government to be no less foolish than the wish to have one's shoes repaired by a tailor or one's health cared for by a quack. Yet Plato provided no reliable criteria for selecting the experts in government and for distinguishing them from quacks. Indeed it would seem that on the whole the self-selected philosopher-kings who have governed mankind in the past have done it more harm than its democratically elected and democratically deposable rulers.

The opposition between Mill's doctrine of democracy, which admits the need for experts, though only in determining and organizing the means to political ends, and Plato's doctrine that there are philosopher-kings who should determine also the political ends, is perhaps the most fundamental opposition within political philosophy. It affects most other political issues. *Even if* we admit that the despotic government of a savage tribe may in some circumstances be justified, we must distinguish between two kinds of despotism: a despotism which guides the tribe towards democracy and a despotism which aims 'at confirming the slaves in their incapacities'. Whoever agrees with Mill (as I do) that democracy is in principle preferable to dictatorship can do so only with the proviso that democracy by itself is no protection against social injustice. Social injustice is curable only by social justice – not by a form of government as such.

The state, like all other human institutions, is merely a transient phase of the changing social universe. The story of this universe is history. It is the historian's task to record it and to make intelligible the ways in which it has unfolded itself through the actions and interactions of people. That this story should be well told, well founded on evidence and relevant, in the sense of containing the answers to more or less specific questions, is generally agreed. Whether or not the story is well told is a matter of aesthetic evaluation, about which a little has been said earlier. The criteria by which we judge whether the story is well founded are similar to those which a reasonable and competent judge in a court of law would apply to the evidence of the available documents and witnesses, including expert witnesses. But there are differences.

The historian, unlike a judge (in canon or common law) is not bound by rigidly formulated rules of evidence. He constitutes together with the other members of his profession a permanent court, which by private and public discussion arrives at judgements all of which are open to an appeal heard by the same court. Again, there is an important difference of scale in the evaluation of evidence. A criminal or civil judge is concerned with relatively small periods of time and the actions of a relatively small number of people. A historian, even if he were inquiring into some aspect of, say, the history of Bristol from 1780 to 1785, would at least implicitly be concerned with a much longer period and larger groups of people. Thus a competent judge transferred from his court to the court of history would not necessarily make an equally competent historian. Lastly, the relevant questions of fact to which the judge has to find the answers are largely determined by the law of the land, whereas relevant historical questions are not similarly codified.

It is mainly by their conception of what constitutes a relevant and answerable historical question that the various philosophies of history differ from each other. Of these I shall very briefly examine three pure types, namely the conceptions of history as a kind of empathy, as a theoretical science and as metaphysics; and one mixed type in which a metaphysical programme for historical research is implemented by scientific theorizing. The selection is of necessity small. Thus – to justify only one omission – a discussion of Toynbee's theory of the growth and decay of civilizations in isolation from his achievement as a historian would very likely give a misleading impression of both.

THE VIEW OF HISTORY AS A KIND OF EMPATHY

This view of history has been worked out, for example, by R. G. Collingwood, who was to some extent influenced by W. Dilthey.[1] The eminently reasonable core of his view is the observation that since the subject matter of history is human action and interaction, and since every action has an objective and a subjective aspect, historical understanding involves true judgements about the agents' beliefs, desires and intentions. 'Suppose, for example,' that 'the historian is reading the Theodosian Code.' In order to know the historical significance of its words 'he must envisage it as that emperor envisaged it'. He must 're-enact in his own mind the experience of the emperor; and only in so far as he does this has he any historical knowledge, as distinct from a merely philological knowledge, of the edict'.[2]

The acceptability of this conception of historical knowledge depends on the interpretation of what it means to 're-enact' other people's experience in one's own mind. It is clearly impossible to re-experience another person's, or even one's own, experience in all its aspects, if only because an experience believed to be a repetition of another would, for this very reason, be different from it. But there are no good grounds for denying that one person's experience may share some aspects with that of another person, and in this sense be a repetition of it. It is also clearly impossible completely to 're-enact' in one mind the simultaneous experiences of many people, e.g. of a cabinet, a revolutionary crowd or two fighting armies. But again there are no good grounds for denying that, e.g., Tolstoy's *War and Peace* describes historical events from the point of

[1] See esp. Dilthey, *Einleitung in die Geisteswissenschaften*, vol. I (Leipzig 1883) and Collingwood, *The Idea of History* (Oxford 1946)

[2] Collingwood, *op. cit.* page 283

view of those involved in them and thereby answers questions which could not be answered by a purely external description. In so far as Collingwood's view of historical understanding implies that some historical phenomena are intentional and require intentional language for their description, it is surely unobjectionable. It raises once more the question of the reducibility of intentional to extensional language. However, this is a question not for the philosophy of history, but for logic.[1]

Whether or not re-enactment in one's own mind – in so far as it is possible – amounts to 'explanation' is largely a trivial matter of the use of this term. Clearly, people often find the actions of others 'explicable' or 'inexplicable' to the extent to which they find themselves able to 're-enact them in their mind' in a non-empty sense of this locution. This sense of 'explanation' is different from the sense used in the natural sciences.[2] But this is no reason for proscribing it, especially as there is little danger of confusing the two. The reason why the empathy-theory is sometimes hotly disputed lies probably in a tendency of some of its proponents to claim that any other method for arriving at true descriptions of past situations and events in human affairs is useless. An engineer's analysis of a tank-battle may throw more light on its course and outcome than re-enacting in one's own mind the experience of the soldiers and commanders who took part in it.

HISTORICAL AS SCIENTIFIC EXPLANATION

It is sometimes said that since history does not, strictly speaking, repeat itself, and since scientific laws and theories presuppose repeatable situations, there can be no laws of history in the sense in which there are physical laws and theories. This is quite unconvincing. An individual spatio-temporally limited situation is in principle unrepeatable whether it is historical or physical. The individual historical situation which consists in

[1] See pages 95 ff
[2] See page 90

my writing down my thoughts on a certain day between 3 p.m. and five minutes past 3 p.m. in room 20 of the Wills Memorial Building in Bristol and the individual physical situation which consists in the movement of my pen at the same time and in the same place are both unrepeatable. Neither of them will ever happen again or happened before *at the same place and at the same time*. Since concrete events are individuated by their particular spatio-temporal location they are unrepeatable. But kinds of situations are repeatable – whether they involve individual human beings, such as myself, or individual fountain-pens, such as the one which I am now using.

It is perfectly possible for a historian to answer the question: 'Why did Napoleon give the order to retreat from Moscow?' by: 'Napoleon was in a situation with such and such features. Everybody in such a situation gives the order to retreat. Therefore, Napoleon gave the order to retreat.' Indeed, it is not difficult to find examples of such explanations in books written by historians. The main reason why some philosophers do not acknowledge that there are general laws of history is not, it seems, the result of some searching philosophical analysis, but the regrettable fact that such laws as are generally accepted by historians are few in number, trivial in content, obvious in their application, and more or less isolated. They are not systematically connected in the manner in which physical generalizations are unified in deductive theories whose deductive fertility is based on their systematic unity.[1]

The modest core of this conception of history is again eminently reasonable: there are historical generalizations which have the same form as empirical generalizations in physics. What makes this kind of view controversial is the tendency of some of its proponents to argue that there is no other sense of 'explanation'. But this is merely a trivial verbal manoeuvre. Re-enacting in one's own mind the experience of the soldiers and commanders who took part in a tank-battle may throw more light on its course and outcome than an analysis carried out by an engineer. If my remarks on the empathy- and the

[1] See chapter 5

'scientific' views of history are correct, I have not so much refuted as deflated them. The deflation consists in replacing their highly interesting but illegitimate claims to exclusive truth by a legitimate claim, of very moderate interest, to be true 'up to a point'. Such is the well-deserved fate of many a philosophical theory.

THE METAPHYSICAL CONCEPTION OF HISTORY

This conception of history which, mainly through its close links with Marxism, has been most influential in modern thought is to be found in the work of Hegel. In order to explain some of its fundamental features I must for the moment make three enormous assumptions, which Hegel claims to have established in his other works. Their examination will have to be postponed to the fourth part of this book, which deals with metaphysical theories. The assumptions are, first, that philosophical speculation can by itself arrive at the absolute truth about the essence of the universe; second, that Hegel has succeeded in discovering and systematically exhibiting this truth; third, that the inner essence of the universe includes, in one of its aspects, the inner essence of human history.

'*The only thought which philosophy brings with it* [to the study of history] *is the simple thought of Reason, that Reason governs the world and that what happened in history happened in accordance with Reason.*'[1] This sentence from Hegel's *Philosophy of History* might, by itself, be interpreted as a rather oratorical overstatement to the effect that the historian, like the natural scientist, must assume that the phenomena which he tries to apprehend and represent are capable of being 'rationally' understood. But Hegel asserts much more, namely that Reason, or the Spirit, is both the 'substance' of the world 'by which and through which all reality has its being and existence' and '*the infinite power*' by which Reason realizes itself.[2] The 'logical'

[1] *Philosophie der Geschichte*, Reclam edition (Leipzig 1907), page 42. The work was published posthumously
[2] *loc. cit.*

structure of Reason has, so Hegel says, been shown by him to be dialectical, i.e. to be a system of categories none of which can be thought clearly without merging into its antithesis and together with its antithesis into a new category which constitutes the synthesis of the original category and its antithesis. This 'logical' process from thesis and antithesis to synthesis, which as a new thesis again merges into its antithesis and together with it into a new synthesis, starts with the poorest category of 'Being' as such, and ends with the richest category of 'the Absolute' which embraces all reality.

Let us say that the thesis 'dialectically implies' the antithesis and that thesis and antithesis 'dialectically imply' the synthesis. Then whatever dialectical implication may mean, it is, as Hegel saw, unlike logical implication since the antecedent of a dialectical implication is poorer in content than its consequent. In this respect it is like the Cartesian implication, which I examined earlier.[1] However, dialectical implication has the further characteristic that its consequent is either the 'opposite' of the antecedent if the antecedent is a thesis, or the reconciliation of two opposites if the antecedent consists of a thesis and its antithesis. The following example of dialectical reasoning is found in the first section of the first chapter of Hegel's *Logic*:[2] pure Being dialectically implies pure Nothingness, and pure Being and pure Nothingness dialectically imply Becoming. Hegel reasons that pure Being is being without any determination and thus Nothing. Indeed they are the same, so that 'each vanishes into its opposite'. Hegel then goes on to say that 'their truth is thus this movement of the immediate vanishing of the One in the Other: Becoming'. I shall later consider the Hegelian dialectics in more detail and examine its claims.[3] Whatever we may think of it, it is in any case presupposed by Hegel's conception of the historical process.

The logical structure of reality, or what for Hegel amounts

[1] See page 23
[2] *Wissenschaft der Logik* (Nürnberg 1812, 1816)
[3] See chapter 13

to the same thing, of Reason or of the Spirit, is neither spatial nor temporal, but has both a temporal and a spatial 'manifestation'.[1] World history, according to his philosophy of history, is *'the manifestation of the Spirit in time, just as the Idea as Nature manifests itself in space'*.[2] The Spirit is in its very essence freedom. Indeed, if the Spirit is reality, then it cannot be bounded by or restricted by anything else. The manifestation of the Spirit in time is the progress in the consciousness of freedom. The vehicle of this progress is peoples. The various stages of this progress are manifested by the spirit of certain peoples. The spirit of a people, however, has only a limited existence which dialectically implies the emergence of another historical stage realized by the spirit of another people. The passions and actions of men are, as it were, used by the Spirit as means for its self-realization. This feature of historical development, which Hegel calls 'the cunning of history', implies that the dialectical historian understands the plan of history, which must remain obscure to the historian who looks merely at human plans and actions.

Since on Hegel's view the essence of the historical process has been established beyond doubt by speculative philosophy, the actual course of history cannot but conform to it. He sees in oriental history the childhood of mankind, in Greek history its youth, and in Germanic culture its old age – the wise old age of fulfilment, not the senility of the Spirit in its temporal manifestation. In the progress toward the consciousness of freedom the oriental peoples only knew that the despot is free, the Romans and the Greeks that some men are free, the 'Germanic world' that everybody is free. Hegel's work on the philosophy of history ends with a description of the sovereign German states of his day. Of these absolute monarchies he says that in view 'of clearly determined laws and a fixed organization of the state whatever is left to the monarch's sole decision is substantially of little account'. The German states of his day

[1] The German word is *Auslegung* which means interpretation and display and is used by Hegel deliberately in both senses at once

[2] *Wissenschaft der Logik*, page 117

are regarded as the ultimate (or very nearly ultimate) realization of the Spirit in history.

The irrefutability of Hegel's metaphysical conception of history by the actual course of history is guaranteed by the flexibility of his philosophical terms. Thus if somebody were to argue that post-Napoleonic Prussia was further from manifesting the consciousness of freedom than post-Napoleonic England, he would be told that he has misunderstood the meaning of freedom, because 'freedom' is not a characteristic of individuals, but of states. Indeed, it seems no easier to distinguish between genuine and merely apparent progress towards the realization of Hegelian freedom than to distinguish between Rousseau's general will and his will of all. Hegel's own political ideal was constitutional monarchy. But constitutional lawyers who, like the unforgettable Herr Huber, tend to justify tyranny and cruelty by metaphysics would not find it too difficult to use Hegel's philosophy of history for their own ends.

THE MARXIST PHILOSOPHY OF HISTORY

This theory owes much to Hegel's metaphysics. It was created by Karl Marx in collaboration with Friedrich Engels and is to some extent the mirror-image of Hegel's philosophy of history. Marx, like Hegel, holds that both nature and history are dialectical in their essence. But he replaces Hegel's 'dialectical idealism' by a 'dialectical materialism'. In his view, he says, 'the mental (*das Ideelle*) is nothing but the material as transferred and translated into the human head'.[1] The substance of reality is not spirit, but matter in dialectical movement. History is the temporal manifestation of material reality which is merely reflected in human minds or, more precisely, in human brains. The ultimate stage of the historical process is, in the words of Engels, not a state which 'governs persons' but the mere 'administration of things and the guidance of processes of produc-

[1] *Das Kapital* volume 1, postscript to 2nd edition (Hamburg 1872) 1st edition Hamburg 1867; Marx-Engels, *Werke*, volume 23, page 27

tion'. 'The state', which according to Hegel is the highest form of human organization, *'withers away'*.[1] The vehicles of dialectical historical progress are not peoples, or the spirit of peoples, but social classes. History in its essence is the history of class struggles. It is these class struggles which are used by the 'cunning of history' to lead through thesis, antithesis and synthesis to the class-less society, i.e. perfect communism – 'from each according to his abilities, to each according to his needs'.

The following often-quoted passage from Marx's preface to his *Critique of Political Economy*[2] conveys the central points of his theory of history:

In the social production which men carry on they enter into definite relations that are indispensable and independent of their will; these relations of production correspond to a definite stage of development of their material forces of production. The sum total of these relations of production constitutes the economic structure of society – the real foundation, on which rises a legal and political superstructure and to which correspond definite forms of social consciousness. The mode of production in material life determines the social, political and intellectual life-processes in general. It is not the consciousness of men that determines their being, but, on the contrary, their social being that determines their consciousness. At a certain stage of their development the material forces of production in society come in conflict with the existing relations of production, or – what is but a legal expression for the same thing – with the property relations within which they have been at work before. From forms of development of the forces of production these relations turn into their fetters. Then begins an epoch of social revolution. . . . In broad outlines we can designate the Asiatic, the ancient, the feudal, and the modern bourgeois modes of production as so many epochs in the progress of the economic formation of society.

[1] *Herrn Eugen Dührings Umwälzung der Wissenschaft* (Stuttgart 1894); Marx-Engels, *Werke*, volume 20, page 262

[2] *Zur Kritik der Politischen Ökonomie* (Berlin 1859), Marx-Engels, *Werke*, volume 13, page 8

The parallels between this summary of the marxist philosophy of history and the Hegelian are fairly obvious. The irrefutability of the marxist conception of the historical process by the actual course of history seems again guaranteed by the flexibility of its philosophical concepts. There is, however, another way of considering Marx's philosophical pronouncements, namely not as dogmatic, but as programmatic or regulative. This is what some marxists seem to mean when they say that marxism is 'not a dogma, but a method'. On this interpretation the principles of marxist philosophy regulate the construction of testable, predictive theories, in particular economic and sociological theories.

The most important theory conforming to the marxist philosophical programme is Marx's own economic theory. Few economists today would deny that this theory constitutes a significant contribution to their discipline, even though some of its specific predictions have not been fulfilled. Among these are, for example, that socialist revolutions will occur in highly developed industrial countries, such as Germany, before they occur in feudal countries such as Russia or China; and that the so-called middle class is bound to be absorbed, on the one hand, into an industrial proletariat which is only just subsisting on its wages, and on the other, into the class of capitalist monopolists who own all the means of production. The first of these predictions appears to have been falsified in the first half of the twentieth century, and the second appears, at the present time, to be far from confirmed. Yet, the need for theoretical revision of marxist economics no more amounts to a refutation of the marxist regulative principles than the need for theoretical revision of a physical theory amounts to a refutation of the regulative principles to which it conforms. Regulative principles, as I have argued,[1] are rules and thus neither true nor false. And only true-or-false propositions are directly testable by experience.

[1] See page 33

10. The Philosophy of Religion

The theories, doctrines and commonsense beliefs which have so far constituted the subject matter of our philosophical reflections are accessible to almost everybody through experiences which he either has had or can bring about at will. Almost everybody has some acquaintance with the difference between valid and invalid deductive arguments and thus a starting point for a journey into formal logic and its philosophy. Experience at first hand of simple mathematical operations marks the beginning of the systematic study of mathematical theories which in turn leads to philosophy of mathematics. Roads to the philosophy of science, the philosophy of action and value, of social life and of history also start from generally accessible first hand experiences. The case is different with the subject matter of the philosophy of religion. We all have, of course, access to some religious doctrine and tradition and to metaphysical arguments which support them. But many people have never experienced, and lack the capacity to induce in themselves or in the external world, the kinds of occurrence which are the original, as opposed to the merely recorded, sources of a religious faith. In this chapter I shall, after a brief discussion of the sources of religious faith and their relation to religious doctrine, make some remarks about the structure of religious statements. I shall then consider the relation between religious and metaphysical doctrines, between religion and science and between religion and morality. In conclusion, I shall outline the tenets of a tolerant agnosticism.

THE PRIMARY SOURCES

The primary sources of any religious faith are neither religious tradition nor religious authority, but experiences which somehow transcend the limitations of personality and events which allegedly transcend the limitations of nature. Religious tradition merely reports such experiences and events while religious authority is derived from their real or alleged occurrence. The most characteristic experiences which allegedly transcend the limitations of personality are so-called 'mystical' experiences. They have been reported in such different cultural contexts that their occasional occurrence can hardly be doubted. From the point of view of philosophical analysis the following characteristics of mystical experiences are worth noting. I have inferred them from my limited reading of personal reports by mystics, from books on mysticism[1] and from experiences of my own, which are probably quite common and seem to be mild or degenerate forms of mystical experience.

Let me first conjecture what a mystical experience is not. It is not being, or becoming, aware of something given as differentiated into individual objects and attributes. It is in particular not perceiving, imagining, judging or desiring. It is indescribable in the strict sense, in which to describe the content of an experience is to apply specific attributes to distinct concrete or abstract individual objects. Yet mystics have often tried to convey the content of their mystical experiences by describing them, since even a misdescription may be a better guide than the mere assertion of indescribability or ineffability. This is the answer to Dr. Johnson who asked why Jacob Böhme, if he had seen the unutterable, should have tried to utter it.[2] In accepting Dr. Johnson's dictum with qualified

[1] See especially Evelyn Underhill, *Mysticism*, 12th edition (London 1930)

[2] *Boswell's Life of Johnson* (Oxford 1927), volume I, page 417

approval only, we permit ourselves the positive conjecture that
a mystical experience is *somehow* a merging of the mystic's individuality into oneness with a whole which is, or includes,
everything that is real and a consequent disappearance of the
somehow illusory distinction between different persons and
more generally between every this and that. Underhill[1] says
that the 'One' which is experienced by the mystic is for him
'not merely the Reality of all that is, but also a living and
personal object of Love'. My own, as I must emphasize again,
limited reading makes me object to this characterization of
mystical experience as directed to a personal object of love. It
does not, I think, accord with the reports by mystics whose
religious background did not include a belief in a personal
god.

From mystical experiences proper we must distinguish the
experience of religious awe in the face of a power in, or behind,
nature on which one is ultimately dependent. Attempts to
describe such experiences are not hopeless, since they do not
involve the radical breakdown of common distinctions and
oppositions which is typical of mystical experiences. They are
also more common.[2] There is, I think, little reason to believe
that both mystical experiences and experiences of religious
awe will not continue to occur. Although I do not pretend to
have characterized them in the clearest possible manner what
I have said about them will be sufficient for my present purpose.

The other important primary source of religious faith is the
alleged occurrence of miracles, i.e. of events transcending the
limitations of nature. The concept of a miracle is, of course,
dependent on the state of the believer's knowledge of nature,
in particular his scientific knowledge. The so-called 'miracles'
of modern technology are not miracles, since they are brought
about by the application of science. To believe in a miracle is
to believe that a certain event has occurred, to judge that the
occurrence of this event is physically impossible, i.e. contrary

[1] *loc. cit.* page 81
[2] For a phenomenological description, see in particular Rudolf Otto,
Das Heilige (Breslau 1917)

to the laws of nature, and yet, in spite of this acknowledged incompatibility, to abandon neither the belief in the event's occurrence nor the beliefs about the laws of nature. A miracle is thus quite different from a highly improbable event, since the occurrence of highly improbable events is compatible with the laws of nature.

To these primary sources of religious faith there might possibly be added a further one, namely a purely intellectual belief in the validity of arguments, by which from premisses believed to be true the existence of supernatural beings, of one supernatural being, or at least a supernatural order, is inferred. Yet it is doubtful whether one would call a person religious if his intellectual conviction were not also accompanied by a belief in miracles, or by experiences of religious awe or by a belief in the possibility of mystical experiences in some people, not necessarily including himself. The primary sources of religious faiths must be distinguished from their interpretation in religious doctrine. Different religions place different emphases on the relevance of these primary sources. To the Christian religion, for example, the belief in miracles is – or has been until recently – essential, whereas in Buddhism they play hardly any role at all.

RELIGIOUS DOCTRINES

Religious doctrines are the formulations, interpretations and explanations of the primary sources, in particular of mystical experiences and of miraculous events. The historical and scientific appraisal of the primary sources, though it is no part of religious doctrine, may nevertheless influence its development, e.g. by demoting a cosmogony, which has formed part of a religious doctrine, from the status of a literal to that of a metaphorical truth. Some modern writers, who wish to hunt with the scientific hounds and run with the religious hares, tend to overemphasize the analogy between religious doctrines and scientific theories. It is certainly true that a religious doctrine, just like a scientific theory, is intended to explain the evidence in virtue of which it is accepted.

But the differences between religious doctrines and scientific theories are very great. Every creed contains dogmata or articles of faith which are fundamental in the following senses: they state, or indicate, man's relation to the universe as a whole. They are understood as having precedence over any statements with which they appear incompatible. They require an unconditional assent which makes them immune from any doubt, test or criticism. The belief in fundamental dogmata of the kind described must be distinguished from the manner in which the dogmata are discovered, promulgated or enforced. A person who does not believe in a religious dogma may still have a religious temper, but he has no religion in the sense of a religious doctrine.

I have said of fundamental religious dogmata that they 'state *or indicate*' man's relation to the universe as a whole. My reason for caution was the logical peculiarity of religious discourse which, roughly speaking, stems from an attempt to deal with extraordinary experiences and events in a linguistic and conceptual framework which is, or at least appears to be, more suited for ordinary experiences and events. The difficulty is greatest in the case of the mystics who try to express in a language which they share with their fellows experiences which they do not share with them. In trying to express an experience which, whatever else it may be, is not statable by the application of attributes to distinct individuals by a person who is aware of himself as a separate individual, the mystic must rely on paradox and even absurdity, on hints rather than statements. A paradox or absurdity may, so to speak, hit one over the head and thus make one see stars which one would not otherwise see. Examples of this use of language in religious discourse are very frequent. Let me choose two, almost at random. One is the apparent contradiction of the Brahman religion which asserts 'That art thou', i.e. that the self and the nonself are 'in reality' identical. The other is contained in a book by Nicolaus Cusanus entitled *On the Learned Ignorance*[1] in

[1] Published in 1440; see edition by P. Rotta (Bari 1913)

which he expresses the conviction that it is the aim of all human intellectual and spiritual endeavour to attain 'that simplicity where contradictories coincide'.

Some, though perhaps not all, alleged miracles present similar obstacles to linguistic formulation and conceptualization. We may be convinced, for example, that the dead cannot be brought back to life after a certain time. Having heard from reliable sources that some people have been revived by doctors after being technically dead for a short time, we can imagine the temporal gap between death and revival to become 'miraculously' greater. But a person who tries to assimilate the natural to the supernatural in this manner has an attitude to miracles which is not characteristically religious. The point of a miracle for a religious person is not that it is located on a continuum between the natural and the supernatural, but that it is a clear manifestation of the supernatural in nature. And to speak in this manner is, as in the case of mystical experiences, to use paradox or absurdity. The miracles which are essential to Christian belief, in particular the resurrection, are of this kind and cannot be construed – except by agnostic bishops – as 'almost' natural events.

The recognition of paradox and absurdity in religious discourse, which results from the use of 'ordinary' notions like 'that', 'thou', 'contradictory', 'coincidence', etc., presupposes a more or less clear distinction between the natural and the supernatural. Such a distinction is absent from the so-called primitive cultures studied by anthropologists. Although much can be learned from their analysis of 'magical', 'mystical' and 'pre-scientific' thinking which is relevant to a better understanding of both religious doctrines and scientific theories, we must limit ourselves to cultures in which, as in our own, a conception of nature as opposed to the (possibly spurious) supernatural has developed. In such cultures the task of religious doctrine is not only to formulate religious dogmata and to guard their apparent paradoxicalities and absurdities against misinterpretations, but also to explain them as expressing the relation between nature and the supernatural.

The complex development of Christian religious doctrine has been summarized by Harnack in the Prolegomena to his monumental *History of Dogma*[1] as follows: 'Dogma in its conception and development is a work of the Greek spirit on the soil of the Gospel. .... The Gospel itself is not a dogma, for belief in the Gospel provides room for knowledge only so far as it is a state of feeling and course of action, that is a definite form of life.' Just as Greek philosophy brought an already available conceptual framework and way of thought to the interpretation of events reported in the New and the Old Testament, so Indian philosophy brought different concepts and modes of thinking to the interpretation of the Vedas. The resulting religious doctrines are very different – not least because the primary sources of Christianity are mainly miraculous events while those of Brahmanism are mainly mystical experiences. According to Christianity the supernatural and the natural are two orders of real existence which are in a mysterious way linked by its founder who is both God and also a man. According to Brahmanism there is one supernatural reality, and nature is only an illusion, dispelled by mystical experience and by the final merging of the individual soul into oneness with the supernatural.

Insofar as religious thinkers relate religious doctrine about the supernatural to the world of nature, they are exposed to intellectual pressures from growing, or at least changing, beliefs about nature. They must account for the apparent paradoxicality and absurdity of dogmata not merely by asserting it to be apparent, but by arguing that and why it is only apparent. In this respect they are like other philosophers. But unlike other philosophers they are committed to the deliberate and unconditional acceptance of the dogmata of their religion. The philosophy of religion, as opposed to any particular religious philosophy or theology, is free from any such commitments. One of its tasks is the analysis of the structure of religious doctrines, e.g. of the relation between the primary religious sources

[1] English translation from 3rd German edition of *Dogmengeschichte* (Freiburg 1900)

and their conceptual formulation and interpretation. Other tasks are the examination of the relationship between science and religion and between religion and morality.

THE CONFLICT BETWEEN SCIENCE AND RELIGION

This conflict arises with very different intensity for different religions. It hardly arises at all for a religion which, like Brahmanism, is based mainly on mystical experiences and interpreted, after the fashion of Sankara's commentaries on the Vedanta, in terms of a sharp distinction between the natural world as it appears in perception and is conceptually organized and the world as it is 'in itself', i.e. unperceived and not subsumed under concepts. This was seen very clearly by Schopenhauer, whose *World as Will and Idea*[1] constitutes an original metaphysical synthesis of Sankara's interpretation of Brahmanism and Kant's transcendental philosophy. If one accepts that the world as perceived and conceptually organized by human beings is, to use Kant's expressions, 'phenomenal' and not 'noumenal', then science is wholly restricted to the former. Whether and how the noumenal world is accessible is a different question, to which Kant, Schopenhauer and – under Schopenhauer's influence – Wittgenstein gave different answers. Yet in so far as the supernatural is indicated, e.g. as 'the thing in itself' (Kant), 'the Will' (Schopenhauer), 'the mystical' (Wittgenstein), no contradiction between these indications and scientific statements can ever arise.

The situation is far less clear when we compare scientific theories with religious doctrines which, like Christianity, contain as dogmata beliefs in the occurrence of miracles. A very simple but, I should think, heretical solution is the following: if taken literally, statements about the occurrence of miracles are paradoxical or absurd. They indicate, however, a truth which cannot be gathered from their literal meaning. This truth must be compatible with the best available empirical knowledge. If this solution is adopted, then all dogmatic beliefs in

[1] *Die Welt als Wille und Vorstellung* (Leipzig 1819)

miracles become metaphorical or 'symbolic' at the cost of being deprived of their original content. More bluntly stated, all references to apparent miracles do not really refer to miracles at all.

Other equally implausible solutions have been suggested. One is that the reports on apparent miracles are really disguised formulations of mystical experiences. The Christian beliefs in the incarnation and resurrection, for example, become a way of indicating a mystical oneness of all men with reality as a whole. Another answer is that the allegedly factual dogmata are really disguised practical precepts. They tell us not what was the case, but enjoin us to live *as if* what is reported as apparently having happened did happen. I have called these interpretations implausible, not because I can make no sense of them. I can. They are implausible as interpretations of the sincere belief in miracles which is essential, e.g. to traditional Christianity.

A more subtle approach to the apparent conflict between science and a belief in miracles might start with an analysis of scientific theories and their relation to experience on roughly the lines of chapter 4. One might point out that scientific theories are logically disconnected from sense-experience, which they do not describe but idealize. The nature of this idealization has been characterized in some detail under the headings of deductive unification (i.e. the modification of empirical discourse on being incorporated into the framework of classical logic and its mathematical extensions) and of deductive abstraction (i.e. the elimination of concepts, which are not relevant to the area covered by the theory, from the conceptual network of empirical discourse). One might then, again on the lines of the analysis of chapter 4, point out that the bridging of the logical gap between scientific theory and experience – the 'application' of the theory to experience – consists in the identification of (theoretical statements describing) an ideal world with (empirical statements describing) the world of experience. This identification is, as we have seen, not the assertion of an identity, but merely the assertion that *for certain specified purposes and within certain specified contexts* idealized and unidealized experience can be treated *as if* they were identical. It might then be argued that in order to make use of this analysis in establishing the consistency between science and a belief in miracles only one further step need be taken: namely, to require that the context in which the identification is permissible should exclude the occurrence of a miracle.

But such a requirement is incompatible with the manner in which scientific theories are tested, since it would make their harmony or disharmony with experience dependent on the individual scientist's religion. An alleged event which would otherwise discredit a theory, or be discredited by it, would nevertheless be regarded as being in harmony with the theory, if the event is among the individual or generic miracles attested by the scientist's religion. The multiplicity of religions, attesting different miracles and classes of them, would make the agreed evaluation of some experiments difficult, if not impossible. It would, in any case, make scientific theory, practice and co-operation into something that is quite different from what it is in fact. In this sense the belief in miracles runs counter to the spirit of science.

Nor will it do to allow a limited intrusion of miracles into the course of nature, e.g. by holding that nature leaves room for random events, some of which could be miracles. For just as the assumption that the course of nature can be limited by supernatural events occurring in nature runs counter to the spirit of science, so the assumption that the manifestations of the supernatural in nature is limited by nature runs counter to the spirit of most, if not all, religions. It certainly violates the spirit of all major Western religions. The truth-claims of science and of religious belief in miracles are such that one of them must be subordinated to the other. Other religious beliefs about the supernatural, for instance the belief in a perfect being who is the creator and sustainer of nature, are not incompatible with science, as was clearly seen by Kant and other metaphysicians before and after him.

METAPHYSICAL AND RELIGIOUS DOCTRINES

Thus the same propositions may be asserted by metaphysical and religious doctrines. Yet religious doctrine differs radically from what might be called 'open metaphysics', even though all the great metaphysicians of the past pursued dogmatic rather than open metaphysics.[1] Open metaphysics exempts no region of experience *deliberately* from critical examination. It exhibits, examines, modifies, and speculatively proposes frameworks of principles and concepts which are assumed, or intended, to constitute the underlying structure of all experience and belief. It proceeds by argument, is corrigible, and seeks out confrontations which enforce the correction of its theses. It may try to delimit the region of the unutterable but, unlike religion, music or poetry, does not try to utter it. Dogmatic metaphysics differs from open metaphysics chiefly by accepting certain propositions as absolute. If it accepts the dogmata of a certain religion it becomes religious apologetics or dogmatic theology. Dogmatic theology may contain ideas and arguments which prove fruitful in open metaphysics and generally in philosophy. But it is neither.

RELIGION AND MORALITY

Religion is in many ways intimately connected with morality. A person who is committed to a religious doctrine is, obviously, committed to the moral teaching which forms part of the doctrine. Mystical experiences, whether or not interpreted by an official religious doctrine, have profoundly changed moral attitudes. They have made an Indian king exchange his kingdom for a life of poverty and contemplation, and an Edwardian university don abominate the English public school system. The decline or rise of religious fervour in a society has often changed its moral standards. These and similar psychological and anthropological observations, which range from platitudes to surprising statements of fact, throw no light on the question

[1] See Part 4

of the logical dependence or otherwise of moral obligation on religious belief, especially on a religious belief in God.

Does 'I am morally obliged to conduct myself in a certain manner in a certain situation' logically imply 'God exists'? Variants of the following argument for an affirmative answer are fairly common. 'To be obliged' is an elliptical locution for 'To be obliged by a law'. The proposition that a law exists logically implies that a law-giver exists. The proposition that I am morally obliged thus logically implies that a moral-law-giver exists. But God is by definition the moral-law-giver. Hence 'I am morally obliged' logically implies 'God exists'. The argument would, if it were valid *and* if its premises were true, prove not only the logical dependence of morality on religion, but also the existence of God.

The validity of the argument can be easily secured by a suitable definition of its key-concepts. However, to define a concept is not to guarantee its applicability in the actual world. Thus the mere definition of the concept of a centaur is no guarantee that the animal kingdom includes a single animal to which the concept is applicable, i.e. that a centaur exists There are, it seems, two main reasons why people regard the key-terms of our moral argument for the existence of God to be applicable. First, they construe every concept of obligation after the fashion of legal obligation. To be legally obliged is, of course, to be obliged by a law. They then argue that every law issues as a command from a sovereign. This is, however, not true, since many societies have no sovereign and since even in societies in which a sovereign power is more or less clearly defined the members of the society may be legally bound by e.g. customary law. The Roman lawyers derived the binding force of customary law from long-established custom and from the conviction of its social necessity (*consuetudo longa et opinio necessitatis*). The justification of customary law in other societies is substantially the same. The second reason is to be found in the sacred scriptures of the Jewish, Christian, Mohammedan and other religions in which God as the sovereign of the universe is reported to have promulgated the fundamental moral laws. Now a person who is committed to the dogma of God as the legislator of the moral laws needs no independent philosophical argument which would establish his belief in the dogma. But if he, nevertheless, wishes to provide such an argument, the dogma must not be among its premisses.

Other arguments 'from morality to religion' are similarly defective. Thus analysis of *the* concept of moral obligation is supposed to reveal that the existence of moral obligations logically implies the existence of absolute justice. Such justice is not always apparent in the lives of morally good persons who suffer undeservedly and of wicked people who undeservedly prosper. Since, however, moral obligations and, therefore, absolute justice exist, the domain of nature, in which a person exists from one birth to one death, must be extended into a supernatural domain, which is so conceived as to allow each man an immortal soul, more than one life, or other similar features described or indicated by a religious doctrine. It is perfectly possible so to define a concept of moral obligation that it carries these or other religious implications. But it is simply not true that a concept of moral obligation which is free from them is therefore inapplicable. On the contrary, if the religiously enriched concept is applicable, then so is the original one. (If the concept of a white horse is applicable, so is the concept of a horse.) Moreover, the only ground for asserting the applicability of the religious component of the enriched concept of moral obligation is acceptance of the religious dogma, which describes or indicates the supernatural domain of which the religious component is supposed to be an attribute. The argument is circular.[1]

In practice a religious believer and a non-believer may acknowledge the same moral obligations (towards human beings), which neither of them has chosen or can discard as a matter of choice. Their motives for fulfilling their moral obligations may be different, but it is by no means clear that the mot-

[1] Other arguments for the existence of God are explained and examined in chapters 11 and 13

ives of one of them will be stronger than those of the other. Moral inadequacy might be enhanced not only by rejecting a religion, but also by accepting it, especially if it contained a doctrine of absolution from sin and a ritual procedure for attaining this. It is probably true that the more intense a person's moral convictions are, the greater will be his courage to stand by them. But the convictions of a secular morality can be as strong as those of a religious morality. Again, the decay of a religion as a social force is frequently accompanied by a decay of the morality which it incorporates. Yet such a decay need not amount to 'demoralization', since it may be accompanied by the emergence of a new morality. But these are empirical questions which – though talked about endlessly by all kinds of professionals and amateurs – are far from having been answered. The philosophical point which I have tried to make is simply that a non-religious morality is not a contradiction in terms.

AGNOSTICISM

Agnosticism is the rejection of any claim made by religious doctrines to any knowledge of the supernatural. Like Goethe's Faust on his Easter walk, the agnostic 'hears the message, but lacks the faith' and may remark – if the religious message is essentially that of a miracle – that a 'miracle is the dearest child of faith'.[1] He does not deny the possibility and occurrence of mystical experiences, and may even believe himself to be acquainted with such experiences. But he is incapable of believing unconditionally what he cannot organize conceptually. He does not reject as mere verbiage the mixture of factual statements, paradoxes and absurdities, by which religious doctrines point to an alleged supernatural reality which he does not apprehend. He does not deny that what cannot be perceived, imagined or brought under concepts may nevertheless exist. Nor is he necessarily a stranger to the mood in which birth and death, good and evil, and even the existence of whatever exists, appear a dark mystery. But – unless he is unfortunate enough

[1] *Faust* part I, scene I

174

to be in danger of brutal persecution for his views, and possibly not even then – he sees no reason for pretending that the religious doctrine of his neighbour or some other doctrine illuminates this darkness for him. He may, helped by the metaphysical speculations of the great philosophers, undertake his own speculative voyage on what Kant called 'the wide and stormy ocean' of the noumenal, which surrounds the island of possible experience, and is 'the seat of illusion where many a fogbank and many a quickly melting layer of ice creates the false impression of new lands'.[1] But he will expect to bring back, at best, no more than a thought-possibility and never an unconditionally acceptable truth.

The agnostic is not an atheist, who unconditionally, uncritically and by an act of faith accepts the doctrine that reality is identical with what is accessible to 'ordinary' experience and theorizing. (The definition of 'ordinary' may vary, but nowadays usually implies compatibility with science.) An *unconditional* acceptance of any doctrine about the universe as a whole and of man's place in it, whether theistic as in Christianity, or atheistic as in some forms of Buddhism, is itself a religious acceptance or (to avoid a needless quarrel about words) very similar to it. The agnostic refuses to turn science into religion by accepting any scientific hypothesis as an article of faith; or to turn religion into science by regarding any article of faith as an empirically confirmed hypothesis. Atheists are prone to the former confusion; some recent philosophers of religion to the latter.

[1] *Kritik der reinen Vernunft*, B. 294

Part 4

METAPHYSICS

Introduction

At the beginning of this book when examples of philosophical problems and methods were given, and later in the course of discussing specific philosophical problems, the term 'metaphysics' was occasionally used in referring to questions and answers which were neither logical nor empirical, and which did not belong to the philosophy of natural science, mathematics or some other non-philosophical inquiry. Metaphysics seemed to loom larger in the philosophy of history and of religious doctrines. Yet metaphysical assumptions are tacitly made in all regions of commonsense and scientific thought. It is their very generality, pervasiveness and familiarity which hides their presence from us in the same way in which we fail to notice the air we breathe or the weight of our bodies, unless for some good reason we direct our attention to them. This may appear very implausible to many people who have glanced at the pages of books containing the word 'metaphysics' in their title and have been repelled by their apparent abstruseness and remoteness from common modes of thinking. The impression vanishes when we formulate and examine, not the metaphysical assumptions of a forgotten historical period or the proposals of an unsuccessful metaphysical innovator, but the metaphysical assumptions of our own culture and age.

In the following four chapters I shall explain and criticize some characteristic conceptions of metaphysics and, as a result of my criticisms, suggest a different account of metaphysical systems (chapter 11). Next I shall examine the extent to which metaphysical assumptions are corrigible, and the manner in which they are in fact corrected (chapter 12). I shall then discuss whether an absolute, incorrigible metaphysics is possible (chapter 13). The concluding chapter of this part will be devoted to the metaphysical problem of freedom and natural necessity (chapter 14).

11. Some Conceptions and Types of Metaphysics

The Greek words of which 'metaphysics' is the translation originally meant no more than the treatise which came after ('meta') the Physics in the compilation of Aristotle's works by his pupils. It did not, as does 'metamathematics', mean a theory which has another theory as its subject matter. I mention this mildly interesting circumstance only because the name 'metaphysics' has acquired, among a variety of other connotations, that of being a theory of theories including physics. Aristotle, who wrote the first systematic treatise on metaphysics, defined it as the science of 'Being *qua* Being'. This real or alleged science has since been called 'ontology' (since 'onta' means 'beings' in Greek) in order to distinguish it from 'metaphysics' in its other senses.

In the present chapter I shall, first of all, consider three important conceptions of metaphysics, namely the Aristotelian conception of metaphysics as ontology, the Kantian conception of metaphysics as epistemology, and Collingwood's conception of metaphysics as a historical science whose aim it is to uncover the ultimate presuppositions which, as a matter of historical fact, are, or have been, made by the people of some community, especially its scientists, theologians or other theorists. I shall then, picking up some earlier threads from Chapter 2 briefly develop a new conception of metaphysics as the exhibition, modification and speculative proposal of categorial frame-works. This approach, it will be argued, does justice to what is unobjectionable in the ontological, epistemological and histori-cal points of view and will allow us to determine the logical status of metaphysical propositions more clearly and more definitely than was feasible when the problem first confronted us in chapter 2.

METAPHYSICS AS ONTOLOGY

Every science has some subject matter the existence of which it takes for granted. Thus zoology is about existing animals or, to put it in a less usual fashion, about animal existence, physics about physical and anthropology about human existence, etc. According to Aristotle, there is also a science which studies existence as such, i.e. 'Being *qua* Being and the properties in-herent in it in virtue of its own nature.' This science 'is not the same as any of the so-called particular sciences, for none of the others contemplates Being *qua* Being; they divide off some portion of it and study the attributes of this portion, as do for example the mathematical sciences'.[1] The metaphysician searches 'for the first principles and the most ultimate causes' which are 'the elements of Being not incidentally, but *qua* Being'. A few brief examples will illustrate Aristotle's concep-tion of ontology, though not its wealth or depth.

Although 'Being' is used in many senses, e.g. as the Being of substances, of the modifications of substances, of processes directed towards the emergence of substances, of the destruc-tions or privations of substances, the fundamental Being is the Being of substances on which all other senses of 'Being' depend. 'If then substance is this primary thing, it is of substances that the philosopher must grasp the first principles and causes'.[2] Aristotle distinguishes elsewhere[3] between 'primary substance' and 'secondary substance' which 'is asserted of a subject but not present in a subject'. Examples of primary substances,

[1] *Metaphysics*, book IV, 1003 a ff
[2] *ibid.* 1003 b 15 ff   [3] *Organon (Categoriae)* 2 a 11

which following a frequent usage of Aristotle I shall simply call substances, are individual material things, such as particular men or chairs. Examples of secondary substances are the species and genera under which the primary substances are subsumed, such as the human species and the genus of mammals.

The nature of those substances which are material things is understood in terms of Aristotle's doctrine of the 'four recognized kinds of cause'. This doctrine is developed at length in the *Physics* and is briefly repeated in the *Metaphysics*.[1] It was no doubt considered less strange in the Athens of the fourth century B.C. than it seems from the point of view of today's commonsense and science. Of the four causes 'one is the essence or essential nature of the thing . . . ; the second is the matter or substratum; the third is the source of motion; and the fourth is the cause which is opposite to this, namely the purpose or "good"; for this is the end of every generative or motive process.' The essence of a thing is that aspect of it in virtue of which it is an individual thing. It is not spatio-temporal location which, as e.g. Kant held, 'individuates' Callias; but 'Callias is in virtue of himself Callias and the essence of Callias'.[2] Aristotle's notion of the essential nature of things is obscure, controversial and – as far as it can be grasped – not indispensable to everybody's way of thinking about material things. The notion of final cause is much clearer, and clearly dispensable. For one can think of things as having no final causes, i.e. ends or purposes of their existence.

According to Aristotle the principles of logic, in particular the laws of contradiction and excluded middle, are also ontological truths.[3] Even if he had not expressed this view explicitly, it is implicit in the use which he makes of the principles in his attempt to refute the ontologies of Parmenides, who asserts Being to be changeless, and of Heraclitus, who asserts it to be ever-changing. Aristotle does not merely accuse them of

[1] Book 1, 983 a 20 ff   [2] *Metaphysics*, book V, 1022 a 25 ff
[3] *Metaphysics*, book IV, 1105 a 15 ff

violating these principles by committing logical fallacies, but of proposing theses which, because they are incompatible with these principles, express ontological falsehoods. In this connexion it is well to remember that the intuitionist philosophers of mathematics consider the principle of excluded middle to be false in mathematics.[1]

Aristotle's ontology is also a theology[2], although developed quite independently of any religious doctrine. It contains, for example, the following argument from the essence of Being to the existence of an eternal prime mover: 'There is something which is eternally moved with an unceasing motion. . . . This is evident not only in theory, but in fact. . . . Therefore, there is something which moves it. And since that which is moved while it moves is intermediate, there is something which moves without being moved; something eternal which is both substance and actuality.'[3] The argument presupposes both the physical fact that there is eternal movement ('of the heavenly spheres') and the physical law that 'an object in motion must be under the present influence of something that is acting upon it'.[4]

This Aristotelian law of motion is incompatible with the first of Newton's 'axioms or laws of motion' which in Motte's English translation of 1729 reads as follows: 'Every body continues in its state of rest or uniform motion in a right line, unless it is compelled to change that state by forces impressed upon it.'[5] Yet Newton's first law of motion is proposed as an axiom of the Being of physical substances in the same way as the Aristotelian axiom with which it is incompatible.[6] The philosopher who accepts the Aristotelian ontology cannot ignore this incompatibility if he takes Aristotle's conception of metaphysics seriously. For 'there are just as many divisions of

[1] See page 54   [2] e.g. *Metaphysics*, book VI, 1026 a 15 ff
[3] *ibid.*, book XII, 1072 a ff   [4] *Physics*, book VIII, 254 b 25
[5] Quoted from Newton, *Mathematical Principles of Natural Philosophy* ed. by F. Cajori (University of California Press 1947)
[6] For a discussion of the incompatibility and related matters see e.g. I. B. Cohen, *The Birth of the New Physics* (London 1961)

philosophy as there are kinds of substance . . .'[1] and what is true in metaphysics cannot be incompatible with what is true in any of the other divisions of philosophy. Aristotle's conception of metaphysics as ontology implies that it and what we now call the 'sciences' are logically connected with each other. In the case of an inconsistency between them one of them must be corrected. As a matter of historical fact the Aristotelian axioms of motion have yielded to Newtonian physics.

Aristotle makes two important assumptions, which are fundamental to his metaphysical enterprise as a whole, namely (i) that the theses which he puts forward in the metaphysics are absolute and not, e.g. corrigible hypotheses and (ii) that Being, as it is 'in itself', is accessible to human beings without suffering any modification through perception and the application of concepts. He does not claim that these assumptions are justifiable by some special metaphysical insight or method; the metaphysician must rely on ordinary perception and hard thinking, which alone can reveal the 'essential nature' of the substances in virtue of which they are what they are and Being is what it is. Since he gives no reasons for his assumptions of absolute ontological truths and the accessibility of Being 'in itself', they must stand or fall without such support. Once brought to light they appear highly implausible, if only because many of Aristotle's metaphysical theses have been abandoned, and their abandonment has not impeded theoretical thought in the various 'divisions of philosophy', in particular the natural sciences. Indeed, the abandonment of the doctrine of the four causes, of the axiom that there can be no unmoved moving substance, and of other Aristotelian principles has been accompanied by theoretical progress.

METAPHYSICS AS EPISTEMOLOGY

Although many of the great metaphysical thinkers before and after Aristotle share his assumption of the accessibility of 'Being *qua* Being', they do not regard the relation between

[1] *Metaphysics*, book IV, 1004 a 5 ff

Being on the one hand, and perception and thought on the other, as unproblematic. In fact, the nature of this relation became one of the major philosophical problems of the modern era. In attempting its solution Kant was led to a new conception of metaphysics as capable of discovering absolute truths, *not* about Being *qua* Being, but Being *qua* known or knowable. The theory which contains these absolute truths can, therefore, no longer bear 'the proud name of an ontology'.[1]

Kant agrees with Aristotle that the principles of metaphysics are common to all sciences and that they differ in character from the special principles which belong to the various particular sciences. An example of a metaphysical principle is the proposition that every change has a cause; and I shall use it in illustrating Kant's definition of metaphysical principles. They are (i) *a priori* in the sense of being 'independent of all experience and even of all impressions of the senses'.[2] At least part of Kant's meaning can be expressed by saying that no proposition describing a mere sense-impression logically implies either an *a priori* proposition or its negation. As regards our example, Kant agrees with Hume that the concept of a causal connexion does not describe any sense-impression; and that no proposition describing a sense-impression – in particular not a proposition describing a succession of events – logically implies either the principle of causality or its negation. The principle is *a priori*. A proposition which is not *a priori* is *a posteriori*. Metaphysical propositions are (ii) synthetic in the sense that the principle of contradiction is not 'sufficient to determine their truth'.[3] This definition may in the light of later developments in formal logic, but still in the spirit of Kant, be given in the following corrected form: metaphysical propositions are synthetic in the sense that the principles of logic are not sufficient to determine their truth.[4] Kant had no

---

[1] *Kritik der reinen Vernunft*, 2nd edition (Riga 1787), page 304
[2] *ibid*. page 2   [3] *Kritik der reinen Vernunft*, page 190
[4] Perhaps we should say 'the principles of logic *and* explicit verbal definitions' – such as: 'vixen' means the same as 'female fox'; or 'father' means the same as 'male parent'

reason to consider the problem of alternative logics.[1] A proposition which is not synthetic is analytic. The principle of causality as understood by Kant is clearly synthetic. If it were analytic, i.e. true in virtue of logic alone, it could not be incompatible with quantum mechanics in which the occurrence of uncaused changes is asserted. Metaphysical principles are (iii) *non-mathematical*. Kant – unlike Leibniz and the logicists, but like the intuitionists and some formalists – regards the axioms and theorems of mathematical theories as synthetic and *a priori*.[2] But he wishes, as did Aristotle, to distinguish metaphysical from mathematical propositions.

According to Kant the main tasks of metaphysics are: (i) to isolate and to exhibit systematically the mathematical and non-mathematical (i.e. metaphysical) synthetic *a priori* propositions which are employed in commonsense and scientific thinking; (ii) to demonstrate the indispensability of those that are indispensable, and the dispensability or spuriousness of the others. Kant calls these tasks, by analogy to legal usage, the *quaestio facti* (question of fact) and the *quaestio iuris* (question of law).

It is Kant's approach to the *quaestio iuris* about the synthetic *a priori* propositions which turns metaphysics into epistemology. The core of his answer is expressed in the following famous passage from his preface to the second edition of the *Critique of Pure Reason*.[3] I shall divide it into two separate parts. (A) 'If intuition must conform to the nature of the objects, then it is not at all clear to me how one could know anything *a priori* about it; but if the object (as object of sensation) conforms to the nature of our faculty of intuition, I find this possibility quite intelligible.' (B) 'Since, however, I cannot rest content with these intuitions, if they are to become knowledge, but must relate them as representations to something as their object – and must determine the object by the representations – I am again confronted by two possibilities: I can either assume that the *concepts* by means of which I determine the object conform to the object, in which case I am in the

---

[1] See pages 55 ff   [2] See pages 64 ff
[3] *Kritik der reinen Vernunft*, page 17

same perplexity as before. . . . Or else I can assume that the objects, or, what amounts to the same, the *experience* in which alone (as given objects) they are known, conforms to these concepts, in which case I can see a way out. . . .'

(A) by itself contains the central idea of Kant's philosophy of mathematics. The synthetic and *a priori* character of the axioms of geometry and arithmetic is explained by the thesis that they describe, not the sensory content, but the formal structure of perceptions. Kant identifies this structure with a pure intuition of (Euclidean) space and (Newtonian) time. I have already discussed Kant's philosophy of mathematics in the restricted form in which it has been taken over by the intuitionist philosophy of mathematics; and have criticized it mainly on the ground that it does not do justice to the apparent multiplicity of competing geometries, set-theories and arithmetics.[1]

(B), together with (A), contains the central idea of Kant's epistemological conception of metaphysics as the science of the fundamental – perceptual and conceptual – structure of Being *qua* known or knowable. To apply concepts to the 'manifold of impressions'[2] is either to describe what is found, or to interpret, connect or organize it. In so far as the application of concepts to this manifold is the connexion or organization of impressions into external objects, it is the objects which conform to the concepts, rather than the concepts which conform to the objects. Concepts by whose explicit or implicit application to the manifold of impressions these impressions are connected into objects Kant calls '*a priori* concepts'. Concepts by whose application to the manifold of impressions these impressions are merely described he calls '*a posteriori* concepts'. *A posteriori* concepts are both abstracted from the manifold of impressions and applicable to it, whereas *a priori* concepts, though not abstracted from the manifold of impressions, are nevertheless applicable to it. Their application transforms the manifold of mere impressions into a manifold of external objects – it transforms mere subjective experience into 'objec-

[1] See chapter 4   [2] *Kritik der reinen Vernunft*, page 129

tive experience' or, as Kant often simply says, 'experience'. Kant holds that all *a priori* concepts are derivable from twelve fundamental concepts which he calls 'the Categories'. I need not enumerate them here.[1] Since Kant uses the term 'category', which usually designates merely a highest kind (*summum genus*) of entities, in a special, technical sense, I spell it with a capital.

'We cannot', says Kant, 'think of an object without Categories',[2] i.e. without applying at least one of them to the manifold of impressions. An example is the Category of causality – the *a priori* relation between cause and effect. Its application to the manifold of impressions must, therefore, account for at least one feature of objective experience. More particularly, Kant argues that a merely subjective experience of an alteration in the manifold of impressions is an *objective* experience of an alteration (= an alteration of an object) if, and only if, the Category of causality is applicable to it.[3] But to state this epistemological condition of objective experience is to state the metaphysical principle of causality, which is a non-mathematical, synthetic *a priori* proposition. Kant formulates it as follows: 'All alterations (of objects) occur in accordance with the law of the connexion of cause and effect.'

The same line of reasoning is adopted for all Categories: every Category is an *a priori* concept by whose application to the manifold of impressions, i.e. subjective experience, an aspect of this manifold becomes objective, i.e. an aspect of objective experience or the experience of objects. To state a true metaphysical proposition is, on the one hand, to state a non-mathematical, synthetic *a priori* proposition; and, on the other hand, to state that the applicability of a Category to subjective experience is a necessary and sufficient condition for some feature of it to be objective. The justification of a true metaphysical principle, i.e. a synthetic *a priori* proposition, is that it expresses a condition for the transformation of merely subjective into objective experience. Kant believes himself to have listed not only all the Categories, but also all the corres-

[1] *Kritik der reinen Vernunft*, page 106
[2] *ibid.* page 165   [3] *ibid.* 232 ff

ponding metaphysical principles which express the function of these Categories in conferring objectivity. Just as the axioms of Euclidean geometry and of arithmetic determine the *a priori* perceptual, spatio-temporal structure of objective experience so the metaphysical principles determine its *a priori* conceptual structure. The mathematical and the non-mathematical synthetic *a priori* principles thus together determine the formal structure of Being *qua* known or knowable.

Though rejecting as 'arrogant' the claim of metaphysics to knowledge of Being in itself, Kant replaces it by an equally absolute claim to knowledge of the *a priori* structure of objective experience. Yet the development of post-Kantian science casts as much doubt on Kant's epistemological metaphysics as did the development of post-Aristotelian science on Aristotle's ontology. In both cases the doubt affects not only the detailed working out of a conception of metaphysics but the conception itself.[1] The mere fact that the general theory of relativity is embedded in a non-Euclidean four-dimensional space-time continuum shows that Euclidean geometry, which is in any case an idealization rather than a description of the manifold of impressions, is not an indispensable presupposition of any objectively true scientific theory. And the mere fact that the principle of causality is, at least in its unrestricted Kantian form, rejected in orthodox quantum mechanics shows that causality is not an indispensable category.

METAPHYSICS AS HISTORY

Even if no metaphysical assumption is indispensable to commonsense and scientific thinking, it may still be true that such thinking cannot proceed without some metaphysical assumptions. Collingwood[2] not only recognizes this possibility, but regards it as an unalterable fact. He argues that the thought of different people, societies and periods rests necessarily on metaphysical principles. But these principles are not exempt from change, obsolescence and replacement; and their change, like

[1] See chapter 13   [2] *An Essay on Metaphysics* (Oxford 1940)

all other historical change, is a proper subject for historical investigation. According to Collingwood metaphysical principles are ultimate, as distinct from proximate, presuppositions. (In order to avoid misunderstandings, I have substituted 'ultimate' and 'proximate' for Collingwood's 'absolute' and 'relative'.) His conception of metaphysics can best be explained by keeping closely to his own words.[1]

'Every statement that anybody ever makes is made in answer to a question.' The question and the statement may be tacit and occur in a monologue. 'Let that which is stated (i.e. that which can be true or false) be called a proposition, and let stating it be called propounding it.' 'Every question involves a presupposition', by which is meant the 'one presupposition . . . from which it directly and immediately "arises".' The fact 'that something causes a certain question to arise' is called 'the logical efficacy of that thing'. A presupposition 'is either proximate or ultimate'. A proximate presupposition 'stands relatively to one question as its presupposition, and relatively to another question as its answer. An ultimate presupposition is one 'which stands, relatively to all questions to which it is related, as a presupposition, never as an answer'. Ultimate presuppositions are not propositions in the sense of not being true or false answers to any question. 'Metaphysics is the attempt to find out what ultimate presuppositions have been made by this or that person or group of persons, on this or that occasion or group of occasions, in the course of this or that piece of thinking.'[2]

This conception of metaphysics is both too narrow and too wide. It is too narrow in its delimitation of metaphysical thinking, which it defines as a species of exhibition-analysis, aiming at the discovery of ultimate presuppositions. It thus excludes any kind of metaphysical speculation. For example, those pre-Socratic philosophers of nature, who held that the universe consists of one kind of stuff only, the metaphysical atomists, who held that it consists of material atoms, and

---

[1] *An Essay on Metaphysics* (Oxford 1940), page 20 ff
[2] *ibid.* page 47

Leibniz, who held that it consists of spiritual ones, did not necessarily exhibit the ultimate presuppositions of their contemporaries. Nor did they necessarily consider their principles as ultimate presuppositions of their own. Leibniz and other metaphysicians admitted that their proposed metaphysical principles could be called into question, e.g. on empirical and logical grounds. They often engaged in discussions about their speculative proposals, and recognized their corrigibility by the manner in which they answered criticisms. For example, the atomistic metaphysical principle that there are absolute simples in nature may be proposed speculatively as an answer to the question whether or not infinite divisibility is logically possible, and justified by arguments concerning the relation between mathematics and nature. Yet even though the metaphysical principle is proposed as an answer to a question, and is therefore not an ultimate presupposition in Collingwood's sense, it would in accordance with most common and philosophical uses of the term still be called 'metaphysical'.

Collingwood's conception of metaphysics is too wide in its demarcation of the class of metaphysical principles. Any kind of principle could conceivably be accepted as an ultimate presupposition. Examples of propositions which at one time or other have been accepted by some people as ultimate presuppositions are: principles of logic, such as the law of excluded middle, principles of mathematics, such as the postulates of Euclidean geometry, principles of physics, such as the Aristotelian principle that every moving body is moved by something, principles of morals, such as Bentham's principle of utility, and, of course, all kinds of religious dogmata. Collingwood's definition of metaphysical principles by the manner of their acceptance rather than by their content or logical status thus blurs too many traditional and useful distinctions. The historical science of ultimate presuppositions is too different from traditional metaphysics to be called by its name. Yet 'historical dogmatics', as it might be renamed, is a perfectly feasible type of inquiry, which is not only interesting in itself, but useful to general history, anthropology, sociology and philosophy.

METAPHYSICS AS THE EXHIBITION, MODIFICATION AND SPECULATIVE PROPOSAL OF CATEGORIAL FRAMEWORKS

It was one of the central aims of Aristotle, Kant and many other metaphysicians to discover the most general concepts which are jointly characteristic of Being *qua* Being or Being *qua* known or knowable, and to formulate principles expressing the applicability of these concepts to their subject matter. In pursuing this aim they had to differentiate the universe into categories (highest kinds, *summa genera*) of entities, to distinguish these categories from each other, to exhibit their relations to each other, and to explain their relevance to commonsense and scientific thinking. By concentrating on this concern with categorization, and at the same time relinquishing any claim to absolute knowledge, we are led to a new, relativistic conception of metaphysics. It covers, I think, more adequately than Collingwood's historical dogmatics, the variety of inquiries which have traditionally been pursued under the name of metaphysics. But it does not cover them all, since there is hardly a branch of philosophy which has not at one time or another been regarded as metaphysical. I am, therefore, content to say that I am here trying to define 'metaphysics' in a narrow sense of the term. (A possible widening of the definition will be considered below, pp. 209 f.)

Any categorization of the universe is merely the highest level of a classification. It determines the highest genera of entities – other than the universal genus 'entity' to which every entity belongs – and is compatible with different subclassifications of these genera into species, subspecies, etc. In an analogous manner a zoological division of all the animals into highest genera is compatible with different subclassifications. Concerning each category of entities – e.g. the category, *if any*, of external phenomena, of facts, processes, of mental acts, etc. – the metaphysician asks two questions, namely what constitutes an entity of the category, and what individuates an entity of the category, i.e. what makes an entity of the category a distinct individual, belonging to it. He thus aims at a determination of what may be called the constitutive and individuating attributes of a category of entities.

I shall say that an attribute is *constitutive* of the entities belonging to a category if, and only if, (i) the attribute is applicable to some entity, i.e. is not empty and (ii) the entity's belonging to the category logically implies the applicability of the attribute to the entity. (Metaphysicians often search for a set of constitutive attributes, such that an entity's belonging to the category not only logically implies the applicability of each of the attributes, but is also logically implied by the applicability of their conjunction.) I shall say that an attribute is *individuating* for the entities belonging to a category if, and only if, (i) the attribute is applicable to every entity of the category and (ii) the applicability of the attribute to an entity of the category logically implies, and is logically implied by, the entity's being a distinct, individual entity of the category. So as not to complicate these definitions, I make no explicit mention of the underlying logic by reference to which the relation of logical implication is used. (See, however, chapter 12.) To every constitutive or individuating attribute, associated with a category of entities, there corresponds what might be called a constitutive or individuating principle expressing the applicability of the attribute to the entities. A categorization of the universe together with the constitutive and individuating attributes and principles which are associated with each category of entities will be called a *categorial framework*.

As an example of a partial categorial framework we might consider Kant's account of the structure of external phenomena. They form a category of entities. The Kantian Categories are their constitutive attributes. Their individuating attribute is their determinate spatio-temporal location in a space of Euclidean and in a time of Newtonian structure. The constitutive principles are the statements asserting the applicability of the Kantian Categories to all external phenomena. The individuating principle expresses the applicability to all external phenomena of the attribute of determinate spatio-temporal location in Euclidean space and Newtonian time. Thus what makes this movement of my fountain-pen an external phenomenon is, among other things, the applicability to it of the Category of causality, according to which the movement is the effect of another external phenomenon which is its cause. And what individuates this movement, and the fountain-pen itself, is its definite spatio-temporal location, or, if we prefer, its path through Euclidean space during an interval of Newtonian time.

The categories of entities belonging to a categorial framework may stand in a variety of relations to each other. Thus, 'being an entity belonging to a certain category' may logically imply, but not be logically implied by, 'being a plurality of entities belonging to a certain other category'. In the Kantian framework, for example, 'being an external phenomenon' logically implies, but is not logically implied by, 'being a plurality of impressions'. The former concept is, one might say, a unifying or objectifying interpretation of the latter. Again, concepts applicable to entities belonging to one category may, though mutually exclusive, for certain purposes and within certain contexts be identified with each other. Thus, as we have seen,[1] the concept of a physical triangle may in scientific reasoning be identified with the concept of a geometrical triangle, as defined in some geometrical theory. The former concept is, we have said, an idealization of the latter. The inter-categorial relations of unifying interpretation and idealization will be considered in more detail in the subsequent two chapters. Lastly, the employment of the constitutive concepts and principles associated with different categories of entities may lead to real or apparent conflicts, of which the conflict between natural necessity and moral freedom is a famous example.[2]

The metaphysician may be concerned with categorial frameworks in a number of ways, of which the following three are of special interest. He may, first of all, approach a categorial framework from the outside, with the aim of exhibiting the

[1] See page 72   [2] See chapter 14

individuating and constitutive principles employed by a group of thinkers. This *external or historical approach* results, if successful, in true empirical statements to the effect that such and such individuating or constitutive principles, e.g. the principle of causality, are employed by such and such people or groups. He may, secondly, examine his own categorial framework from the inside, with the aim of formulating its constitutive and individuating principles. This *internal approach* results, if successful, not in empirical statements about the acceptance of these principles but in the statement of the principles themselves, e.g. of the principle of causality. As we have seen, this principle appeared to Kant, who considered it from the inside of his own categorial framework, synthetic and *a priori*. Why all constitutive and individuating principles, when considered from the inside of the categorial framework to which they belong, give rise to this impression will be explained in more detail in chapter 13. The metaphysician may, thirdly, for a variety of reasons try to construct a new, or radically modified, categorial framework. This *constructive or speculative approach* results, if successful, in proposals for a new categorization of the universe together with new constitutive and individuating principles. The principles may be proposed for acceptance (*a*) as incorrigible synthetic *a priori* propositions, (*b*) as corrigible regulative principles, or (*c*) as 'relative' synthetic *a priori* propositions. The conception of a corrigible metaphysics may seem strange. I shall, however, presently argue, not only that it is perfectly reasonable, but also that it conforms to the traditional practice of metaphysicians – as distinct from their methodological pronouncements.

12. The Corrigibility of Metaphysics

By calling an internally consistent proposition, a set of beliefs or a theory 'corrigible', we do not simply imply that it is changeable or admits of alternatives. We also imply that it may conceivably come into conflict with experiences or considerations which are external to it; that the conflict can be resolved by abandoning or modifying it; and that this resolution can be supported by rational argument. Simple empirical generalizations – e.g. 'All swans are white' – are corrigible in this sense and are abandoned when they come into conflict with observations. But even there the conflict is not always resolved in favour of the observations, which sometimes may be reassessed and demoted to the status of illusions. Scientific theories – e.g. the Ptolemaic theory of the universe – are also corrigible in the light of observation, although the determination and resolution of conflicts between theory and experience may be a much more delicate matter.[1]

In the present chapter I shall argue that categorial frameworks and their associated principles are also corrigible. Conflicts, ranging from real or apparent incompatibilities to implausible or merely uncomfortable divergences, may arise between a categorial framework on the one hand, and various commonsense beliefs and experience on the other. Such a con-

[1] See chapter 5

flict may be resolved by abandoning or radically modifying the framework, and the resolution supported by rational argument. The conflict may concern the categorization of the universe as well as the constitution or the individuation of the entities falling within the various categories of the framework.

Indeed the conflict may go even deeper. It may affect the system of logic in which the categorial framework is embedded and thus force us to recognize *the corrigibility of systems of logic*. That every categorial framework presupposes a logic became clear when the notions of a constitutive and an individuating attribute were defined by means of the relation of logical implication, which differs for different logical theories, e.g. those discussed or mentioned in chapter 3. The dependence of a categorial framework on its underlying logic also becomes obvious when we remember that every categorial framework consists in a categorization of 'all entities' and thus presupposes the universal – as it were, transcategorial – concept of an entity. It presupposes that some propositions are true about any entity whatsoever. Such truths include the principles of logic. Yet a principle of one logic need not be a truth of another. The principles of excluded middle and double negation are truths of standard classical, but not of intuitionist logic. Again, the concept of 'all entities' is conceived by some logicians, e.g. Frege and Brentano, as a totality and thus an object; by others, e.g. Aristotle and Russell, as a mere plurality. The difference in these conceptions affects the structure of the corresponding logical systems.

I have tried to show earlier the possibility, availability and actual employment of alternative logics,[1] and shall in the next chapter give reasons for rejecting a rather tempting 'transcendental' argument to the contrary. The possibility of conflict between the logic underlying a categorial framework and some other area of thought or experience external to it is by no means far-fetched. Thus, as we have seen, the intuitionists have resolved the conflict between classical logic and their mathematical intuition by abandoning the former. And we must surely

[1] See pages 55 f

admit that they have supported their resolution of the conflict by rational arguments – even if we do not find these arguments convincing. Again, as has also been mentioned, some quantum-physicists have proposed the abandonment of standard, classical logic in favour of a different logical theory in order to resolve a conflict between their conception of quantum physics and classical logic. Lastly, it has been argued (especially in chapter 5), that a particular three-valued logic is more adequate to empirical discourse than standard classical logic. Once the corrigibility of a logical system which underlies one or more categorial frameworks is admitted, one might feel inclined so to widen the concept of a categorial framework that its underlying logic becomes part of it. Whether or not one decides to follow this inclination is, however, of little consequence.

THE CORRIGIBILITY OF CATEGORIZATIONS

There can, I think, be little doubt about the corrigibility of categorizations. There are plenty of examples in the works of social anthropologists of categorizations which, when looked at from the outside by a modern Westerner, seem bizarre. Yet a categorization made by a primitive people may occasionally seem less strange than one proposed by a modern meta-physician. Thus the Hanunóo of the Southern Phillipines exclude, we are told,[1] persons and animals from the class of material things, whereas Descartes, who regarded animals as complex automata, includes animals, but not persons, in that category. An adherent of Darwin's theory of evolution might reasonably argue that the Cartesian categorization conflicts with that theory and that the conflict should be resolved by adopting a different categorization. He might, in particular, argue that consciousness and intentional phenomena are not peculiar to men, but are found also on lower evolutionary levels. The general point, which hardly needs further elaboration, is that a categorization may come into conflict with new theories and new experiences, and that a resolution of the con-

[2] C. Lévi-Strauss, *La Pensée Sauvage* (Paris 1962), chapter 5

flict by abandoning or radically modifying the categorization may be supported by reasonable arguments. Such a conceptual change would, of course, affect every classificatory scheme based on the original categorization of entities, without necessarily affecting the logic underlying the categorial framework.

THE CORRIGIBILITY OF INDIVIDUATING
ATTRIBUTES AND PRINCIPLES

Taking the category of external entities or objects as an example, I assume that neither the logic underlying the categorial framework as a whole nor the question which objects are external objects is in dispute. Thus I assume that, say, a Leibnizian, a Kantian, an Einsteinian and a Bohrian would agree about what is to count, and what is not, as an individual external object. They find, for example, no difficulty in identifying the table around which they are to gather for a philosophical discussion. Yet they disagree about its individuating attribute. For Kant it is its location in space and time which, as pure intuitions, are quite distinct from their material content. As against this Leibniz argues that any such absolute conception of space and time is mistaken, that they are inseparable from the things in them, and that the notions of empty space or empty time are absurd. He regards space as an order of co-existences and time as an order of successions of things, whose individuality has nothing to do with their spatio-temporal location.[1] What according to Leibniz' individuates external objects is the 'principle of the identity of indiscernibles', i.e. that 'there are no two individuals which are indiscernible from one another'.[2] In other words, the attribute 'possessing at least one feature not possessed by any other entity' is applicable; and 'being an individual entity (of any category whatever)' logically implies, and is logically implied by, 'possessing at least one feature not possessed by any other entity'.

[1] *Correspondence with Clarke* (London 1717), third letter, section 4
[2] e.g. *ibid.* fourth letter, section 4

Leibniz rejects the Newtonian and thus implicitly the Kantian principle of individuation, because it conflicts with the general 'principle of sufficient reason', namely 'that nothing exists without a sufficient reason why it is thus rather than otherwise'.[1] This principle, which expresses the constitution of all existent entities, is closely connected in Leibniz's philosophy with the principle that God never acts without sufficient reason for acting as he does. Leibniz's argument for the rejection of absolute time is as follows:

Suppose someone asks why God did not create everything a year sooner; and that he wants to infer from this that God did something for which He cannot possibly have had a reason why He did it thus rather than otherwise, we should reply that this inference would be true if time were something apart from temporal things, for it would then be impossible that there should be reasons why things should have been applied to certain instants rather than to others, when their succession remained the same.[2]

A similar theological argument is used in rejecting the notion of absolute space.

Within an agreed category of external entities the individuating principles of such entities may conflict not only with a (perhaps nowadays rather remote) theological theory, but also with a scientific theory. I have already mentioned that the Newtonian and Kantian manner of individuating external phenomena through their location in a three-dimensional Euclidean space and an independent one-dimensional time is incompatible with the principle of individuation of the general theory of relativity, which replaces them by a four-dimensional Riemannian space-time with variable curvature. One cannot play down the seriousness of the conflict by saying that the general theory of relativity is after all only a theory. For just as Newton's individuating attributes and principles have seeped into commonsense, replacing older modes of commonsense thinking, so Einstein's principles might – and if they remain unchallenged for a long time very likely will – become

[1] *ibid.* third letter, section 7   [2] *ibid.* section 6

part, first of the educated, and later of the more common commonsense of future generations. Because the logical structures of theoretical and commonsense thinking are different, the theoretical concepts and principles will, of course, be received by commonsense in a loosened form.[1]

THE CORRIGIBILITY OF
CONSTITUTIVE ATTRIBUTES AND PRINCIPLES

As regards the problem of the corrigibility of constitutive attributes and principles the position is very much the same. An obvious example is the conflict between quantum mechanics, in the form given to it by Bohr, Heisenberg and others, and the constitutive principles of Kant and Newton. Quantum theory arose from an attempt to explain certain phenomena in the ordinary, macroscopic world – observed spectra, specific heats, radioactivity and the behaviour of light – which could not otherwise be explained. The new theory conflicts much more radically with the old categorial framework than does the general theory of relativity. As Einstein says of its interpretation by Bohr, it forces us to renounce the assumption 'of the independent existence of the physically real as located in the various parts of space'.[2] As has been mentioned earlier, in the opinion of some experts the new theory conflicts even with classical logic. It also conflicts with a common feature of the Kantian and Einsteinian principles of individuation by making the spatio-temporal position of some external phenomena dependent on a choice between mutually exclusive conditions of observation,[3] and it replaces the Kantian concept of causality as constitutive of external phenomena by the concept of a probable connexion. I cannot enter into a detailed discussion of the manner in which orthodox quantum theory tends to disrupt the older categorial framework, and how the framework

[1] See pages 86 f
[2] See the papers by Niels Bohr and Albert Einstein in *Dialectica*, volume 2 (Basle 1948)
[3] *ibid.*

can be preserved, for example, by a decision to regard the theory as false, or as a merely provisional instrument of prediction. The latter escape is neither inconceivable nor without precedent. It was suggested to Galileo Galilei on the authority of Cardinal Bellarmin and, ultimately, of Thomas Aquinas.[1]

It is worth mentioning that the abandonment of the principle of causality in favour of a principle of a merely probabilistic connexion between external phenomena had been suggested by C. S. Peirce long before the advent of quantum mechanics. He argued that the apparent unavoidability of experimental error in applying Newtonian physics is due, not to a defect in our measuring techniques, but to nature itself, whose laws are not strictly causal, but probabilistic.[2] This Peircean modification of the Kantian framework is much less drastic than the modifications brought about by Bohr's interpretation of quantum mechanics. It may, thus, serve as an example of a simpler and readily intelligible correction of a constitutive principle for an otherwise unchanged category of external phenomena. Kant, we remember, argued that the applicability of the Category of causality to the manifold of impressions is a necessary condition for an objectifying interpretation of it. But the abandoning of his Category does not, as he thought, imply the impossibility of physics and commonsense objective experience. It merely implies the replacement of Newtonian by a non-Newtonian physics.

The question of the corrigibility of constitutive principles arises also in mathematics. I have argued earlier (in chapters 4 and 5) that to apply a geometry to perception is not to describe perception, but to identify perceptual with geometrical notions within certain contexts and for certain purposes. Thus, e.g. both Euclidean and non-Euclidean triangles are not identical with, but are idealizations of, perceptual or physical triangles. More generally, entities of mathematics – and of all theories

[1] See G. de Santillana, *The Trial of Galileo* (London 1958)

[2] C. S. Peirce, 'The Doctrine of Necessity Re-examined', *Collected Papers*, ed. Hartshorne and Weiss (Harvard University Press 1931–5), volume 6

embedded in mathematics – do not belong to the category of external objects. They fall into a separate category, or separate categories, of entities and have their own individuating and constitutive attributes.

Gödel has stressed the analogy between, on the one hand, the constitution of new mathematical objects belonging to one category out of pluralities belonging to another and, on the other hand, the constitution of physical objects out of pluralities of sense perception.[1] 'It should be noted' he says

that mathematical intuition need not be conceived as a faculty giving an *immediate* knowledge of the objects concerned. Rather it seems that, as in the case of physical experience we *form* our ideas also of those objects on the basis of something else which *is* immediately given. Only this something else here is *not*, or not primarily, the sensations.[2]

What unifies a mere plurality of mathematical entities into an object is the application of the concept of a set to the plurality.[3] Gödel remarks that there is a close relationship between the concept of the set and the Kantian Categories, namely that 'the function of both is "synthesis", i.e. the generating of unities out of manifolds (e.g. in Kant, of the idea of *one* object out of its various aspects)'.[4]

Yet just as the constitutive attributes associated with the Kantian Category of external phenomena admit of alternatives and are corrigible in the light of, e.g. developments in physics, so the constitutive attributes of mathematical entities are also not unique: set-formations which are permitted in one type of set-theory are not permitted in another type. In Gödel's view this multiplicity is only apparent, since there is *one* mathematical reality which will eventually be described by *one* obviously true set-theory. But this philosophical conviction of a great mathematician is, I think, not at present well supported.

[1] See 'What is Cantor's Continuum Problem?' *American Mathematical Monthly*, 54, (1947). Revised and expanded version in *Philosophy of Mathematics – Selected Readings*, ed. by P. Benacerraf and H. Putnam (Englewood Cliffs, N.J. 1964)

[2] *ibid.* page 271   [3] *ibid.* page 262   [4] *ibid.* page 272, footnote 40

His appeal to the analogy between set-formation and the application of the Kantian Categories to pluralities of impressions is particularly unconvincing, since the Kantian constitutive principles are, as we have seen, corrigible.

I have said nothing about individuating principles in mathematics, since all mathematical theories employ the Leibnizian principle of the identity of indiscernibles for the individuation of mathematical entities. It is conceivable that this principle too might be replaced or modified. But I can adduce no example of an actual mathematical theory which makes use of a different principle of individuation.

The foregoing arguments and illustrations should be sufficient to show that categorial frameworks are corrigible. Yet a conflict between the demarcation of a category of entities and their constitutive or individuating principles on the one hand, and some other set of propositions on the other, need not be resolved by correcting the categorial framework. The conflict, for example, between the general theory of relativity and the Kantian principle of individuation can be resolved by reconstructing the theory. The general nature of such reconstructions has been explained early on in this book under the heading of replacement-analysis. Its task is, we remember, to solve problems of the following form: given an *analysandum A*, a criterion of defectiveness *D*, by which *A* is defective, and a replacement-relation *R* – to find or construct an *analysans X* such that, (1) *A* is not defective by the criterion *D* and (2) *A* stands to *X* in the replacement relation *R*. In our example *A* is the general theory of relativity, *D* a straight incompatibility with the Kantian principle of individuation for external phenomena, and *R* the requirement that *A* and *X*, i.e. the analysed and the analysing theory, should have equal predictive power. The problem is solvable.[1]

In the discussion of replacement-analysis it was pointed out that some of its problems possess no solution. However, even if a conflict between the principles associated with a categorial

[1] See e.g. R. d'E. Atkinson, 'General Relativity in Euclidean Terms', *Proceedings of the Royal Society* (series A), volume 272 (1963)

framework and some other proposition or set of propositions is not solvable by a particular kind of replacement-analysis because the conditions D and R are too strict, it is always open to the obstinate adherent of a categorial framework to weaken the conditions. Thus an intelligent person who, after having been brought up in a 'primitive' society and within a categorial framework pervaded by magical notions has obtained a degree in one or more of the natural sciences, might experience a strong conflict between his magical framework and his scientific knowledge. But he can, by suitable replacement-analyses of his scientific beliefs, adjust them to his original categorial framework. He can, if all else fails, subordinate science to magic, just as a scientist whose religion includes the belief in miracles, may subordinate science to his religion.

A GENERAL PATTERN OF ARGUMENTS
IN SUPPORT OF A CATEGORIAL FRAMEWORK

In order to exhibit a general pattern of arguments supporting one categorial framework in preference to another, it will be useful to start by considering an example. Let us imagine a nineteenth-century scientist who is also a Kantian defending the Kantian categorial framework, especially the Kantian concept of causality, against the Aristotelian categorial framework, especially the Aristotelian concept of final cause. Though imaginary the example is not implausible, since at that time many eminent scientists, e.g. Gauss, were Kantians. Our scientist might, first of all, simply assert that the Kantian framework is more in accordance with the spirit of science than the Aristotelian. If asked to formulate more clearly what he regards to be the spirit of science he might say that science has the twofold task of predicting and explaining natural phenomena. To the question as to what he means by 'explaining' natural phenomena, he might answer – for he is a typical nineteenth-century scientist – that a scientific explanation consists in showing that, and how, nature works as a mechanical system. He might supplement his answer by a general characterization of a mechanical system or by examples of such systems. In either case it would soon become obvious that he is drawing heavily on Newtonian physics.

At this stage of the imaginary dialogue our scientist's questioner might express the suspicion that the justification will become circular. He might point out that the Kantian categorial framework is itself derived from an analysis of Newtonian physics and a commonsense which is thoroughly imbued by it; and that consequently our scientist's conception of scientific explanation is defined by its capacity to be accommodated in the Kantian framework. If 'scientific explanation' means, among other things, fitting the Kantian framework, then the scientist can easily justify his position. But he will be arguing in a circle, the smallness of whose diameter will make his justification not only circular, but also trivial.

This point has, I think, to be conceded. But it still leaves our scientist with the possibility of justifying the Kantian or, indeed, the Aristotelian categorial framework by reference to the different predictive efficacy of scientific theories fitting one or the other framework. He might argue as follows:

'I take it that all of us desire scientific theories which allow us to predict the course of nature, and that we prefer scientific theories with greater predictive power to scientific theories with smaller predictive power. I admit, of course, that the comparison between the predictive power of two scientific theories is not always easy, and in some cases impossible. But the difference is, in many cases, especially those which are relevant to my argument, overwhelming. I have found that scientific theories which, naturally and without replacement-analysis, fit the Kantian categorial framework, are on the whole predictively much more powerful than scientific theories which fit the Aristotelian framework. This is why everybody who prefers more highly to less highly predictive theories should prefer the Kantian to the Aristotelian categorial framework.'

The argument is pragmatic, inductive and corrigible. It is pragmatic because the criterion by which the categorial frameworks are compared is their usefulness in satisfying a desire of high priority. It is inductive, since it infers the distribution of a certain feature in the class of all scientific theories from its distribution in the subclass of all so far available theories. And it is corrigible for the same reason that all inductive arguments are corrigible: it is in principle always possible that in future an increasing number of theories with high predictive power will fit the Aristotelian framework more closely than the Kantian, so that a future Aristotelian might be able to use a pragmatic, inductive argument of the same form in support of the Aristotelian framework.

Our example also exhibits a connexion between a categorial framework and experience through one or more intervening scientific theories. Experience is linked to a scientific theory by testable reasoning, the structure of which has been examined earlier.[1] A scientific theory is linked to a categorial framework by employing the categorization and the constitutive and individuating principles associated with the latter. Yet it should be noted that an empirical refutation of the theory may leave the categorial framework intact, namely, when the refuted theory is replaced by a new theory which fits the framework no less than did its abandoned predecessor.

Our example of an inductive argument supporting one categorial framework rather than another can be easily generalized. Instead of considering the Kantian and the Aristotelian categorial frameworks we may consider any two categorial frameworks; instead of particular theories we may consider types of theories; and instead of employing the pragmatic criterion of the desired maximum predictiveness, we may employ some other pragmatic criterion. Our criterion need not necessarily be pragmatic. It could, for example, be aesthetic, such as elegant simplicity, so long as it is logically independent of the constitutive or individuating principles associated with the frameworks. Again, we might instead of one criterion employ a whole set of them, in which case we would have to compare their respective weights. All these and other possibilities could be spun out endlessly.

[1] See chapter 5

The inductive argument of our example and its generalizations are, of course, exposed to all the objections which can be raised against induction as a method of reasoning. But even apart from these objections, it does not strike one as particularly convincing. This is due mainly to the paucity of statistical material. We cannot, for example, refer to mortality-tables of scientific theories – much less of other sets of beliefs – in the manner in which we refer to mortality-tables in estimating our expectation of life. The facts which are relevant to our arguments have not been statistically analysed, if indeed they are so analysable. We may, therefore, be inclined to be more modest in our defence of one categorial scheme in preference to another. Transferring this modesty to the nineteenth century Kantian scientist of our example, we allow him to express it by adding some qualifications to his defence of the Kantian categorial framework:

'I see that my inductive argument does not impress you greatly, and confess that I too do not find it convincing. Let me, therefore, simply repeat that in my experience the scientific theories which fit the Kantian categorial framework are on the whole predictively much more powerful than those which fit the Aristotelian framework. This is why everybody who prefers more highly to less highly predictive theories should *for the time being* prefer the Kantian to the Aristotelian framework.' This argument too can easily be generalized.

THE CORRIGIBILITY OF METAPHYSICAL PRINCIPLES IN A WIDER SENSE OF THE TERM

So far I have been concerned only with the corrigibility of metaphysics in the narrow sense of the term in which it comprises principles for the categorization of the universe into categories of entities, their associated constitutive and individuating principles, and the principles of logic underlying each categorial framework.

The principles of the logic in which a categorial framework is embedded are, as has been pointed out, constitutive not of the entities belonging to a particular category, e.g. the category of external objects, but of all objects as such. They are 'transcategorial constitutive principles'. They are not necessarily the only transcategorial constitutive principles associated with a categorial framework.

We have already encountered a non-logical, transcategorial constitutive principle in Leibniz's principle of sufficient reason, according to which whatever exists has a sufficient reason why it is thus rather than otherwise. Another such principle is Berkeley's famous 'to be is to be perceived'.[1] These and similar transcategorial constitutive principles are just as corrigible as are intracategorial ones. The class of corrigible metaphysical principles can be widened further by admitting into it those – non-logical and non-empirical – principles which are logical consequences of principles associated with a categorial framework in conjunction with other assumptions. An example is the principle of the continuity of every change in nature, often expressed by *natura non facit saltus* (nature makes no jumps). Kant deduces it from his constitutive principle of causality and the assumption that 'neither time nor what appears in time consists of smallest parts'.[2] A closely related example is the principle that there is no void in nature, often expressed as *natura abhorret vacuum* (nature abhors a vacuum). Leibniz deduces it from his transcategorial principle of sufficient reason together with his theology in the second letter to Clarke: 'The more matter there is, the more opportunity is there for God to exercise His wisdom and His power; and for this reason, among others, I hold that there is absolutely no void.'[3]

Yet in calling any member of the mixed logical progeny of framework-principles and other propositions 'metaphysical', we are exposing ourselves to rather pointless verbal disputes as to whether it deserves this name. It has in the past been

[1] *A Treatise Concerning the Principles of Human Knowledge* (Dublin 1710), section 3
[2] *Kritik der reinen Vernunft*, page 254
[3] *Correspondence with Clarke* (London 1717), third letter, section 4

awarded so indiscriminately that new stipulations governing its assignment or refusal may be in order. The following requirements, all of which are satisfied by framework principles, would seem reasonable: (i) A metaphysical proposition, to deserve this name, should be corrigible. (ii) A metaphysical proposition should not be logically necessary in the sense of being a substitution instance of some logical principle. This is part of what Kant meant by calling metaphysical propositions 'synthetic'. (iii) A metaphysical proposition should not be empirical in the sense that its truth or falsehood is determined solely by experiment or observation. This is part of what Kant meant by calling metaphysical propositions '*a priori*'. (iv) A metaphysical proposition should be comprehensive in the sense of applying to all entities of at least one category.

These criteria are not only satisfied by framework-principles and their pure or mixed progeny, but also by the corresponding regulative principles. Thus a person who employs the Kantian categorial framework will not only regard the principle of causality as (internally) incorrigible. He will also conform to the corresponding regulative principle that he should employ the concept of causality for organizing external phenomena in his commonsense and scientific thinking. In a similar manner every metaphysical statement supports a corresponding regulative principle. However, people may employ regulative principles which are not so backed in a merely heuristic fashion; and there is no good reason to exclude such principles, if they are sufficiently comprehensive, from the class of metaphysical principles. The possibility of construing metaphysical propositions as regulative principles was suggested very early on in this book as a middle position between the extreme views that metaphysical propositions are absolute truths *sui generis* and that they are nonsensical strings of words.[1] This suggestion, which has been useful on many occasions, has now been both refined and justified.

Our criteria could be made more precise. Even so they

[1] See page 33

would admit of borderline cases to which the name 'metaphys-ical' could be assigned or refused with equal propriety. My main concern in what follows will be with framework-principles.

13. The Problem of
Absolute Metaphysics

Metaphysical beliefs have been no more exempt from change than scientific beliefs. Yet while the ideal of incorrigible, absolute truth has been abandoned in the sciences, it is still very much alive in metaphysics. Metaphysicians no longer believe, as Descartes did, that there is a single method for the discovery of absolute truth in all intellectual inquiries, from the most concrete empirical science to logic and metaphysics. But many of them still hold, with Kant and Hegel, that there exists such a method for the discovery of absolute truth in metaphysics. They are prepared to admit that Kant, in employing the transcendental, or Hegel, in employing the dialectical method, may have been mistaken about some of the details or about the scope of these methods. But these shortcomings, they assert, are easily emended or avoided. It is mainly this faith in the fundamental soundness of the transcendental or the dialectical method which makes metaphysicians search for *the* true metaphysical system among the ruins of the past or inspires them with confidence in their own attempts to lay its foundations. In the present chapter I shall discuss various claims to reach absolute metaphysical truths by means of so-called transcendental deductions and by means of dialectical reasoning. I shall conclude by examining one of the most famous arguments for an allegedly incorrigible metaphysical thesis, namely Anselm's ontological argument for the existence of God.

TRANSCENDENTAL DEDUCTIONS

The conception and the name of a transcendental deduction is due to Kant.[1] The term 'deduction' is, Kant tells us, borrowed from the legal terminology of his day, where it means the justification or validation of a legal claim. The term 'transcendental' is meant to indicate that the claim concerns the necessity and universality of synthetic *a priori* propositions, in particular individuating or constitutive principles associated with his categorial framework. Kant attempts a transcendental deduction of the individuating principles for external phenomena in the Transcendental Aesthetic and a transcendental deduction of the constitutive principles for external phenomena in the Transcendental Analytic of his *Critique of Pure Reason*. Since these principles have been abandoned in post-Kantian mathematics and natural science, they are not universal and necessary, but dispensable. Kant's transcendental deduction has failed.

It may have failed because, although the general idea of a transcendental deduction is sound, the Kantian categorial framework is not, so that a transcendental deduction of some other categorial framework – perhaps one that resembles the Kantian in important respects – might still be feasible. Or else it may have failed because the general idea of a transcendental deduction is unsound. I shall try to justify the second diagnosis by defining a general notion of a transcendental deduction, of which the Kantian is a special case; by setting out necessary conditions for the success of any transcendental deduction; and by showing that one of them cannot be satisfied. Since this fundamental flaw of all transcendental deductions is rather simple, it will be useful to explain why it has escaped Kant and others after him. By providing this explanation,

[1] *Kritik der reinen Vernunft*, 2nd edition, Akademie Ausgabe, page 116

further light is thrown on the logical status of constitutive and individuating principles, especially their apparent incorrigibility when considered 'from inside', and their corrigibility when considered 'from outside' their associated categorial framework.

Let us say that a person 'employs' a categorial framework in his thinking about the objective content of his experience or, briefly, in his objective thinking if, and only if, he categorizes the world in the manner of the framework, applies its constitutive and individuating attributes and, explicitly or implicitly, acknowledges the truth of its associated constitutive and individuating principles. A person who employs e.g. the Kantian categorial framework will, among other things, agree with Kant that external phenomena form a category, that the constitutive attribute 'x causes y' is applicable to them, and that the constitutive principle of causality is true. A transcendental deduction can now be defined as a logically sound demonstration to the effect that a particular categorial framework is indispensable to everybody's objective thinking. A 'logically sound demonstration' need not, as was made clear by Kant, be a deductive argument. But it may contain deductive arguments, and these must not be fallacious.

Before a transcendental deduction of a categorial framework can be attempted, the framework itself must be exhibited or constructed. Kant uncovers the framework which he wishes to justify as indispensable by a brilliant exhibition-analysis of the commonsense and scientific thought of his day. He is on the whole successful in isolating the individuating and constitutive attributes of external phenomena from among the variety of attributes applicable to them, and in formulating the corresponding individuating and constitutive principles.

The analytical or speculative establishment of a categorial framework is, however, not the only precondition for its successful transcendental deduction. For even if we grant the possibility of showing that *some* categorial framework must be employed in everybody's objective thinking, we do not for this reason have to grant that the accepted categorial framework is *the only* available, or possible, categorial framework. (In a similar manner, we may grant the possibility of showing that we must drink some liquid if our thirst is to be quenched, without granting that lemonade is the only available, or conceivable, liquid.) The transcendental deduction of a categorial framework thus presupposes – or, if we prefer, includes – a demonstration of its uniqueness.

Kant and many other metaphysicians take their own categorial framework so much for granted that the need for a uniqueness demonstration does not occur to them. It is in any case difficult, if not impossible, to see how such a demonstration could be given. *Prima facie*, three possibilities seem to offer themselves of demonstrating the framework's uniqueness: first, by comparing it with experience as undifferentiated into individuals and attributes. But this cannot be done since the statements formulating the comparison would involve the application of some attributes. Even a mystic could not, presumably, experience the world and himself both in a differentiated and in an undifferentiated manner, and go on to compare them with each other. Second, by comparing it with all its possible competitors. But this cannot be done, since there is no reason for assuming that the competing frameworks, which someone can conceive at any particular time, exhaust all possible competitors. Thirdly, by an examination entirely 'from within', i.e. by means of statements employing its individuating and constitutive attributes. But such an examination can, at best, exhibit the way in which the framework is employed, not demonstrate its uniqueness.

The need for a uniqueness demonstration may be obscured by confusing the unavailability or inconceivability of alternative frameworks at a certain time or for a certain metaphysician with their impossibility. A closely related confusion consists in mistaking *the merely internal incorrigibility of framework-principles* for incorrigibility. Kant himself fell victim to it in regarding his synthetic *a priori* principles, which are internally incorrigible, as incorrigible without qualification. This has become clear in the case of the principle of causality, which is indeed synthetic, in the sense of not being a truth of logic, and *a priori*, in the sense of being independent of all impressions of the senses[1], but has nevertheless been abandoned, e.g. by Peirce. The point can be established quite generally as follows.

Consider a categorial framework F, a category of entities, say external phenomena, and an attribute S, (e.g. 'x is a substance') which is constitutive of the entities in the category. To assert the corresponding constitutive principle is to assert (i) that S is not empty, i.e. that it is applicable to some entity; (ii) that the entity's belonging to the category logically implies the applicability of S to the entity. The first of these propositions is not a truth of logic, i.e. it is synthetic. The second is a logical implication or, if we prefer, a definition. Their conjunction, which is the constitutive principle, is thus also non-logical. So long as we employ F, any statement about an entity of the category is, by definition, a statement about an instance of S. In other words, every statement about an entity of the category logically implies that the entity is an S. It follows that no statement about an entity of the category can be incompatible with the statement that all entities of the category are instances of S, i.e. with our constitutive principle. The principle is incorrigible, or *a priori, with respect to F.* By a similar argument we can show that any individuating principle for a category of entities associated with F is both non-logical and incorrigible with respect to F. Briefly, so long as we employ F, all statements refer to entities which are constituted and individuated by the framework principles of F. It follows that these principles are incorrigible with respect to F. It does *not* follow that they are simply incorrigible.

Kant's transcendental arguments are the most famous and, because of the many incidental insights they contain, very likely the most profound ones. Yet the tendency towards justifying a categorial framework or part of it by such arguments is not peculiar to the great philosopher who gave them their name. In the preceding chapter I have given examples of framework-principles, which were in fact abandoned or

[1] See page 188

corrected under strong – though never irresistible – pressures from outside a categorial framework. Most categorial frameworks which have in fact been abandoned or revised by thinkers of a later generation were the subject of a transcendental deduction by an earlier metaphysician.

An important example is the attempted transcendental deduction of the principles of standard elementary logic which, as 'trans-categorial' principles, are constitutive of all entities of whatever category, provided that the categorial framework in question is embedded in that logic. It is found in the writings of Frege.[1] In his terminology a linguistic expression, e.g. 'x is a philosopher' or 'x is to the left of y', expresses a function if, and only if, it contains one or more 'unsaturated' places, e.g. those indicated by 'x', or by 'x' and 'y', such that when the places are 'saturated' by suitable names, the expression becomes a true or false statement.[2] He defines a (transcategorial) object as 'everything that is not a function . . . that is to say everything the expression of which contains no unsaturated place'.[3] An object is thus anything that can be correctly named as a substitution-instance of a function, i.e. named as filling the place of an 'x', 'y', etc. The correctness is determined by the principles of logic and the logic in question is the logic employed by Frege, and formulated by him. One of these principles is the law of excluded middle. Let us call 'U' that attribute of any object which consists in its being correctly namable as a substitution-instance of a function. Then we may assert as a constitutive principle for the objects of any category that (i) U is not empty and (ii) 'Being an object of whatever category' logically implies 'possessing U'. The locution 'logically implies' like the locution 'correctly namable . . .' contains an implicit reference to Frege's logic.

Since, *if* one employs Frege's logic, no statement can be

---

[1] See especially 'Funktion und Begriff', (Jena 1891), now reprinted in G. Frege, *Funktion, Begriff, Bedeutung*, ed. G. Patzig (Göttingen 1962)

[2] See page 45

[3] *Funktion, Begriff, Bedeutung*, page 28

incompatible with the constitutive principle, this principle is internally incorrigible. Frege, however, holds that it is incorrigible without qualification. He says that the notion of a (transcategorial) object 'because of its simplicity does not admit of further logical decomposition' and implies that if a particular notion of an object is employed in *his* thinking and is not further analysable in the logic underlying it, then it is indispensable to everybody's thinking.[1] A similarly unsatisfactory argument is put forward by Russell in order to demonstrate the incorrigibility of the principle of excluded middle.[2] It is, he argues, 'necessary for the beliefs which none of us, if we are sincere, is willing to abandon'. There is no good philosophical reason for excluding the intuitionists, much less thinkers of future generations, from the company of those among 'us' who are sincere.

It is interesting to note that Bohr who, as one of the creators of quantum mechanics, showed the possibility of abandoning the principle of causality without thereby abandoning objective, and in particular scientific, thinking, has nevertheless himself fallen victim to the transcendental illusion. He considers his own categorial framework, at least in so far as it replaces the principle of causality by another principle, the so-called 'principle of complementarity', as 'irrevocable'.[3] From the inconceivability to himself and other, though by no means all, physicists of doing without this constitutive principle he infers not its internal incorrigibility, but its incorrigibility *simpliciter*. It is a controversial matter among physicists whether at present any heterodox theory of quantum mechanics is available or feasible. But even in the absence of a counterexample Bohr's arguments are in no way compelling. This point was eloquently and clearly made by Einstein.[4]

One could easily multiply these examples of transcendental arguments, which range from arguments of great subtlety to

[1] *loc. cit.*

[2] P. A. Schilpp, ed. *The Philosophy of Bertrand Russell* (Evanston, Ill. 1946), page 682

[3] *Dialectica*, volume 2 (Basle 1948)   [4] *op. cit.*

simple-minded muddles. Failure to distinguish between the merely internal incorrigibility of a particular categorial framework and its indispensability may lead to the sad spectacle of one philosopher accusing another of confusing *the* categories, when in fact they do not share the same categorial framework. There is, as I have tried to show, room for rational argument between a Hanunóo and a Cartesian about the merits of categorizing animals with things. But the Hanunóo who merely asserts that the Cartesian confuses two different categories with each other is saying no more than that the Cartesian would be confusing his categories if he were a Hanunóo. And this is not saying very much, even if it is said in a very superior tone of voice.

Before leaving the topic of transcendental deductions it might be useful to ask and to answer two rhetorical questions. First, is it really true that every thinker employs a categorial framework? Second, how could one show this except by a transcendental deduction? As regards the first question, I never asserted that everybody employs a categorial framework. What I have argued was simply that if a categorial framework is employed by somebody, then its transcendental deduction is impossible since no uniqueness demonstration is available. I am, I admit, of the opinion that as a matter of empirical fact many people, including many philosophers, employ or have employed categorial systems. This is an empirical statement about some people, not an allegedly incorrigible statement about all people, past, present or future, much less about men or rational beings as such. The second question thus does not arise. It is possible that man will one day apprehend the world in a manner which is as different from what we call 'thinking' as is our thinking when compared with the manner in which, say, an earthworm apprehends his environment. I have no conception of what such super-thinking might be. But what is inconceivable to me may nevertheless be possible.

The Problem of Absolute Metaphysics

THE DIALECTICAL METHOD

The dialectical method, as conceived by Hegel, claims to establish even grander metaphysical truths than the transcendental method and to do so in an even grander manner. Its claims were briefly explained – and, for the sake of argument only, granted – when the philosophy of history was discussed. On that occasion an example of the method in action was given.[1] One way of approaching Hegel's conception of absolute metaphysical thinking is to consider his criticisms of Kant's transcendental method and the conclusions he draws from them. Thus Kant's central idea of replacing ontology by epistemology is in Hegel's eyes a fundamental mistake. Kant considered it possible, and indeed necessary, to examine the faculty of acquiring knowledge in order to find out what is and what is not knowable. One must, as Hegel puts it, 'first acquire knowledge of the instrument before undertaking the work which is to be done by means of it, since, if the instrument should turn out to be unsatisfactory, all effort would be wasted'. But this will not do. 'The examination of the faculty of acquiring knowledge (*des Erkennens*) cannot proceed except by acquiring knowledge (*erkennend*); as regards this so-called instrument, examining it is the same as acquiring knowledge about it.' And, Hegel continues, 'wishing to acquire knowledge before acquiring knowledge is as preposterous as the resolution of a certain scholastic to learn how to *swim* before *daring to enter* the water'.[2]

The conclusion which Hegel draws from this objection to Kant's epistemological metaphysics is not to reject absolute metaphysics altogether, but to revive metaphysics as ontology. 'The older metaphysics had in this respect a superior idea of thinking than has become the rule and fashion in recent times', namely the idea that 'thinking in its immanent determinations

[1] See pages 155 f

[2] *Encyclopädie der philosophischen Wissenschaften* (1st edition Heidelberg 1817) quoted from Philos. Bibliothek edition (Leipzig 1949), section 10

and the true nature of things are one and the same content'.[1] Hegel thus goes back beyond Aristotle to Parmenides who, in about 500 B.C., asserted that thinking and its subject matter are identical. Since thought and Being are ultimately identical, Kant was mistaken (*a*) in opposing the thinking subject to objective being; (*b*) in regarding the Categories as 'formal' concepts by whose application the thinking subject forms objects out of a manifold of impressions; and (*c*) in assuming that Being, as it is in itself, is inaccessible to thinking.[2] If 'thinking in its immanent determinations' and 'the true nature of things' are 'one and the same content', then the subject matter of thinking is *ultimately* thinking. This thinking which reveals itself through itself to itself is the absolute Spirit.

But how, we must ask – overcoming a certain dizziness for which Hegel would not blame us – does the Spirit reveal itself through itself to itself in that part of itself which is the philosopher's conscious mind? The answer is: by dialectical reasoning. Once again reference to Hegel's criticism of Kant and the conclusions he draws from it will help. Kant had argued that when we try to apply the Categories, not to the manifold of impressions the organization of which into objects is their sole legitimate function, but to Being in itself or the 'thing in itself' we involve ourselves in contradictions because Being in itself is not accessible. Hegel, granting that the application of the Categories to Being leads to contradictions, refuses to draw the Kantian inference but concludes instead that Being contains contradictions. He agrees that any application to the same particular of mutually incompatible 'ordinary' concepts, e.g. 'being a mouse' and 'being a lion', would be self-stultifying. But he infers from this that the Categories which apply to (and are) Being are not ordinary concepts. He assigns thinking in terms of ordinary, rigidly demarcated concepts to what he calls the level of the 'understanding', that is to say, the level of commonsense and science; and he assigns thinking in terms of

[1] *Wissenschaft der Logik* (1st edition Nürnberg 1812, 1817) quoted from Philos. Bibliothek edition (Leipzig 1948) volume I, page 25 f
[2] *Wissenschaft der Logik*, pages 66 ff

fluid, developing concepts to what he calls the level of 'reason', on which absolute metaphysical thinking proceeds.

The dialectical method is characterized by Hegel himself as follows:

The one thing needed *in order to achieve scientific progress* – and the quite simple insight into which is essential – is the knowledge of the logical proposition that the negative is at the same time positive, or that the self-contradictory does not dissolve itself into zero, i.e. abstract nothingness, but, essentially, into the negation of a *concrete* content, or in other words that such a negation is not overall negation, but *merely the negation of a concrete thing*, which dissolves itself; that it is determinate negation, so that the result contains that from which it results.[1]

The negation is 'a new concept, but the (*sic*) concept which is higher and richer than its predecessor; because it has been enriched by its negation or opposite, and thus contains it, but also more than it, and is the unity of itself and its opposite'. In this manner, says Hegel, 'the system of concepts has to form itself – and to complete itself in a course which is irresistible, pure and free from external ingredients'.

Any attempt to demonstrate the irresistibility of dialectical reasoning would itself have to proceed by such reasoning and is thus out of the question. Dialectical reasoning, like Cartesian deduction, its philosophical ancestor, must therefore be regarded as self-evident. Yet many philosophers have found Hegel's dialectical reasoning quite resistible. The reason for this lies in Hegel's conception and use of negation: The 'negation of a concrete content' may lead one to the affirmation of a 'concrete content' quite other than that selected by Hegel as '*the* concept which is higher and richer than its predecessor'. Some dialectical steps are moreover not only resistible but by no means 'free from external ingredients'. The dialectical progress, for example, from mechanism to 'chemism' and onwards to teleology, though exhibited as inexorable, is no more than a wrapping up into dialectical terminology of beliefs which

[1] *Wissenschaft der Logik*, pages 35 ff

were widely shared by nineteenth-century scientists and philosophers.[1]

The doctrine that reality reveals itself completely in Hegel's dialectical system was passionately denied by Søren Kierkegaard, who insisted that it has no room for the Category of the *human* individual or human existence. 'Even if a man occupies himself his whole life with Logic', by which Kierkegaard means Logic in the Hegelian sense, 'he does not become Logic, but exists himself in altogether different Categories'.[2] According to Kierkegaard and the later existentialists, human existence has nothing to do with the Category of existence as it occurs in Hegel's Logic, one thesis of which characterizes 'essence as the ground of existence'.[3] They hold that the converse thesis is true because they are convinced that man shapes himself by his choices and decisions. By what is probably a deliberate use of irony Kierkegaard often adopts Hegel's dialectical style of reasoning in order to show that 'there can be no system of human existence'.[4] Yet Kierkegaard's antisystematic dialectic is no less – and no more – resistible than the systematic dialectic of Hegel. Both seem to argue a case when in effect they merely tell us to take or leave the insights which they have to offer.

If we reject, as I think we must, the absolute claims which Hegel makes for his dialectical method, we must still ask wherein its possible value consists, apart, of course, from isolated philosophical insights or stimulating and provocative ideas. The following interpretations have been suggested at one time or another. One is that Hegel simply denies the law of contradiction which, since a contradiction logically implies any proposition whatsoever, allows him to deduce whatever he likes. This interpretation is not merely uncharitable, but does not do justice to Hegel's distinction between 'understanding' and

[1] *Encyclopädie der Philosophischen Wissenschaften*, pages 178 ff

[2] *Concluding Unscientific Postscript* translated by D. F. Swenson (Princeton 1941), chapter 2, section 2, page 75 (1st edition Copenhagen 1846)

[3] *Encyclopädie der Philosophischen Wissenschaften*, pages 126 ff

[4] *ibid.* page 101

'reason'. Another interpretation replaces the charge of absurdity by one of triviality. It accuses Hegel of inflating the commonplace that thoughts and real situations change, into a spurious profundity by an empty pretence to understand the 'inner necessity' of this change. A third interpretation is that the dialectic is an esoteric method which can be understood only by a select few – to be precise, only by those who agree with Hegel. A fourth interpretation, which was mentioned in discussing the Marxist philosophy of history,[1] is to regard the dialectical method as regulative or programmatic. It enjoins the philosopher and the natural and social scientist to take note of internal and external conflicts and of the way in which conflicts are resolved by the adjustment of conflicting aspects to each other in new unities. The advice *to attempt* explanations of change in terms of conflict, and to construct theories in the light of this point of view is reasonable and fruitful. It is neither absurd, nor trivial, nor esoteric; and it is not pointless to give it or to take it seriously.

OTHER TYPES OF ARGUMENT IN SUPPORT OF ALLEGEDLY
INCORRIGIBLE METAPHYSICAL TRUTHS

These other types of argument are not peculiar to metaphysics. The so-called phenomenological method[2] is sometimes called in to bolster a transcendental argument. But, apart from the general criticisms of this method as an attempt to distinguish the uninterpreted given from its interpretations, it seems particularly unsuitable for supplying the uniqueness demonstration which a transcendental deduction presupposes. Thus Kant's transcendental deduction of the principle of causality is based on the distinction between the manifold of impressions as given, and its interpretation as objective experience through applying, among other Categories, that of causality to what is given. A phenomenological description might be possible of what is given without interpretation, and of the interpretation itself. But it could never show that the interpretation (as

---

[1] See page 160   [2] See page 24

phenomenologically described) of the given (also as phenomenologically described) is the only possible interpretation.
Again it might be said that dialectical reasoning is nothing but
a conscious mental activity which is phenomenologically
cleansed of all impurities. But since dialectical reasoning is in
any case regarded as self-justifying, because self-evident, the
phenomenologist assertion is merely a repetition of the same
claim in other words.

If then incorrigible metaphysical propositions are to be
established at all, they must be established by ordinary arguments, i.e. by deduction or induction. But ordinary arguments
establish corrigible propositions only. Deduction proceeds
from corrigible premisses to equally corrigible conclusions,
whereas induction proceeds by its very nature from corrigible
premisses to conclusions which are even more exposed to correction than the premisses. (My statement that all observed
swans are white may be false because I failed to notice that
one of the birds I observed was a black swan. My statement
that all swans are white may be false for this or other reasons.)
Yet absolute metaphysicians have nevertheless attempted to
establish absolute truths by ordinary arguments. The most
interesting and important attempts in this direction are arguments for the existence of God.

The doctrine that the universe has been created by an eternal
being whose power and benevolence are unlimited is a dogma
of many, though not all, religions. It might be claimed that a
religious person who believes in the existence of God needs no
philosophical proof of it. A believing Christian might well say
that the search for a philosophical proof of God's existence
would be only one of those symptoms to which the founder of
his religion referred when he said that 'an evil and adulterous
generation seeketh after a sign'.[1] Philosophical proofs are not
among the primary sources of religious faith.[2] The main
reason why religious, as distinct from metaphysical, theologians
attempted to prove the existence of God was not to still doubts
but to show that faith and reason are in harmony with each

---

[1] Matthew XVI, 4   [2] See pages 162 ff

other. We have already come across such attempts, namely an ethical argument based on the premiss that there is absolute justice,[1] and Aristotle's argument based on an alleged physical fact and an alleged physical law.[2]

Another inference from the observation of nature to the existence of God is the so-called 'teleological argument': in observing nature, especially animals and human beings, we are often faced with states of affairs and processes which appear to have been designed by a higher intelligence. In the absence of any other explanation it must be concluded, with certainty or high probability, that what appears to be designed by a higher intelligence is in fact so designed, so that the designing higher intelligence exists. Just as Aristotle's argument for the existence of a prime mover conflicts with modern physics, so some versions of the teleological argument for the existence of a prime designer conflict with modern biology, in particular with Darwin's theory of natural selection. It should be noted, however, that at least one distinguished post-Darwinian philosopher argues probabilistically that the conflict must be resolved in favour of the assumption of a prime designer of nature.[3]

The metaphysically purest of all attempts to prove the existence of God is the so-called ontological argument to the effect that the concept of God logically implies the existence of God. We owe its original and most famous version to Anselm of Canterbury.[4] 'We believe', says Anselm, 'that You are something than which nothing greater can be thought' and we *understand*, and thus have in our mind, what we believe. This understanding is shared even by the fool who says in his heart, there is no God.[5] But

surely that-than-which-a-greater-cannot-be-thought cannot exist in the mind alone. For if it exists solely in the mind even, it can

---

[1] See page 172   [2] See page 183

[3] See F. Brentano, *Vom Dasein Gottes*, posthumously published, (Leipzig 1929)

[4] *Proslogion*, edited and translated by M. J. Charlesworth, (Oxford 1965)

[5] Psalm LIII, 1

be thought to exist in reality also, which is greater. If then that-than-which-a-greater-cannot-be-thought exists in the mind alone, this same that-than-which-a-greater-*cannot*-be-thought is that-than-which-a-greater-*can*-be-thought. But this is obviously impossible. Therefore there is absolutely no doubt that something-than-which-a-greater-cannot-be-thought exists both in the mind and in reality.[1]

The argument is strengthened by an attempt to show that the existence of the insuperable something is necessary existence:

And certainly this being so truly exists that it cannot be even thought not to exist. For something can be thought to exist that cannot be thought not to exist, and this is greater than that which can be thought not to exist. Hence, if that-than-which-a-greater-cannot-be-thought can be thought not to exist, then that-than-which-a-greater-cannot-be-thought is not the same as that-than-which-a-greater-cannot-be-thought, which is absurd. Something-than-which-a-greater-cannot-be-thought exists so truly then, that it cannot even be thought not to exist.[2]

The argument is all too easily faulted by an objector who makes one of two assumptions which Anselm almost certainly did not make and need not have made: (i) the logic underlying the argument is standard elementary logic. According to this logic the only way of correctly analysing the locution 'There exists' is through the existential quantifier '$\exists x$'. But '$\exists x$' is not a predicate.[3] Our objector concludes that Anselm made the mistake of regarding existence, which is not a predicate, as a predicate. (ii) The logic underlying the argument is an extension of standard elementary logic, according to which the locution 'There exists' is correctly analysed either by '$\exists x$', which is not a predicate, or by a predicate of predicates. For example 'There exists a man' is correctly analysed by 'The predicate "man" is not empty', where the predicate 'not empty' (which analyses 'There exists') is a predicate of the predicate 'man' and not of any individual. Our objector concludes that Anselm made the mistake of regarding existence

[1] *Proslogion,* chapter 2   [2] *ibid.* chapter 3   [3] See pages 45 f

which is a predicate *of predicates* as a predicate of an individual, namely of God.

The objector might continue by pointing out that in the third chapter of the *Proslogion* Anselm adds a further confusion by applying the predicate of necessary existence, which is neither a predicate of individuals nor a predicate of predicates. But a defender of Anselm's argument might point out that we must not first impute to Anselm the employment of a logical theory, which he does not in fact employ, and then refute him in terms of it. It is, he might add, not beyond human ingenuity to devise a logical theory in which the notion of existence is a predicate of individuals and in which a modal operator 'necessarily' occurs so that it becomes permissible to state *meaningfully*, though perhaps falsely, that some entity (other than a predicate or a class) has the property of existence or of necessary existence. Let us then in fairness to Anselm concede the possibility of such theories and assume that he employed one of them and that he cannot thus be accused of a logical confusion, committed in a logic which he did not employ. We, therefore, admit that the following attributes cannot be rejected as confused or ill-formed: 'x exists insuperably in the mind', briefly $M(x)$; 'x exists insuperably in reality', briefly $R(x)$; 'x exists of necessity insuperably in the mind', briefly $NM(x)$; 'x exists of necessity insuperably in reality', briefly $NR(x)$. Not to admit these attributes is to evade Anselm's argument, rather than to face it.

Anselm asks us to concede that, even though we may not agree with it, we *understand* his assertion that something has the attribute $M(x)$. Now, what is it for a hearer to understand a speaker who asserts that something that may be unknown to the hearer has an attribute, say, $P(x)$? At least two senses of understanding might be distinguished. First, a weak sense: the hearer is able to define $P(x)$ in familiar terms and acknowledges that the speaker has – correctly or incorrectly – applied $P(x)$ to something that may be unknown to the hearer. He does *not* acknowledge, thereby, that $P(x)$ is (correctly) applicable to anything whatever. In the weak sense a hearer understands even a speaker who asserts that a something that may be unknown to the hearer has the attribute 'being a ghost', which the hearer regards as inapplicable, the attribute 'being a round square', which the hearer regards as self-contradictory, or the attribute 'being the proof of Fermat's last theorem', about whose applicability the hearer suspends judgement. Second, a strong sense which is admittedly unusual, if not idiosyncratic: the hearer understands the speaker in the weak sense and acknowledges, in addition, that $P(x)$ is applicable, i.e. not empty. Strong understanding implies weak understanding, but not the other way round.

There is no difficulty in understanding Anselm's assertion that something has the attribute $M(x)$ in the weak sense. But to be able to define $M(x)$ in familiar terms is not to acknowledge its applicability. He himself gives no reason why its applicability should be acknowledged. On the contrary, if one were to concede that the Anselmian logical implications between $M(x)$, $R(x)$, $NM(x)$ and $NR(x)$ hold in the logic which implicitly underlies his reasoning, one might be even less inclined to concede the applicability of $M(x)$. In any case no definition, and no logical consequences of it, commit one to acknowledging the applicability of the defined attribute. We need concede no more than that we understand Anselm in the weak sense. It is at this point that his ontological argument breaks down.

Anselm and those who share his faith understand his assertion in the strong sense: they do not only understand the definition of the attribute $M(x)$, but acknowledge that it and the other 'theistic attributes' such as $NM(x)$, $R(x)$ and $NR(x)$ are applicable. Let us then assume – as some theologians think we should do in any case – that Anselm addressed his argument to believing Christians. In that case it could be recast as a transcendental deduction on the following lines: just as the Categories of the Kantian categorial framework do not describe subjective sense-experience, but organize the manifold of sense-impressions into objective experience, i.e. the experience of physical objects; so Anselm's theistic attributes do not describe subjective religious experience, but organize the manifold of 'religious impressions' into objective experience, i.e. the experience of *one* object, namely God. That is to say, just as the Kantian Categories are constitutive of physical objects, so the theistic attributes are constitutive of the theological object; and just as the Kantian constitutive principles, which assert the applicability of the Categories to physical experience, are incorrigible for anybody who employs the Kantian categorial framework; so the constitutive principles which assert the applicability of the theistic attributes, are incorrigible for anybody who employs the Anselmian categorial framework. Yet, just as e.g. a Peircean's objective physical thinking can do without the Category of causality so, e.g. a Buddhist's objective religious thinking can do without Anselm's theistic attributes. Thus, if we interpret or reconstruct Anselm's ontological proof as a transcendental deduction, it will be no worse than all the others. But it will also be no better.

14. The Metaphysical Problem of Freedom

The distinction between mental and physical phenomena is compatible with a great variety of different categorial frameworks, many of which have at different times and in different communities been implicitly employed or explicitly propounded by theologians, scientists and metaphysicians. It is, for example, possible to unify mental phenomena into one mental substance (Spirit, Mind, world-soul) or a plurality of transient or permanent mental substances (spirits, minds, souls), and to unify physical phenomena into one physical substance (matter) or a plurality of physical substances (material objects), so that mental and physical substances form separate, ultimate categories. It is also possible to admit only the category of one or more mental substances of which physical phenomena are dependent aspects; or only the category of one or more physical substances of which mental phenomena are dependent aspects. Each of these possibilities can be worked out consistently. It is – let me emphasize once more – in any case rather naïve for, say, a 'Cartesian dualist' to accuse a modern 'realist' of confusing *his* categories merely because they differ from the Cartesian ones. The categorization as well as the constitutive and the individuating principles associated with each of these different categorial frameworks may, of course, come into conflict with other sets of beliefs – the conflict being resolvable either by abandoning the framework or by adjusting the conflicting beliefs to it (by replacement-analysis).

These points should be borne in mind in any discussion of the ancient, though ever excitingly fresh, metaphysical problem of the relation between the course of nature, of which human bodies are part, and the execution in nature of apparently free choices to interfere with it in one of at least two equally realizable ways. We may expect each of the mentioned types of categorial framework to be able to accommodate this relation in some way; but must not be surprised if each of these accommodations to the different types of framework gives rise to feelings of uneasiness, intellectual discomfort or the impression of serious conflict. In the present chapter I shall, first of all, briefly explain some characteristic metaphysical strategies aimed at incorporating the notion of apparently free choices and that of their execution in nature into categorial frameworks, whether habitually employed or newly proposed in order to accommodate these notions. Having discussed these strategies and drawn some morals from the discussion, I shall then outline a further approach, which concedes the possible occurrence in nature of bodily conduct which is freely chosen in the sense that it realizes one of at least two equally realizable ways of interfering with the course of nature.

The *impression* of such freedom is rarely denied and was noted in analysing the concept of an action.[1] In this connexion we considered two sequences of Events $E\,B\,F$ and $E\,B'\,F'$, where B and B' refer to different kinds of *chosen* bodily conduct, and described a person's apparent freedom to realize one of these sequences in nature as follows: he has the impression (i) that neither B nor B' are predetermined, i.e. determined by preceding Events, which include the Event E; (ii) that the sequence EB predetermines the Event F and that the sequence EB' predetermines the Event F'; (iii) that the choice between B and B' and, consequently, between $E\,B\,F$ and $E\,B'\,F'$ originates *somehow* in himself, in his mind or will, in a manner

[1] See pages 112 ff

which is not wholly determined by his past. These impressions may, of course, be wholly or partly illusory. (i) and (iii) suggest that bodily conduct may not be predetermined, but determined by non-Events. Does this make sense?

THE GRAND-ILLUSION THEORY

The grand-illusion theory, as it might be called, implies that it does not. Although the theory is defended by all empiricists in the classical tradition of British empiricism, its most articulate spokesman is David Hume. He does not quarrel with our description of the impression of freedom or liberty, but speaks of it as of 'a false sensation or seeming experience which we have, or may have, of liberty or indifference in many of our actions'.[1] He holds that 'the long-disputed question concerning liberty and necessity' has for so long been left undecided only because of 'some ambiguous expressions, which keep the antagonists still at a distance, and hinder them from grappling with each other'. Indeed 'all mankind, both learned and ignorant, have always been of the same opinion with regard to this subject' and 'a few intelligible definitions would immediately have put an end to the whole controversy'.[2] The problem, or rather the pseudoproblem, of freedom arises from confusing freedom as opposed to constraint – e.g. the constraint of a prisoner who is not 'free' to leave his prison – with freedom as opposed to that necessity which pervades the universe of which every man is a part.

According to Hume the second opposition, and the concept of freedom or liberty which occurs in it, is spurious. 'Liberty', he says, 'when opposed to necessity, not to constraint, is the same thing with chance; which is universally allowed to have no existence.' Hume's reason for agreeing with this opinion, which is no longer universally held, is his view that every

[1] *An Enquiry Concerning Human Understanding* (Edinburgh 1742), quoted from the edition by L. A. Selby-Bigge (Oxford 1902, etc.), page 94, footnote 1

[2] *An Enquiry Concerning Human Understanding*, page 81

Event is causally predetermined by some of the Events preceding it. Like Kant after him, he holds that the concept of causality is indispensable to all objective thinking since 'by means of this relation alone we can go beyond the evidence of our memory and senses'[1] and since without its applicability and actual application not only the natural sciences, but also history, politics understood as a science, and even 'the foundation of morals', would be impossible.[2] Hume gives no elaborate proof of the indispensability of the concept of causality and of its irreplaceability by some other concept. What he does say might be regarded as an embryonic version of the Kantian transcendental deduction from internal incorrigibility to incorrigibility without qualification.

If all Events, including men's chosen bodily conduct, 'can be traced up, by a necessary chain'[3] at least to Events which precede the existence of life on earth, then some widespread beliefs must be either abandoned or radically modified. Hume is well aware of this need. As we have seen, he demotes the impression of liberty to the status of a mere confusion or, at best, a grand illusion. He reinterprets the common conception of virtuous and vicious actions (as not in *every* case necessitated by Events of a far-distant past) by assimilating them to aesthetic qualities for which their human bearers are morally neither praised nor blamed. 'Why', he asks, 'should not the acknowledgment of a real distinction between vice and virtue be reconcilable to all speculative systems as well as that of a real distinction between personal beauty and deformity?'[4] Lastly he feels, or rather pretends to feel, uneasy that he cannot 'explain distinctly' how 'the Deity can be the mediate cause of all the actions of men without being the author of sin and moral turpitude'. He seems quite content to leave this problem to religious believers as one of the 'mysteries, which mere natural and unassisted reason is very unfit to handle'.[5] His resolution of the apparent conflict between his meta-

---

[1] *ibid.* page 26   [2] *ibid.* page 90   [3] *ibid.* page 100
[4] *An Enquiry Concerning Human Understanding*, page 102
[5] *ibid.* page 103

physics and his non-metaphysical beliefs in favour of the former is a good example of the general thesis that such a solution is always possible.

But the required modifications of beliefs which many people hold, at least in their practical deliberations and moral evaluations, are rather drastic. It is hard to accept that so common and frequent an impression as that of freedom is an illusion which rests ultimately on linguistic confusions. Only an unshakable conviction that the principle of causality applies to all external phenomena, including all bodily movements, could counteract many people's deep-seated belief that human freedom is 'better than the freedom of a roasting jack which, having once been wound up, executes its movements by itself'.[1] Kant, who shares Hume's assumption of the unrestricted applicability of the principle of causality to all external phenomena, nevertheless rejects Hume's account of human freedom as a mere verbal manoeuvre. But his own solution of the apparent conflict between the principle of causality, which he too accepts as a constitutive principle for all external phenomena, and the impression of freedom is hardly less drastic than Hume's. It consists in a modification of the categorial framework rather than in a reinterpretation of practical, moral and religious beliefs.

THE DOUBLE-WORLD THEORY

The double-world theory, as Kant's theory might be called, rests on a radical distinction between the phenomenal world, as apprehended by human beings in their perception and thought, and the world as it is in itself. That the world as we know it is different from the world in itself is, as we have seen,[2] an assumption which is fundamental to Kant's explanation of the possibility of synthetic *a priori* propositions, i.e. incorrigible mathematical and metaphysical propositions. Such propositions

[1] Kant, *Critique of Practical Reason* (Riga 1788), Ac. ed. volume V page 97

[2] See pages 186 f

are possible only because they express the manner in which human beings organize the subjective manifold of impressions into objective experience. They do not describe features of the world, but, strictly speaking, only features of the world as it appears to human beings. 'All objects of an experience which is possible to us' are 'nothing but mere representations ... which outside our thoughts have no independent existence in themselves.'[1] Objective experience and its philosophical analysis imply the existence of a world in itself, the thing in itself or a 'noumenal' world; but they imply nothing about its features.

However, if we also consider our moral experience and submit it to philosophical examination, we can supplement this scant information. We know, on the one hand, that whatever happens in space and time, such as our bodily conduct, and whatever happens in time, such as our thoughts, choices and decisions, 'can be traced up, by a necessary chain', back to a past in which no men existed. We know, on the other hand, that the categorical imperative is absolutely binding upon us[2] and that we therefore are *somehow* free, i.e. not causally determined, to obey or disobey it. The two claims to knowledge seem to contradict each other. But the apparent contradiction can be resolved if we remember that whatever exists or happens in space or time is merely part of the phenomenal world, and not of the world in itself. Since we are free, but are causally determined in the phenomenal world, it follows that we are free in the noumenal world. Man as a phenomenon is causally determined but as a noumenon is free.

The choices of which we are aware, as well as their execution, occur in the phenomenal world as members of temporal and causally related sequences. Our genuine noumenal freedom can thus not be exercised in time, but only extra-temporally. A free choice is, therefore, according to Kant, not a choice within the infinite sequence of happenings which includes our

[1] *Critique of Pure Reason* B. (Riga 1787), Ac. ed. volume III, page 338
[2] See page 130

life. It is a choice of the sequence as a whole. How this extra-temporal choice of an infinite sequence of happenings is to be understood Kant does not pretend to be able to explain. He merely argues that the assumption of such a choice, however mysterious, is internally consistent, consistent with both objective and moral experience, and necessary if the apparent contradiction between man's subjection to the principle of causality and to the categorical imperative is to be resolved.

A mysterious truth is preferable to an easily grasped falsehood. However, in order to attain some understanding of man's noumenal freedom we may resort to analogy or myth. Kant himself frequently uses the analogy of a society of free people under self-given laws, and speaks of a society, or world, of noumenal individuals subject to the categorical imperative. Plato, who also believed in natural necessity and noumenal freedom, falls back on myth. In the tenth book of the *Republic* he tells the story of Er the Pamphylian, who died and lived again to report on what happens to the soul after death. He reports that every soul chooses a life from a limited number of alternatives. To this life the soul is bound by necessity. Plato emphasizes that the choice of a life made by a soul is restricted by the choices of other souls. Kant does not mention this problem of possible conflicts between the noumenal choices made by different individuals.

The notion of noumenal freedom is neither an *a posteriori* concept which describes the manifold of impressions, nor a Category by whose application the manifold is organized into objects. It is what Kant calls an 'Idea'. His accounts of the Ideas and in particular the Idea of noumenal freedom vary throughout his works. He sometimes speaks of freedom as if it were a mere heuristic fiction. Yet, especially in his later works, he regards this Idea as characteristic of the reality to which we have access *only* as moral beings by apprehending the categorical imperative, and never as theoretical thinkers who are separated from reality by the intervening curtain of space and time and the application of the Categories.

The categorical imperative determines the noumenal choices

of all human beings and thus indirectly their intra-temporal choices: for noumenally to choose an infinite sequence of happenings which include one's life is *ipso facto* to choose any happening, and therefore any intra-temporal choice, included in the sequence. The determination is not compelling: for the noumenal choice is a choice between genuine alternatives, i.e. different, equally realizable infinite sequences of happenings. Lastly the determination is not predetermination, i.e. determination by Events preceding the choice or its execution in nature: for the choice is not made in nature or time. Thus Kant agrees with Hume that our impression of (intra-temporal) freedom stands in need of philosophical reinterpretation. But he does not agree with Hume that it is wholly illusory. The illusion consists merely in our transposing extra-temporal, noumenal freedom into time and nature.

THE GRAND-ILLUSION AND THE DOUBLE-WORLD THEORIES IN A PROBABILISTIC FRAMEWORK

Both Hume and Kant accept the metaphysical thesis that the principle of causality as applicable to all natural phenomena is incorrigible. The thesis, as has been argued earlier, is mistaken and it is quite possible to replace the constitutive attribute 'x causes y' by 'x probabilifies y with a certain definite probability' as was done by Peirce and is being done by orthodox quantum theorists. By itself, this replacement does not support the assumption that occasionally the choice between two courses of actions *somehow* originates in ourselves in a manner which is not wholly determined by preceding Events, even though the predetermination would now be probabilistic and not causal. The radiation of a piece of radium is unfree, in the relevant sense of the term, whether it is governed by causal or by probabilistic laws. The apparent conflict between an unrestricted principle of probabilistic predetermination of natural phenomena and our impression of freedom takes the place of the apparent conflict which Hume and Kant tried to resolve in their different ways. There is thus no need to elaborate the corresponding (probabilistic) grand-illusion and double-world theories, especially as an analysis of the concept of probabilification would be necessary and would confront us with controversial issues which are not directly relevant to our problem.

THE DOUBLE-LANGUAGE THEORY

The double-language theory of freedom tries to resolve the apparent conflict between predetermined and free actions by assuming that 'predetermination' and 'freedom' belong to two different vocabularies both of which describe the same phenomena. We have already met this kind of approach in discussing attempts to bridge the gulf between mental and physical phenomena.[1] The double-language theory of freedom stands somewhere between the Humean and the Kantian theories. It follows Hume in trying to resolve the apparent conflict by a linguistic clarification; and it follows Kant in regarding neither predetermination nor freedom as complete illusions. But this theory demands, like the others, a radical reinterpretation of the impression of freedom. For this impression is that it is sometimes in our power to choose between, and execute *in nature*, one of at least *two* equally realizable courses of events, and not just one of them which is describable as freely chosen in one language and as predetermined in another.

THE EXISTENTIALIST THEORY OF FREEDOM

The existentialist theory of freedom trusts the impression of freedom more than it trusts any metaphysical or scientific assumption. Man's existence, as Kierkegaard never failed to assert (or clearly to imply), cannot be captured by the categories of Hegel's Logic or of any scientific system.[2] The impression of freedom, though perhaps sometimes illusory, is in general not misleading. If an assumption clashes with this belief, the assumption has to be abandoned, modified or demoted to a mere heuristic precept. The existentialists reject in particular

[1] See page 99   [2] See page 223

any extrapolation of scientific generalizations, arrived at in situations from which human actions are carefully excluded, to human actions and choices. In their unwillingness to discount the evidence of their subjective experience of freedom they are as obstinate as Hume and Kant are in their unwillingness to discount the testimony of the natural science of their day.

It must, I think, be conceded that each of these theories either is or could be made internally consistent and consistent with experience. It must also be conceded that each of them will appeal to some people. But others will find that the required reinterpretation of their experience and beliefs imposes too great an intellectual strain. They will be equally dissatisfied with Hume's or the two-language theory's terminological re-arrangements, with Kant's transposition of the freedom which they seem to possess in nature into a supernatural world, and with the existentialists' cavalier disdain of the scientific under-standing of nature of which they are a part. Such people (among whom I include myself) will look for another approach which is not only internally consistent and consistent with experience, but demands no radical reinterpretations.

THE THEORY OF FREEDOM IN NATURE

The theory of freedom in nature, which will now be sketched in outline, has a negative and a positive task. The negative task is to show that the principle of universal predetermination has not been established; i.e. that there is room for believing that, at least in some cases, chosen bodily conduct is not wholly pre-determined, i.e. determined by preceding Events and nothing else. The positive task of the theory is to explain and to justify the assumption that in so far as a person's chosen bodily con-duct is not predetermined it may be determined by a non-Event, in such a manner that the conduct can be intelligibly ascribed to the person and not, for example, to chance or to God. Let us tackle these tasks in turn.

The arguments in support of the principle of universal pre-determination, especially of causal predetermination, are (apart from inductive generalizations from common experience, which cut both ways) of two kinds. They are either transcendental deductions to the effect that the principle is indispensable to objective experience, or arguments to the effect that a denial of the principle is incompatible with scientific thinking in its present form. Both kinds of argument must be rejected on the basis of our previous discussions. Transcendental deductions rest, as we have seen, on the tacit assumption that what is inconceivable to some people or at some time is inconceivable to all people at all times. They fail to provide a uniqueness demonstration of the categorial framework in question and fail even to acknowledge the need for it.[1]

As regards scientific thinking, it has been argued[2] that scientific theories are idealizations of experience, resulting from deductive unification by means of their logico-mathematical framework and from deductive abstraction. To apply a scientific theory to sense-experience is to identify some of the theory's concepts and propositions which do not describe sense-experience with concepts and propositions which do. The identification is permissible in some, but not all, contexts and for some, but not all, purposes. It follows that empirical propositions about chosen bodily conduct may in *some* cases not be identifiable with corresponding theoretical propositions of physical, chemical, neurological and other scientific theories, which imply universal predetermination of the (idealized) Events which are their immediate subject matter. But this means that science, in its present form, is consistent with the assumption that chosen bodily conduct is on occasions not wholly predetermined. It is of course possible, indeed likely, that we often wrongly believe that particular actions are not wholly predetermined, when in fact they are. And it is even possible that all human conduct is wholly predetermined, i.e. determined by preceding Events and nothing else. But – and this is the sole point of our negative arguments – it remains possible that the concept of not wholly predetermined chosen conduct is not empty.

[1] See pages 213 ff   [2] See pages 80 ff

We now may turn to the positive task of trying to make sense of the determination of chosen bodily conduct by a non-Event. The most promising approach is to consider 'moral determination', with the impression of which we are familiar in our experience of conflicts between duty and inclination. Consider, for example, a situation in which a person is inclined to make a cruel joke but is aware of the moral principle, which he accepts, that cruelty is to be avoided either in general or in situations of the kind in which he finds himself. The moral principle, in so far as we construe it as non-temporal, is a non-Event – even though its apprehension or expression are, or are features of, an Event. The person is under the impression that his making or refraining from the cruel joke is not completely predetermined by preceding Events. He is also under the impression that in so far as his conduct is not predetermined it is determined by the moral principle. The principle, without being causally or otherwise compelling, determines him not to make the joke, although he has it in his power to make it.

The only reason for distrusting the impression of moral determination on all occasions was the metaphysical principle of universal predetermination. By showing that this principle is not indispensable to objective, especially scientific thinking, we have also made room for the possibility of conduct which is morally determined, in so far as it is not predetermined. We have established a new *possible* balance between the familiar impressions of freedom and moral determination on the one hand, and the equally familiar conviction that all Events are predetermined, i.e. are determined by Events only. Since this balance differs from the balance, or imbalance, implied by the commonly accepted theories of freedom, it must be guarded against misinterpretation.

No more is claimed at present than that – like other theories – it represents a possibility. Moral determination is not analysable in terms of complete probabilistic predetermination, since such probabilistic predetermination consists also in the determination of Events, including chosen bodily conduct, by Events and nothing else. Like complete causal predetermination it leaves no room for determination of conduct by non-Events. In assuming that our conduct is, at least on some occasions, morally determined, we may, but need not, assume that moral principles exist independently of the Events which are, or include, their being apprehended. It is sufficient to assume that in so far as an Event includes the apprehension of a moral principle it leaves room for moral determination, as opposed to predetermination.

By restricting the applicability of the principle of universal predetermination we are enabled to assume that the impression of freedom and moral determination does not always mislead us and need not be reinterpreted in Humean fashion or transposed from nature into a Kantian supernatural world. But, it might be objected, is not moral determination too different from predetermination to be philosophically acceptable? To this question two answers seem appropriate. First, in trying to draw the line between mere impressions (including what Hume calls the 'seeming experience' of freedom) and reliable impressions, we are dependent on the impressions and on a choice between different ways of organizing them into a consistent and plausible system of an objective world. There is no *a priori* reason to distrust the impressions of freedom and moral determination, unless they clash with stronger evidence. Second, there is no *a priori* reason against assuming that just as, e.g., neurophysiological predetermination arose as a novelty at a relatively late stage of the world's history, so moral determination through the apprehension of moral principles arose as a further novelty at a still later stage. But I should hesitate to base the argument on this kind of speculation.

Moral determination is self-determination. A person's moral choices determine his character, by which we understand not only the person's natural dispositions and inclinations, but also his past moral choices in accordance with, or contravention of, moral principles. It will not do, I think, to say that a person's conduct is determined by his past and by his character. If we admit the possibility of freedom and moral determination, we must also admit the possibility of a person's forming his character to the extent to which his choices are morally determined. In Plato's myth and in Kant's philosophy an individual has only one, extra-temporal, moral choice: the choice of a life, or the choice of an infinite sequence of Events containing it. On our theory, which has been sketched in outline, a man might have the occasion for many such choices. Dostoyevsky's tale of the Grand Inquisitor shows why this possibility can be unattractive and burdensome. It may well be that it is not only deference to a mistaken analysis of scientific thinking, but also the burden of limited freedom in nature, which makes legions of philosophers argue for universal predetermination in nature. One need not share Kierkegaard's and the existentialists' disdain for logic, science, and any metaphysics other than their own in order to inquire into the possibility of a moral freedom which would be more than a *façon de parler*.

It is worthwhile to compare our theory with Kant's, with which it has some affinities: in both theories a person has the power to do or to neglect his duty. Moral choice is autonomous; it is self-determination. However, on our theory moral choices are made and executed in nature by natural human beings. Again, the categorical imperative, which, as has been argued,[1] does not in any case serve as a necessary and sufficient criterion of the morality of an action, is replaced by a multiplicity of possibly incompatible moral points of view. Yet much that Kant says about moral experience and noumenal choice can be adapted to our sketch, once his views are freed from the fetters which the transcendental deduction of the principle of causality in the *Critique of Pure Reason* imposes on the *Critique of Practical Reason* and his other ethical works.

If we admit the possibility of moral determination of conduct by non-Events, we are justified in admitting the possibility of other kinds of determination by non-Events. Thus a person may apprehend some morally indifferent aesthetic ideal to which he may choose to approximate by his conduct, e.g. the life of a scholar, a man of action, etc. By restricting the

[1] See page 131

universal applicability of predetermination one makes room for determination by accepted non-moral ideals. There is no need to elaborate these possibilities. Instead, I shall consider the questions of how moral determination and natural pre-determination can be in harmony with each other and how, if at all, the assumption of moral freedom can be justified as a guide to action.

Many people believe – at least when engaged in practical pursuits – that their actions are partly predetermined and partly morally determined. They believe that in their journey from birth to death they very often lack the power to choose between alternative routes, but that they sometimes possess this power, although they admit that they may be mistaken on particular occasions. If they sometimes have the power to choose, then the principle of universal predetermination is not true. But this does not mean that the course of nature is not governed by strict laws. It may simply be that what is predetermined is not a single narrow route, but a somewhat broader avenue within which they have the power to choose their own paths. I may be causally predetermined to walk from my home to my office between eight and nine tomorrow morning, but free to choose whether to wear a green or a blue tie. I may be probabilistically predetermined with a probability of $\frac{1}{2}$ to take this walk, but free (even from probabilistic determination) to choose my tie.

Again, my life might be represented as a directed network of routes all of which start at the same point, my birth, and end at the same point, my death. I may be predetermined to proceed within the network of routes from birth to death, but have it in my power to choose the routes on which I proceed at any intersection. Both these pictures and some combinations of them can be expressed in less metaphorical terms. They corres-pond well to the way in which some people look back on their life and forward to their death, and to the way in which lives are recorded in biographies and autobiographies. The assumptions which correspond to the various metaphorical road maps and imply that at any moment a man has only one realized past, but more than one realizable future, do not conflict with science. They conflict, of course, with a number of metaphysical theories, especially those which extrapolate science into a metaphysical system.

Our theory of freedom, especially moral freedom in nature, undoubtedly stands in need of further elaboration, modification, and safeguards against all sorts of misunderstandings. It can, like the other theories of freedom so far considered, be squared with the best available empirical knowledge. If accepted, it can be incorporated into a categorical framework which acknowledges a category of choices (between real alternatives) capable of execution in nature and a category of natural Events. A constitutive attribute of the former entities would be 'being determined by moral principles', or more generally 'being determined by non-Events'. A constitutive attribute of the latter entities would be 'being predetermined by Events, not including the apprehension of moral principles (or other choice-determining non-Events)'. The theses of our theory then become, like the theses of the Humean and Kantian accounts, framework-principles and, *with respect to* the categorial framework with which they are associated, incorrigible.

It is, however, possible to argue for the acceptance of our kind of theory of moral freedom on pragmatic grounds. Pragmatic arguments for a thesis presuppose that it is undecidable on logical or empirical grounds, and are addressed only to people who would prefer one state of affairs to another, even though they have no evidence about its realizability in nature. Such pragmatic arguments, of which the following is an example, are much older than the philosophy of so-called pragmatism, of which the main representatives were C. S. Peirce and William James.[1]

The argument is addressed to a person who prefers a world containing more to one containing fewer moral actions, and who would act in accordance with this preference if it were in his power to do so. He has on some occasions the possibly

[1] See especially 'The Will to Believe', *The Will to Believe and Other Essays in Popular Philosophy* (New York 1898)

wrong impression of his power to realize his choice between a moral and an immoral option in nature. *If* at every time of his life at most one of his options is realizable, whether it is moral, immoral or indifferent, then no choice of policy and none of his beliefs would make any difference to the course of nature and to his life in it. It would in particular not matter whether he assumed that he has at every moment of his life, as well as only one realized past, only one realizable future; or whether he assumed that at some times of his life he has more than one realizable future. It would not in either case be in his power to take or miss opportunities to act morally. Hume and Kant argued in favour of the one-future assumption. But we have seen that their arguments are not compelling and that either the one-future or the many-futures assumption may *possibly* be true.

If, however, at some moments of his life he has it in his power to realize his choice between a moral and an immoral option in nature, then it may well make a difference to the course of nature and his life in it, whether he assumes that he has this power or whether he makes the one-future assumption. Making the latter assumption may make him disregard his intention to act morally. It may, for example, serve him as a welcome excuse to spare himself the effort towards realizing a moral option, which he would not spare himself if he made the former assumption. Briefly: if there is no moral freedom, he can miss no moral options. If there is moral freedom, he can miss moral options by assuming that there is no such freedom. On balance the assumption that he is free (if he is free to make it and to act on it) is more in accord with his moral intentions than its negation.

The pragmatic argument does not establish that the concept of moral freedom is not empty in the same sense in which the concept of, say, 'lion' or of 'prime number' is not empty. It merely justifies making an assumption, and acting on it, for people who have a certain preference and have no empirical means for deciding whether they can or cannot realize it. Thus we could not produce a cogent pragmatic argument to support the assumption that living in a house with the street number thirteen brings bad luck, even if we addressed it to people who prefer good luck to bad. For the assumption, like other superstitions, is not empirically undecidable but false. On the other hand, the pragmatic argument does not establish a mere practical fiction, which bids us to act as if a proposition were true which – like the useful assumption that all other drivers are drunk – we know to be false. Lastly, it should be noted that the assumption of moral freedom in nature may even without this rather tenuous pragmatic support appeal to some people, as doing more justice to their objective and moral experience than the other alternatives which have been considered.

The constructive metaphysician is like a builder who builds a new house for satisfactory living. He hopes that the categorial framework which he has constructed will give its prospective tenants all modern intellectual and, possibly, emotional comforts. He hopes that the framework has been built with due logical care and fits in well with the landscape of the best available empirical knowledge and other beliefs which he shares with his fellows. But he knows that it is not the only habitable framework, that people have different intellectual and emotional preferences, that the landscape is continuously changing, and that the most modern comforts may become obsolete. He also knows that he has much to learn from his predecessors and competitors, and that a monopoly in the speculative building of categorial frameworks is just as undesirable as a monopoly in the speculative building of houses. What has been said about moral freedom in nature does not, of course, amount to more than a very rough sketch of part of a categorial framework which is intended to do justice to many people's moral convictions and to their equally strong conviction that the scientific understanding of nature is superior to every other understanding of the physical universe.

Part 5

THE PAST OF PHILOSOPHY AND THE CONTEMPORARY SCENE

Introduction

A bird's eye view of the past and a worm's eye view of the present share an unavoidable feature with the most detailed and circumstantial descriptions of the same landscape: progress and retrogression, achievement and failure lie largely in the eye of the beholder. This is particularly so in writings on the history of philosophy. In looking, as he must, through his own categorial framework at those of others, the historian will naturally see them as more or less defective approximations to his own. A degree of historical and human empathy may temper, but not conquer, this tendency. The point of view of the concluding two chapters on the past and present of philosophy has been developed in the earlier parts of this book. It is not the only possible one. But without some point of view no viewing is possible.

15. The Past of Philosophy

The original aim of philosophy was systematic knowledge of everything that is knowable. In pursuing it, philosophers had to make use of all available help that commonsense and specialist inquiry could provide. Western philosophy, and we are not here concerned with any other, took its first steps by reacting to mathematical and scientific discoveries, some of which may have reached the Greeks through their commercial and other contacts. Burnet's assertion that the development of Greek philosophy depended on the progress of scientific, and especially mathematical, discovery more than on anything else can hardly be contested.[1] Reflection on commonsense beliefs and the available scientific knowledge, and the adaptation of these beliefs to the search for total knowledge or its first principles leads, on the one hand, to the emergence of different philosophical movements and traditions and, on the other, to the emergence of new special sciences and scientific traditions. The history of philosophy is the history of a continuous discussion which goes on within the various philosophical traditions, between these traditions, and between philosophy and the sciences. Indeed, the history of philosophy is in some respects like political history. Discussion within its various traditions is analogous to political discussion within the parties

[1] J. B. Burnet, *Greek Philosophy* (London 1943), page 2

of a state, discussion between the traditions to discussion between the parties, and discussion between philosophy and science to discussion between neighbouring states. Philosophical like political life has its authoritarian phases, its great leaders as well as its demagogues and opportunists; and relations between philosophy and science have, in spite of their interdependence, like the relations between neighbouring states, varied greatly between friendship and hostility and between equality and domination.

GREEK PHILOSOPHY

Greek philosophy is, first of all, philosophy of nature. Its founder is Thales of Miletos (640 – 550 B.C.). He is reported to have predicted successfully a solar eclipse and to have introduced geometry into Greece.[1] He taught that everything in nature consists ultimately of water. This idea may have been prompted by the fact that water exists also in the solid and gaseous state, that it is essential to life, and by his belief that the earth is surrounded by water. He was probably the first to ask the question of the ultimate constitution of physical nature and of reality in a philosophico-scientific rather than in a mythological sense, though at that stage of intellectual development it is not easy sharply to separate philosophy and science from mythical cosmogonies. The other two Milesian philosophers – Anaximander and Anaximenes – developed and refined the cosmology of Thales.

Pythagoras of Samos (*ca*. 540 – 500 B.C.) was probably influenced by the Milesian school. The attribution of the mathematical theorem which bears his name, whether or not he was its first discoverer, suggests that he was one of the greatest mathematicians. He was probably also the first to recognize the spherical shape of the earth. His doctrine that 'things are numbers' must be understood, on the one hand, in the light of his distinction between the unlimited – the amorphous substratum – and the limit, which gives it form or

[1] Burnet, *op. cit.*

structure; on the other hand, in the light of his conception of numbers as exhibiting geometrical patterns and their combinations. Pythagoras was the first thinker who explicitly identified the 'real nature' of existence with its (mathematical) structure or form, and made mathematics both an object of philosophy and an instrument of philosophical understanding.

If the Milesian and Pythagorean speculations can claim to be the ancestors of physics and of metaphysics, Heraclitus and Parmenides (fifth century B.C.) may be regarded as the first pure metaphysicians in the ontological sense of the term. For Heraclitus Being as such is a continuous flux from opposite into opposite: 'You cannot step twice into the same river.'[1] 'Conflict is the father of everything.'[2] The metaphysics of Parmenides is the antithesis of that of Heraclitus: according to Parmenides Being as such is free from coming into existence and from ceasing to exist; it is changeless, neither spatial nor temporal and, therefore, indivisible; and it is identical with thought. Whatever does not have these characteristics is mere appearance. As was mentioned earlier,[3] Zeno of Elea (fifth century B.C.) probably developed his paradoxes of motion in order to prove that the rejection of the Parmenidean doctrine of Being implies logical contradictions. Heraclitus and Parmenides have been the inspiration of many metaphysicians from Plato to Hegel and beyond.

Scientifically the most fruitful reconciliation between the changeless reality of Parmenides and the everchanging reality of Heraclitus is the atomism of Democritus of Abdera (*ca.* 460 B.C.). The atoms are the smallest indivisible parts of the physical world. They are invisible, though not necessarily of the same shape and size. Being indivisible, they cannot change. Perceived objects are constellations of atoms in otherwise empty space; and physical change is explained as their rearrangement according to laws of combination, based on difference of shape and size of different kinds of atoms. Only atoms

[1] H. Diels, *Die Fragmente der Vorsokratiker* (Berlin 1903), fragment 41
[2] *ibid.* fragment 44   [3] See page 9

and the void have real existence. The atomistic theory of Democritus (and of his teacher Leucippus) is one of the most famous examples of a metaphysical theory which, long after it was first thought of, was woven into the fabric of empirically testable, scientific theories.

The age of cosmological speculation was followed by a period which, with some justice, has been compared to the European age of enlightenment, an age of criticism in all spheres, of scepticism and of real and spurious polyhistors. The teachers and thinkers of this age are called 'sophists', a name which only later acquired its derogatory connotation. 'Sophistry', says Aristotle, 'seems to be philosophy, but is not.'[1] The first of the sophists was Protagoras of Abdera (born about 500 B.C.). The core of his doctrine is contained in his famous saying that 'man is the measure of all things, of things that are that they are, and of things that are not that they are not'. The statement must, I think, be interpreted as expressing an extreme subjective relativism and not, e.g. in Kantian fashion, as implying that what is knowable is modified by the structure of human perception and conceptual organization.[2]

This subjective relativism extended also to ethics and political philosophy and finds expression in the doctrine of Thrasymachus that 'justice is the interest of the stronger'.[3] Another famous sophist was Gorgias who tried to show '(i) that there is nothing, (ii) that even if there is anything, we cannot know it, and (iii) that even if we could know it, we could not communicate our knowledge to anyone else.'[4] The sophists ranged from those who in contemporary terms would be university teachers of established academic subjects to those who teach the technique of making 'the weaker thesis to appear stronger', or of making friends and influencing people. Hippias of Elis was located somewhere in the middle of this spectrum. He made some genuine mathematical discoveries, was a man of scholarship and a superb showman; he should be living in this day of television personalities.

[1] *Metaphysics*, book IV, 1004 b 25   [2] Burnet, page 115
[3] See page 186   [4] Burnet, page 120

The life and death of Socrates (*ca.* 470 – 399 B.C.) form one of the great chapters in the history of mankind. His philosophy is an out-and-out reaction against the sophists, although he owed much to their techniques of argument and – at least in his later life – shared their distrust in the truth and usefulness of cosmological speculation. Classical scholars have for years been trying without obvious success to disentangle the Socratic philosophy as it appears in Plato's dialogues from the philosophy of the historical Socrates. It seems safe to assume that he anticipated the theory of Forms which Plato developed throughout his life and which – whether or not Plato in the end abandoned it – exerted a profound influence on later thought. He emphasized the philosophical need for the analysis of commonsense beliefs in a systematic fashion in order to arrive at the meaning of abstract nouns, especially moral terms such as justice, virtue, goodness, and through the establishment of their meaning at moral truths. His is the characteristically Greek doctrine that moral virtue is a kind of knowledge and vice a kind of ignorance. A historian's assessment of Socrates' philosophy will depend on his assessment of Plato's work and on his conjecture as to what in this work is due to Socrates.

Plato's (428 – 348 B.C.) central and most influential doctrine represents a new attempt to solve the problem – posed by Thales and answered in different ways by his successors – of the difference between appearance and reality. In order to understand the ever-changing perceptual and physical world and in order to act morally in it, one must know the unchanging reality which underlies the changing appearances. Apart from being unchanging, this reality must be mind-independent and capable of precise definition and of being grasped by reason. Part of this reality is revealed by mathematics. Thus the world of perception and physical nature contains many circular objects, which we can easily order according to their more or less perfect circularity. But such ordering is possible only because we grasp the mind-independent Form of a circle, which is defined as the locus of all points equidistant from a given point. No perceptual circle is perfect. It merely more or less approximates to – 'partakes in' – the Form of the circle. Apart from mathematical Forms, there are also other Forms in particular the moral Forms, e.g. Justice and Virtue. Not every class of things or actions is related to a Form as is the class of perceptual circles to the Form of the circle; and Plato's views as to the classes which correspond to Forms changed during the course of his life. The dating of his dialogues, on which the possibility of tracing the history of the theory of Forms depends, is, like the attempt to solve the problem of distinguishing the historical and the Platonic Socrates, a favourite occupation of classical scholars. The vitality of Plato's thought in all branches of philosophy reaches through Greek and medieval times into our own day. The theory of Forms, as the demand to employ mathematics in the explanation of nature, strongly influenced Galileo. The philosophy of mathematics and science sketched earlier in chapters 4 and 5 could be regarded as a Platonism deprived of the ontological claim that mathematical and theoretical structures are unique and mind-independent.

The thought, if not always the name, of Aristotle (384 – 322 B.C.) is ever-present in philosophy, in the subject of logic which he created, and in many other sciences. If we compare his philosophy with that of his teacher Plato in terms of their overriding scientific interests, we might well say that Plato's thought was mainly directed to and modelled on mathematics and mathematical physics, especially astronomy, whereas Aristotle's thought was mainly directed to and modelled on biology and the social sciences. It has been said that something like this is true of all philosophers; that they all are either natural Aristotelians or natural Platonists. Aristotle's philosophy of infinity, of the moral and political life, as well as his conception of metaphysics are of such fundamental importance, that they confront us at every stage of philosophical thinking on these matters. His rejection of Plato's theory of Forms and his own conception of the function of universal notions is the source of the unending, and often fruitful, controversy about the nature and function of general terms. According to

Aristotle universals do not exist independently of particulars, but *in* the particulars as features of them.[1]

MEDIEVAL PHILOSOPHY

Medieval philosophy has, especially since the seventeenth century, been widely regarded as a period of protracted philosophical stagnation. It has often been assumed that the philosophy of that era lacked the stimulus of new mathematical and scientific ideas and degenerated into mere verbal quibbles and sterile exegeses, first of a decadent Platonism, and later of a petrified Aristotelianism. This depressing picture has had to be revised in many respects. Historians of science have shown that many of the scientific ideas of the Renaissance had already been considered by medieval thinkers. Historians of logic have shown that many logical theories of medieval thinkers partially anticipated modern theories and can be better understood in the light of them. Lastly, the view – always rather implausible – that modern philosophy started with a complete rejection of medieval philosophical thought has proved untenable.

Medieval philosophy, unlike Greek and modern philosophy, concentrated its main attention on Christian, and to a lesser extent on Jewish and Mohammedan, religious doctrine. Religion and theology in the Middle Ages played a similarly overpowering role to that played by science in our own day. And it is just as likely that a philosopher of that time would, honestly and naturally, try to reconcile his speculations and conceptual innovations with religious dogma, as that a present-day philosopher would, from genuine respect for science, adapt his philosophy to the best available scientific knowledge. The interaction between religion and theology on the one hand, and philosophy, on the other, was moreover not one-sided, and the development of Christian dogma has frequently been influenced by philosophical thought. It must, however, be admitted that a society in which the fight against heresy is

[1] See e.g. *Metaphysics*, book XIII, 1086 a 25 ff

backed by political power can hardly fail to dampen the spirit of innovation.

Maurice de Wulf, one of the exponents of modern Catholic scholasticism, describes the relation between the orthodox medieval philosophy, for which he reserves the name 'scholasticism', and theology, as follows:[1]

Amongst the problems of scholastic philosophy *very many* had their origin in theology in this sense, that they arose *on the occasion* of theological controversies. In the ninth and tenth centuries, the quarrel about predestination raised the question of human liberty and its relation to divine providence and divine justice; the Paschasian controversy on the real presence of Jesus Christ in the Eucharist brought forth dissertations on substance and accident; the dogma of the Trinity suggested discussion on the notions of nature and person and individual; transsubstantiation and the divine simplicity provoked the study of change. . . .

If our own scientific age should give way to an era dominated by some non-scientific ideology, we may well imagine a future defender of modern philosophy arguing on similar lines. He might point out that just as medieval philosophy was not merely 'the handmaid of theology', so modern philosophy was not merely the handmaid of science – even though many of its problems arose on the occasion of scientific controversy. He might add that just as medieval philosophy had its share in the formation of religious orthodoxy, so modern philosophy had its share in the formation of scientific orthodoxy.

Much of medieval philosophy appears, at least from our bird's eye view, as a dispute between a Christian Platonism and a Christian Aristotelianism. The latter becomes in the work of Thomas Aquinas (1225 – 1274) the dominant philosophy of Catholicism. Even apart from logic, medieval philosophy contains a wealth of fruitful ideas. But to an age in which theology as 'systematization of certain doctrines that a positive revelation

[1] *Introduction à la Philosophie Néo-scolastique* (Louvain 1904), quoted from English translation by P. Coffey, *Scholasticism Old and New* (London 1910), page 57 ff

has delivered to us'[1] has ceased to be a prevalent intellectual and social force, the ideas which arise from the interaction of philosophy with theology will seem less important than those which arise from the interaction of philosophy and science, and from philosophical speculation unfettered by theological restrictions.

MODERN PHILOSOPHY

Modern philosophy starts as an explicit rejection of scholastic philosophy of which it nevertheless is in many ways a continuation. Its main external stimulus is mathematics and physics, and the great thinkers who inaugurate it are also mathematical innovators of genius and original scientists. Descartes[2] was the inventor of the geometry which bears his name. Leibniz together with Newton founded the differential and integral calculus. Berkeley's critique of the calculus[3] was only appreciated in the nineteenth century. Kant's theory of the origin of our planetary system[4] is still taken seriously. But all these philosophers were also deeply concerned with the place of God in the scheme of things, accepting a conception of God which had been formed in medieval theology and philosophy.

Speaking in very broad terms and subject to many qualifications, we might say that the dispute between Platonism and Aristotelianism is replaced by an analogous dispute between rationalism and empiricism. The rationalists, like Plato, derived much of their philosophical inspiration from mathematics and mathematical physics, whereas the empiricists derived much of it from the empirical sciences. It was – as one is wont to say when engaging in such broad historical generalizations – no accident that John Locke was by profession a medical man. But unlike their Greek predecessors the modern rationalists and empiricists put great emphasis on the epistemological, as

[1] de Wulf, *op. cit.*, page 8   [2] See page 21
[3] *The Analyst* (Dublin 1734)
[4] *Allgemeine Naturgeschichte und Theorie des Himmels* (Königsberg and Leipzig 1755)

opposed to the ontological approach, i.e. on the question of the content and limits of knowledge.[1]

The rationalist conception of a science (and of philosophy as either the fundamental science or as the total science) rests on the assumption that it can be compressed into a finite number of propositions, which a methodical thinker can recognize as self-evidently true and from which he can by self-evidently correct steps of reasoning infer *all* propositions which are true of the subject-matter of his science. The classical statement of this position is due to Descartes.[2] Perhaps the most beautiful examples of a rationalist metaphysical system are Leibniz's *Monadology* which is based on the assumption that all philosophical truths can be deduced from the principle of contradiction and the principle of sufficient reason, and Spinoza's *Ethics, demonstrated in geometrical order*.[3] Descartes' method has been criticized earlier on; and that Leibniz's two principles cannot bear the burden which he puts upon them has become quite clear in the light of modern logic, of which he, among others, laid the foundations.

According to the rationalists 'the fluctuating assurance of the senses', as Descartes calls it, obscures rather than reveals the truth about anything. All truths, even though we may not be conscious of them, are innate and are brought to consciousness by systematic thinking. The doctrine of innate ideas has been taken to mean almost everything from the absurd view that human beings are born with the explicit awareness of, say, the truth of Pythagoras' theorem to the reasonable view that a man, unlike a dog, is born with a disposition to become aware of this truth. It is anathema to the empiricists for whom sense-experience is the ultimate source and test of truth. John Locke, therefore, starts his *Essay Concerning Human Understanding*,[4] the first work of modern empiricism, by attacking the doctrine 'that there are in the understanding certain innate principles;

[1] See pages 185   [2] See page 21 f

[3] *Ethica, ordine geometrico demonstrata.* Published posthumously; see e.g. edition by van Vloten and Land (The Hague 1882–3)

[4] London 1690

some primary notions . . . . characters, as it were stamped on the mind; which the soul receives in its very first being; and brings into the world with it'. Locke's argument is more effective against the less plausible versions of the doctrine than against the plausible assumption of innate dispositions, especially as his own doctrine implies that man has certain innate cognitive dispositions.

The empiricist conception of philosophy sees its function neither in laying the foundations of all knowledge, as Plato, Aristotle, Descartes and Leibniz saw it, nor in serving as the handmaiden of theology. 'In an age', says Locke in his Epistle to the reader of his Essay,

that produces such masters as the great Huygenius and the incomparable Mr. Newton, with some others of that strain, it is ambition enough to be employed as an under-labourer in clearing the ground a little and removing some of the rubbish that lies in the way of knowledge.

To fulfil this ambition, one must inquire into the two fountains of knowledge, namely our observation of external sensible objects and our observation of the internal operations of our minds.[1]

Among the results of Locke's inquiry two views in particular have been subjected to criticism by his empiricist successors. One is his distinction between primary qualities which are 'utterly inseparable from the body in what state so ever it may be', such as solidity, extension, shape, motion, rest, number; and secondary qualities which are 'nothing in the object itself, but powers to produce the various sensations in us by their primary qualities'.[2] The other is his doctrine of abstraction according to which 'the mind makes the particular ideas received from particular objects', e.g. chalk, snow, milk, 'to become general', e.g. by forming the idea of whiteness.

As Berkeley showed, Locke's distinction between primary and secondary qualities is incompatible with Locke's teaching

[1] *ibid.*, book II, chapter 1

[2] *Essay Concerning Human Understanding*, book II, chapter 8, sections 9, 10

about 'the two fountains' of knowledge: in order to know which qualities are inseparable from sensible objects we would have to be able to compare sensible objects as they are apart from our observation with the same objects as they appear in it. But this, according to Locke himself, is impossible. Berkeley also rejects the doctrine of abstraction. There are, according to him, only particular ideas. 'Whatever hand or eye I imagine it must have some particular shape or colour.'[1] There are no general ideas, only words used generally, i.e. as referring to many things. A word 'becomes general by being made the sign, not of an abstract idea, but of several particular ideas, any one of which it indifferently suggests to the mind'.[2] Berkeley's rejection of abstract ideas is easily understood if one recognizes that he tacitly identifies all ideas with images, since clearly every image, however schematic, is a particular image. His explanation of generality as a function of a use of words (without any reference to mind-dependent or mind-independent universal entities, or universals) was developed earlier by the so-called 'nominalists' of the Middle Ages.

To assume the existence of colour without shape is, Berkeley maintains, to fall into the fundamental error of the theory of abstraction. Colours and shapes as such have no existence. A coloured object exists with a particular colour and having a particular colour entails having a particular shape. Just as the separation of colour from shape so also, according to Berkeley, the separation of existence from perception is a false abstraction. 'To be is to be perceived'.[3] Strictly speaking, this famous dictum of Berkeley is, if not a false abstraction, at least incomplete. Its completion is: to be is to be perceived by some mind or spirit.

Locke's unperceived external world and 'matter' (which Berkeley regards as unperceived existence) are contradictions in terms due to false abstraction. The world consists of nothing but spirits (percipients) and their perceptions. But the pen

[1] *A Treatise Concerning the Principles of Human Knowledge* (Dublin 1710), section 10
[2] *ibid.*, section 11   [3] *ibid.*, section 3

which I now perceive does not cease to exist when it is unperceived by me or any other finite mind, since whatever exists is perceived by an eternal spirit, namely God. The principle 'to be is to be perceived' leads thus quickly and easily – all too quickly and all too easily – to a demonstration of the existence of God. By reference to God's perception illusory perceptions are distinguished from those that are not. 'A spirit is a simple, undivided active being – as it perceives ideas, it is called the understanding, and as it produces or otherwise operates them it is called the will.'[1] This central conception of Berkeley is very similar to Leibniz's conception of a monad and implies, as in the *Monadology*, that spirits – being indivisible and simple – are immortal.

Only spirits are causally effective in producing ideas and in affecting other spirits. The ideas produced by God and perceived by other spirits are the world. God's power to produce ideas is analogous to, but infinitely greater than, man's power to produce, say, the idea of a blue elephant in his mind. Ideas are causally ineffective. Because they occur in regular sequences, though without being necessarily connected, prediction is possible. Science consists in searching for regularities in the sequences of ideas; it describes how, not why, events in nature take their course. To reason why is the task of metaphysics and the theology to which Berkeley, as a Christian bishop of the eighteenth century, was committed.

Hume's most radical modification of Berkeley's philosophy is his rejection of the Berkeleyan doctrine of spirits. In Berkeley's view everybody is acquainted with at least one spirit, namely himself. But, says Hume,[2] 'For my part, when I enter most intimately into what I call *myself*, I always stumble on some particular impression or other, of heat or cold, light or shade, love or hatred, pain or pleasure. I never can catch *myself* at any time without a perception, and never can observe anything but the perception.' Hume, I think incorrectly, fails to

[1] *A Treatise Concerning the Principles of Human Knowledge*, section 27
[2] *A Treatise of Human Nature* (1st edition London 1739), part IV, book I, section VI

observe that, as Brentano[1] pointed out, in having a perception I am, at least sometimes, also aware of *my* having the perception, i.e. that it is *I* who am aware of heat or cold, etc. Consequently, Hume affirms that, apart from some metaphysicians whose reports he obviously distrusts, 'the rest of mankind' are nothing but 'a bundle of or collection of different perceptions, which succeed each other with an inconceivable rapidity, and are in a perpetual flux and movement'.[2]

If there are no spirits but only sense-impressions, their memory-images and their combinations, we can have no knowledge of any necessary connexion in nature, but only of regular sequences of impressions. It follows that induction cannot be justified in terms of such necessary connexion, and the road is clear to Hume's famous argument that induction admits of no philosophical justification whatever.[3] The relation of causality, without which no thinking about matters of fact is possible, is simply based on habit. There is nothing to the concept of causal connexion 'except only a present object and a customary transition to the idea of another object, which we have been accustomed to conjoin with the former'. And, Hume goes on, 'this is the whole operation of the mind, in all our conclusions concerning matter of fact and existence'.[4] The outcome of Hume's argument anticipates the antimetaphysical position of the logical positivists, and is open to the same objections.[5] A caricature of the development of empiricism which nevertheless bears some resemblance to the original might read as follows: Locke *minus* the external world equals Berkeley. Berkeley *minus* spirits equals Hume.

The rationalist conception of the philosopher as a supermathematician who provides science with its axiomatic foundations and the empiricist conception of the philosopher as an underlabourer who clears away the rubbish which hinders

[1] See page 92   [2] *A Treatise of Human Nature, loc. cit.*
[3] See page 88
[4] *An Enquiry Concerning Human Understanding* edited by Selby-Bigge, page 54
[5] See page 33

experimental research each emphasize an important aspect of scientific thinking. That these views are onesided is affirmed in Einstein's introduction to Galileo Galilei's *Dialogue Concerning the Two Chief World Systems.*[1]

To put into sharp contrast the empirical and the deductive attitude is misleading, and was entirely foreign to Galileo. . . . The antithesis Empiricism *versus* Rationalism does not appear as a controversial point in Galileo's work. Galileo opposes the deductive methods of Aristotle and his adherents only when he considers their premises arbitrary or untenable. . . . Galileo himself makes considerable use of logical deduction. His endeavours are not so much directed at factual knowledge as at comprehension.

By itself neither the rationalist nor the empiricist conception of scientific thinking can account for the achievement of Galileo, Newton and their successors, in which the world of experience was described in the language of mathematics. In order to understand the kind of conceptual organization of the perceptual content which constitutes science and in particular physics, a synthesis of empiricism and rationalism is required. The Kantian philosophy was meant to be such a synthesis. This synthesis, as we saw, is not a mere putting together of the Humean emphasis on the role of sense-experience and the Leibnizian emphasis on the role of logic in our thinking. It exhibits a further element which escaped the notice of both empiricists and rationalists, namely the role of non-logical and non-empirical concepts and principles in objective experience. As I have argued earlier, Kant's exhibition of the individuating and constitutive concepts and principles associated with his and his contemporaries' categorial framework was an important step forward, although his attempt at demonstrating the indispensability of his Categories and the incorrigibility of his framework-principles later proved an obstacle to progress.

Fichte, Schelling and Hegel developed what they regarded as the true core of the Kantian philosophy into speculative systems which lost contact with the natural sciences. They all rejected

[1] Edited by Cajori (Berkeley 1953), page XVII

Kant's doctrine that the world in itself is unknowable. Hegel's dialectics of Reason, Nature and History is one of these systems which is still alive.[1] Schopenhauer's philosophy is another. It presupposes, as has been pointed out, a thorough acquaintance with the *Critique of Pure Reason* and represents in many respects a synthesis of Kant's transcendental philosophy with the philosophy of Sankara, the Indian commentator on the Vedanta, which is the metaphysical part of the sacred scriptures of the Hindus. A more orthodox development of the Kantian philosophy is found in the works of J. F. Fries and Leonard Nelson who follow Kant in paying close philosophical attention to mathematics and physics.

The empiricist line of thought was importantly developed by J. S. Mill, who, undismayed by Hume's rejection of any inductive logic, tried to revive Bacon's attempt to place a *Novum Organon*, an inductive logic, alongside Aristotle's old *Organon*, his system of deductive logic. Mill's interest in social problems also prompted him to refine Bentham's utilitarianism and to analyse the methods of the social sciences.[2] Brentano's philosophy is in many respects an extension of Hume's empiricism, to which he adds his own theory of intentional phenomena – a theory whose roots go back to medieval thought.

The nineteenth and the beginning of our own century also gave birth to anti-intellectualist movements which not only emphasize man's irrationality, the evidence for which has never been less than plentiful, but extol it as the legitimate guide of human action and thought. To Kierkegaard's Christian rejection of systematic metaphysics and science there corresponds Nietzsche's anti-Christian rejection of traditional thought and morality. The ideal society should be ruled by an aristocracy whose 'will to power' must not be stifled by the Christian slave-morality and religious superstition. The wrong kind of men 'have with their "all are equal before God" dominated the destiny of Europe; until in the end a dwarfed, almost ridiculous species has been produced, a gregarious

[1] See pages 220 f
[2] See *System of Logic* (London 1843), book VI

animal, something well intentioned, sickly and mediocre, the contemporary European'.[1] Nietzsche's works read like passionate sermons exhorting the fit to take a hand in bringing about the survival of the fittest. They are spiced with psychological aphorisms which vary from profound observations on human nature to pompous banalities. Much of what he says could – after translation into their peculiar idiom – have issued from the mouths of the National Socialist leaders. But Nietzsche *cannot* be considered an early National Socialist – if only because his contempt for nationalism and his occasional high praise of Jewish achievements would probably have earned him a place in a concentration camp.

[1] *Jenseits von Gut und Böse* (Leipzig 1886) end of section 30

16. The Contemporary Scene

'Even though we almost always see the Gorgiases and Hippiases uppermost . . . the genuine works possess nevertheless a quite peculiar, quiet, slow and powerful influence; and as if by a miracle we see them in the end emerge out of the bustle like a balloon, which rises from the thick atmosphere of this earth into purer regions, where having once arrived it remains so firmly anchored that no one can ever drag it down.'[1] To try to identify those of one's contemporaries, if any, whose philosophical work is destined to survive the bustle of their lifetime is impossible – unless one makes the arrogant assumption that one's own philosophical point of view is the measure of all philosophizing. Even the comparatively modest task of separating the sophists from the serious philosophers is better left to future historians. In order to avoid any misunderstandings which might arise from my mentioning the works of some contemporary philosophers and not of others, the following impressions of the contemporary philosophical scene will be restricted to brief remarks on those traditions and those thinkers of the recent and more distant past whose influence is still felt as a living force.

[1] Preface to the 2nd edition of Schopenhauer, *Die Welt als Wille und Vorstellung* (Leipzig 1844)

THE ANALYTICAL TRADITION

The analytical tradition in its modern form has been strongly influenced by Bertrand Russell. On the one hand, he provided in *Principia Mathematica*, of which he and A. N. Whitehead were the joint authors, a logico-mathematical system which for a time was regarded as the only framework, and therefore as a necessary criterion, of all sound thinking. On the other hand, he extended certain techniques, which the authors of *Principia Mathematica* had found useful in welding logic and mathematics into one unified system, in such a way as to make them applicable to other than logico-mathematical concepts and propositions. One of these techniques is the 'method of logical constructions', the first application of which outside mathematics is due to Whitehead. Russell describes it as follows:

Given a set of propositions nominally dealing with supposed inferred entities we observe the properties which are required of the supposed entities in order to make these propositions true. By dint of a little logical ingenuity, we then construct some logical function of less hypothetical entities which has the requisite properties. This constructed function we substitute for the inferred entities, and thereby obtain a new and less doubtful interpretation of the body of propositions in question.[1]

Russell used this method in the service of an empiricist philosophy, in particular for the reduction of propositions about physical objects to propositions about so-called 'sense-data', a more sophisticated version of Hume's impressions and ideas.

It soon became clear that the method of logical constructions and the apparatus of *Principia Mathematica* were not powerful enough for the detailed execution of Russell's empiricist programme, since, for example, dispositional properties, such as 'brittle' or 'magnetic', resisted the reductive treatment. Contemporary empiricism is quite content to acknowledge as legitimate the employment of concepts which are not analysable into characteristics of sense-data or of other observable

[1] 'The Relation of Sense-Data to Physics', *Scientia* (1910), republished in *Mysticism and Logic* (London 1917)

entities. Russell's method of logical constructions must nevertheless be regarded as a prototype of the philosophical method which was described earlier in this book as replacement-analysis – even though the analytical philosophers who pursued this type of analysis did not, on the whole, make their method explicit. Russell's own analytical work covered a wide field of philosophical problems, to whose treatment he brought much more than 'a little logical ingenuity'.

Russell – like Aristotle, Leibniz, and his more immediate predecessor Frege – inquired at various periods of his philosophical activity into the relation between logic, which constitutes a standard of correct thinking about the world, and the world itself. But it was Ludwig Wittgenstein's *Tractatus Logico-Philosophicus* which became the classical work relating modern logic to the knowable world. According to Wittgenstein there corresponds to every true or false atomic proposition (in the framework of standard elementary logic) a possible fact. Thus if we select one member from every pair of contradictory atomic propositions – e.g. 'This pen is black' and 'This pen is not black' – we get a sequence of propositions, say, p_1, p_2 .... Each sequence constitutes the description of a possible world. The sequence in which every member is true describes the (actual) world: 'The world is everything that is the case.'[1] A compound proposition[2] which is true in all possible worlds is, as in Leibniz's philosophy, a principle of logic. There are no other such principles. All atomic facts are independent of each other. There is no necessary connexion – of Berkeleyan, Hegelian, or any other kind – between facts. Propositions are in a very special sense 'pictures of' possible or actual facts.

It is not possible to describe the categorial framework of the *Tractatus* in detail. But some similarities with Kant's approach are worth mentioning. The world is theoretically knowable only through language or, as Kant would say, through the application of concepts. 'Of the will as the bearer of the ethical we cannot speak',[3] i.e. we can have no theoretical knowledge of it.

---

[1] *Tractatus Logico-Philosophicus*, 1   [2] See page 41
[3] *Tractatus Logico-Philosophicus* 6.423

Beyond the world of facts as pictured by propositions is the mystical, a conception which bears some resemblance to the Kantian thing in itself. In the preface to the *Tractatus* Wittgenstein claims, as did Kant before him, that 'the *truth* of the thoughts communicated' in the work seems to him 'unassailable and definitive'. The claim is moderated by the qualification that, if it is justified, then the value of the *Tractatus* consists secondly 'in the fact that it shows how little has been done when these problems have been solved'.[1]

Wittgenstein's later philosophy differs from the philosophy of the *Tractatus* in many important respects. The incorrigibility claim for its categorial framework and underlying logic is abandoned. He admits that there is a multiplicity of different languages and linguistic activities, just as there is a multiplicity of games which cannot be precisely delimited but bear a 'family-resemblance' to each other: 'How should we explain to someone what a game is? I imagine that we should describe *games* to him, and we might add: "This *and* similar things are called 'games'". And do we know any more about it ourselves?. . . . We do not know the boundaries because none have been drawn. To repeat, we can draw a boundary – for a special purpose. Does it take that to make the concept usable? Not at all! (Except for that special purpose.)'[2]

Another central point of Wittgenstein's later philosophy is his emphasis on the impossibility of a private language. Using such a language would consist in conforming to rules without the possibility of justifying the correctness of their application by 'an appeal to an independent authority' (*eine unabhängige Stelle*).[3] The sense in which a language is a social phenomenon is made clear by a thorough investigation into what it is to conform to a rule. This investigation and Wittgenstein's closely related analysis of so-called private experiences has had a strong influence on later 'linguistic' philosophers. These however,

[1] *ibid.*, page 29

[2] *Philosophical Investigations* translated by G. E. M. Anscombe (Oxford 1953), No. 69

[3] *ibid.*, No. 265

unlike Wittgenstein, who distinguished between 'surface grammar' and 'deep grammar', have tended to restrict themselves to ordinary English usage. *One* possible means of distinguishing between the two kinds of grammar might be to assign those features of a language which vanish on translation (at least into a .closely related language) to its surface grammar.

Wittgenstein's method in his later philosophy is 'exhibition-analysis.'[1] However, the use of this method is once again combined with a claim to exclusiveness: 'Philosophy may in no way interfere with the actual use of language; it can in the end only describe it.'[2] There are many examples of philosophical attempts at 'interfering with language', some of which have been successful even in the sense that they have become part of ordinary languages. Yet, although the employment of exhibition-analysis to the exclusion of any other mode of philosophizing must in the end impoverish philosophy, Wittgenstein's own use of it has greatly enriched it. The same is true of G. E. Moore's and C. D. Broad's detailed analyses.[3]

PRAGMATISM AND MARXISM

Pragmatism and Marxism have, in spite of many great differences, more in common than their enormous influence on contemporary non-philosophical thinking. They both rightly acknowledge their indebtedness to Hegel. The close relations between Marxism and Hegelianism have been mentioned earlier. C. S. Peirce, one of the leaders of pragmatism and its profoundest thinker, does not see the core of the Hegelian approach in its rigid and artificial progress from thesis to antithesis and onwards. The importance of Hegel's way of philosophizing is, according to Peirce, that he 'simply launches his boat into the current of thought and allows himself to be

[1] See pages 26 f   [2] *Philosophical Investigations*, No. 124
[3] See e.g. Moore, *Philosophical Studies* (London 1922) and Broad, *The Mind and Its Place in Nature* (London 1925)

carried wherever the current leads.' The central meaning of Hegel's dialectic is 'that a frank discussion of the difficulties to which any opinion spontaneously gives rise will lead to modification after modification until a tenable position is attained'.[1]

Another common feature of pragmatism and Marxism, or more accurately Marx's Marxism, is the insistence on praxis as the test of theorizing – a praxis which is not an aspect of a wholly predetermined course of nature but allows genuine choices within the limits set by nature. A rational person, according to Peirce,

not merely has habits, but also can exert a measure of self-control over his future actions; which means, however, *not* that he can impart to them any arbitrarily assignable character, but, on the contrary, that a process of self-preparation will tend to impart to action (when the occasion for it shall arise), one fixed character, which is indicated and perhaps roughly measured by the absence (or slightness) of the feeling of self-reproach, which subsequent reflection will induce.[2]

According to Marx 'social life is essentially *practical*. All mysteries which tend to deflect theorizing into mysticism find their rational solution in human praxis and in the understanding of this praxis.'[3]

For Peirce too praxis is a social activity: a man's 'circle of society (however widely or narrowly this phrase may be understood) is a sort of loosely compacted person, in some respects of higher rank than the person of an individual organism'. Indeed 'a person is not absolutely an individual. His thoughts are what he is "saying to himself", that is saying to that other self that is just coming into life in the flow of time.'[4] If the first of these quotations links Peirce with Hegel and Marx,

[1] 'The Fixation of Belief' in Coll. Papers edited by C. Hartshorne and P. Weiss (Harvard University Press 1931–5), volume V, sections 358–87

[2] *ibid.*, sections 411–34

[3] 'Thesen über Feuerbach', Marx-Engels, *Werke* (Berlin 1960–66), volume 3, pages 533 ff

[4] 'The Fixation of Belief'

the second links him with the existentialist conception of a person as determining himself freely. These affinities cannot, however, be pursued here.

Peirce distinguishes clearly between the pragmatist and the other philosophical ingredients of his thought. Pragmatism, for him, is a method of ascertaining the meaning of what he calls 'intellectual concepts', i.e. those concepts 'upon the structure of which arguments concerning objective facts may hinge'.[1] Such concepts 'carry some implication concerning the general behaviour either of some conscious being or some inanimate object, and so convey . . . the "would-acts", "would-dos" of habitual behaviour. . . '. The *total* meaning of the predication of an intellectual concept is 'contained in an affirmation that under all conceivable circumstances of a given kind (or under this or that more or less indefinite part of their fulfilment . . .) the subject of the predication would behave in a certain way. . .'.[2] He quotes a wider definition of pragmatism by William James which 'in practice' comes very near to his own. For our purposes here James' definition seems more illuminating: 'Pragmatism is the doctrine that the "meaning" of a concept expresses itself either in the shape of conduct to be recommended or of experience to be expected'.[3]

Pragmatism implies for Peirce the doctrine of 'fallibilism', i.e. 'the doctrine that our knowledge is never absolute, but always swims as it were in a continuum of uncertainty and of indeterminacy'.[4] Fallibilism, in this sense, was never a feature of Marxism, even though Marxism emphasized the dependence of all (non-Marxist) ideologies on the economic structure of the society in which they arise. Where Marxism has become the official philosophy, it has tended to play a role rather similar to that of orthodox Catholic theology in the Middle Ages – the role of being always the standard, and never the object, of philosophical criticism. But this might happen to any philosophy and must not blind us to its philosophical content. It is very doubtful whether Marx himself would have approved of

[1] 'The Fixation of Belief', section 467   [2] *ibid.*   [3] *ibid.*
[4] *ibid.*, volume 1, sections 171–5

attempts to remove any of his theses from free philosophical discussion.

EXISTENTIALISM

Existentialism in the widest sense of the term is the insistence on the obvious and important truth that no theory can describe concrete human existence in its full concreteness. The truth is obvious because even those theories which, like zoology or physiology, get by with a minimum of idealization[1], describe individuals *qua* members of certain kinds of things only. It is important because in forgetting it we might give way to the tendency to confuse our own simplifications with non-existent simplicities in the natural or human universe. Individual happiness and suffering slip through the nets of conceptual generalization and idealization and are more successfully caught in poems, novels, paintings or music. Indeed existentialist philosophers, *qua* philosophers, often fail in their search for concreteness because they in fact replace one set of generalizations by another. 'Concreteness' itself is after all a highly general term.

Existentialist philosophy has its more recent roots in the philosophy of Brentano and Husserl and in what one is almost tempted to call the 'anti-philosophies' of Kierkegaard and Nietzsche. It has also been influenced by such great novelists as Dostoyevsky, Proust and Kafka and has some affinities with Wittgenstein's later philosophy and Peirce's pragmatism. If Wittgenstein sees the legitimate function of philosophy in the description, without modification, of language, so the existentialists see it in the description, without modification, of the mental activity of man. Phenomenology, which is the method of existentialist philosophy[2] consists, in the words of Merleau-Ponty[3], in 'describing, not in explaining or analysing'. The description is of all intentional phenomena in Brentano's and Husserl's sense and not merely of linguistic phenomena. Yet

[1] See pages 80 f   [2] See page 24
[3] *Phénoménologie de la Perception* (Paris 1945), preface

even so, it aims at a description of what is interpersonal rather than idiosyncratic – a distinction which is not easy to make since, for example, Kafka's K. in *Das Schloss* is as personal a person as the narrator of Proust's *A la recherche du temps perdu*. The danger of extrapolating idiosyncratic moods into characteristics of man as man has not always been avoided.

The main value of the work of Merleau-Ponty and those existentialists who, like him, strive after philosophical clarity, lies in detailed descriptions of mental phenomena, rather than in methodological pronouncements of which the following is an example: 'The phenomenological world is not the explication of a pre-existing being (*d'un être préalable*), but the foundation and constitution of being (*la fondation de l'être*), it is not the reflection of a pre-existing truth but, like art, the realization of a previously non-existent truth.'[1] In trying to describe mental phenomena Merleau-Ponty draws not only on the works of Husserl and his closer pupils, but also on the writings of psychologists, especially of the so-called *Gestalt*-school.

What unites all existentialists is the doctrine that man is free in the sense that his life consists in determining himself. Their fundamental tenet is that the impression of our freedom is in no way illusory but that a careful phenomenological description of it reaches the very foundations of human existence. I cannot do better than let Merleau-Ponty speak for himself in order to convey at least the flavour of an existentialist philosophy which is free from linguistic contortions:

If it is said that my temperament inclines me to sadism or masochism, then this too is merely a *façon de parler*, since my temperament exists only for that secondary knowledge that I gain of myself in seeing myself, as it were, through the eyes of others. By accepting it, I confer value on it and in this sense choose it. What is wont to mislead us here is that we often look for freedom in the voluntary deliberation which examines our motives in turn and which seems to submit to the strongest or most convincing one. In reality, however, deliberation follows decision, namely my secret decision which makes the motives

[3] *Phénoménologie de la Perception*, page xv

appear in my mind, since without a decision which confirms or opposes a motive one would have no conception whatever of its force. . . .[1]

What chiefly divides the existentialists are their different religious commitments. There are catholic, protestant, jewish and atheist existentialists, and their religion is not separable from their philosophy. Nietzsche's 'God is dead'[2] is as much a fundamental presupposition of one wing of the existentialist movement, as Kierkegaard's affirmation of the existence of the God to whom Abraham was prepared to bring his son as a sacrifice is of another. Religious doctrines, including atheism, are not phenomenological descriptions but interpretations of experience. A study of the existentialist writers shows that their works are deeply influenced by the thoughts of their metaphysical predecessors. Antimetaphysics to the existentialists – as to the positivists, marxists, 'purely scientific scientists', etc. – means no more than rejection of other people's metaphysical assumptions.

THE CLASSICAL TRADITIONS

The classical traditions most noticeable in contemporary philosophy are Thomistic Aristotelianism, which is still the orthodox Catholic philosophy, and Kantianism, as modified by British empiricism and American pragmatism. The aim of Kant to determine definitely the limits and conditions of objective experience is being vigorously revived among analytical philosophers and others. Leibniz's monadology lives on in logic, metaphysics, and even in physics, where e.g. his criticism of physical atomism is taken seriously. Medieval logicians are not only being credited with the anticipation of much modern logic, but are being studied anew. Platonism is much in evidence in the philosophy of mathematics, the philosophy of science and metaphysics. Thus Whitehead, who once called Western philosophy a series of footnotes on Plato, has himself

[1] *ibid.* page 497
[2] *Die Fröhliche Wissenschaft* (Leipzig 1882), section 18

provided by his work a major footnote to Plato's main dialogues. Even the pre-Socratics have found advocates among modern metaphysicians.

THE FUTURE

The future of philosophy is, like its past, inextricably bound up with the whole of man's intellectual life. Philosophy develops by giving birth to new disciplines or acting as Socratic midwife, by internal criticism, by reacting to changes in its social and intellectual environment and by the independent exploration of new possibilities of thought. There is no reason to assume that philosophy has lost the power to produce – alone or with already existing disciplines – new forms of systematic inquiry. When Frege, in the footsteps of Leibniz and in the company of Dedekind, Cantor, Boole and others, laid the foundations of modern logic, he complained that his work was unlikely to be read by either philosophers, who would regard it as mathematics, or by mathematicians, who would regard it as metaphysics. Today mathematical logic is an independent subject or, at least, a thriving branch of mathematics. At about the same time as mathematical logic, experimental psychology became a subject of its own, having been nursed in laboratories founded by philosophers and fed mainly on the philosophical views of British empiricism and the school of Brentano.

Today there are signs of a new science of general linguistics emerging from the interaction between logic, philology and the philosophy of language created by Wittgenstein and pursued by his successors as a painstaking inquiry into the philosophically interesting features of their mother tongue. There are also signs of a similar interaction between a hitherto mainly descriptive anthropology and the philosophico-historical approach to ideology on marxist and Collingwoodian lines. In this context the approach to categorial frameworks, outlined earlier in this book, might prove fruitful. Philosophers are likely to continue their traditional pioneering in the no-man's-lands between established disciplines – e.g. between history and the natural sciences – and to open them up to intensive cultivation by later settlers.

In order to appreciate fully the role of internal philosophical criticism one must study the history of philosophy in some depth. Still, even the brief remarks (in chapter 15) on the development of British empiricism from Locke to Hume may be of some help. Obscurities and possible confusions in Locke's philosophy are removed by Berkeley. The empiricist position is further refined and purified by Hume in such a manner that its implications and limitations become equally intelligible to both empiricists and their opponents. Only then does it become clear that a radical empiricism leads to philosophical scepticism about the external world and thus about the natural sciences, to whose service it had been dedicated by Locke. To explore an avenue of thought as persistently as possible is fruitful even if in the end it turns out to be a blind alley. A more recent example of internal philosophical criticism is the philosophical analysis of philosophical analysis, which started out as an apparently autonomous, anti-metaphysical inquiry and led to deeper insights into the relations between analysis and metaphysics.

The continual reaction of philosophy to its social framework shows itself in the manner in which philosophy brings to light the moral assumptions made by a community and in the manner in which it criticizes them. Aristotle's recognition of the need to justify slavery and his inability to provide a cogent justification of the institution, as it in fact existed, prepared the way for the moral condemnation of all kinds of slavery by later philosophers. The same applies to Mill's wholly honest justification of colonial rule in very special circumstances, which nowadays obtain hardly anywhere.

About philosophy as reflection on non-philosophical thinking – commonsense, logical, mathematical, scientific, historical and religious – nothing need be added at this stage. When a new discipline emerges, its subject matter does not necessarily cease to be of interest to philosophy. Thus in spite of the emergence of psychology as a branch of the biological sciences, philosophical psychology continues as a branch of philosophy. Even if, as in the case of the physical sciences, the new discipline takes over from philosophy, philosophy gains as well as loses territory. For example, in so far as philosophy ceases to be philosophy of physical nature, it becomes philosophy of the science of physical nature, i.e. philosophy of physics.

There is no reason why philosophical speculation and conceptual innovation should cease. Philosophical genius of the order of a Plato, Aristotle, Leibniz or Kant is perhaps even more rare than creative genius in the arts and sciences. But the intimate connexion of all aspects of intellectual life makes it appear very unlikely that the source of philosophical inspiration has dried up. What the next stroke of philosophical genius may be is, of course, wholly unpredictable.

Only a rather uninformed and unreflective person could say with any conviction that philosophy has run its course: that it started as the successor of mythical thinking, spent a millennium as the handmaid of theology and three centuries as an underlabourer of modern science, gave birth to vigorous offspring and is now ripe for honourable (or perhaps even dishonourable) retirement. Philosophical reflection will cease only when non-philosophical reflection too is at its end. Although I have argued that there is no perennial philosophy – no hard unchangeable core of philosophical truth – philosophy is perennial. Its inner life and its intellectual environment confront the philosopher with a continually changing constellation of problems and never absolve him from his duty to think again.

Select Bibliography

The following books, all in English and easily available, are relevant to the problems discussed in the text. I have starred those which to me seem particularly suitable for further reading.

Part 1: Austin, J. L., *Philosophical Papers* (Oxford 1961); Ayer, A. J., *Language, Truth and Logic* (2nd edition London 1956); Beck, L. W., *Philosophic Inquiry* (Englewood Cliffs, N.J. 1963)★; Hospers, J., *Introduction to Philosophical Analysis* (London 1959)★; Moore, G. E., *Lectures on Philosophy* (edited by C. Lewy, London 1966); Nakhnikian, G., *An Introduction to Philosophy* (New York 1967); Pap. A., *Semantics and Necessary Truth* (Yale University Press 1958); Russell, B., *The Problems of Philosophy* (London 1912)★.

Part 2: Alexander, P., *Sensationalism and Scientific Explanation* (London 1963); Anscombe, G. E. M., *Intention* (Oxford 1963); Ayer, A. J., *The Problem of Knowledge* (London 1956)★; Braithwaite, R. B., *Scientific Explanation* (Cambridge 1953)★; Beth, E. W., *Mathematical Thought* (Dordrecht 1965); Carnap, R., *Introduction to Symbolic Logic and its Applications* (New York 1958); Chisholm, R. M., *Theory of Knowledge* (Englewood Cliffs, N.J. 1966)★; Chisholm, R. M., *Perceiving* (Cornell University Press 1957); Feigl, H., *The 'Mental' and the 'Physical'* (Minnesota Paperbacks, Minnesota University Press, 1967)★; Geach, P. T., *Reference and Generality* (Cornell University Press 1962); Hempel, C. G., *Aspects of Scientific Explanation and Other Essays in the Philosophy of Science* (New York 1965); Kneebone, G. T.,

Select Bibliography

Mathematical Logic and the Foundations of Mathematics (London 1963)*; Körner, S., *The Philosophy of Mathematics* (London 1960); Körner, S., *Experience and Theory* (London 1966); Kneale, W. C., *Probability and Induction* (Oxford 1949); Lorenzen, P., *Formal Logic* (translated from German, Dordrecht 1965); Nagel, E., *The Structure of Science* (London 1961); Nidditch, P. H., *Elementary Logic of Science and Mathematics* (London 1960); Popper, K. R., *The Logic of Discovery* (translated from German, London 1959)*; Prior, A. N., *Formal Logic* (Oxford 1955); Quine, W. V., *The Methods of Logic* (2nd revised edition, London 1962)*; Reichenbach, H., *Experience and Prediction* (Chicago 1947); Ryle, G., *The Concept of Mind* (London 1949); Salmon, W. C., *The Foundations of Scientific Inference* (Pittsburgh University Press 1967)*; Toulmin, S. E., *The Philosophy of Science* (London 1953); Weyl, H., *Philosophy of Mathematics and the Natural Sciences* (translated from German, Princeton University Press 1949)*; Wilder, R. L., *Introduction to the Foundations of Mathematics* (2nd revised edition, New York 1965).

Part 3: Acton, H. B., *The Illusion of the Epoch* (London 1962); Baier, K. E. M., *The Moral Point of View* (Cornell University Press 1964); Berlin, I., *Historical Inevitability* (Oxford 1955); Braithwaite, R. B., *An Empiricist View of the Nature of Religious Knowledge* (Cambridge 1955); Broad, C. D., *Five Types of Ethical Theory* (London 1930); Dray, W. H., *Laws and Explanation in History* (Oxford 1950); Field, G. C., *Moral Theory* (2nd edition, London 1966)*; Frankena, W. K., *Ethics* (Englewood Cliffs, N.J. 1963)*; Gallie, W. B., *Philosophy and the Historical Understanding* (London 1964)*; Gardiner, P. L., *The Nature of Historical Explanation* (Oxford 1952); Gombrich, E. H. J., *Art and Illusion* (London 1962); Hare, R. M., *The Language of Morals* (Oxford 1952); Hare, R. M., *Freedom and Reason* (Oxford 1963)*; Hart, H. L. A., *The Concept of Law* (Oxford 1961); Hampshire, S. N., *Thought and Action* (London 1959); Kenny, A., *Action, Emotion and the Will* (London 1963); Nowell-Smith, P. H., *Ethics* (London 1954 etc.)*; Popper, K. R., *The Open Society and Its Enemies* (London 1945); Smart, R. N., *Reasons and Faiths* (London 1958); Toulmin, S. E., *Reason in Ethics* (Cambridge 1950); Walsh, W. H., *An Introduction to the Philosophy of History* (London 1951)*; Wright, G. H. von, *Norm and Action* (London 1963).

Part 4: Bergman, H., *Realism* (Madison 1967); Campbell, C. A., *In Defence of Free Will* (London 1967); Cohen, L. J., *The Diversity of Meaning* (London 1962); Emmet, D. M., *The Nature of Metaphysical Thinking* (London 1945)*; Findlay, J. N., *Hegel* (London 1958)*; Hartshorne, C., *Anselm's Discovery* (La Salle 1965); Lazerowitz, M., *The Structure of Metaphysics* (London 1955); Strawson, P. F., *The Bounds of Sense – An Essay on Kant's Critique of Pure Reason* (London 1966); Strawson, P. F., *Individuals, An Essay in Descriptive Metaphysics* (London 1959)*; Walsh, W. H., *Metaphysics* (London 1963)*.

Part 5: Bocheński, I. M., *The Methods of Contemporary Thought*, (translated from German, Dordrecht 1965); Gallie, W. B., *Peirce and Pragmatism* (2nd edition, New York 1966); Körner, S., *Kant* (London 1955); Manser, A. R., *Sartre* (London 1966); Warnock, G. J., *English Philosophy since 1900* (Oxford 1958).

Index of Persons

Index of Persons

Index of Subjects

Index of Subjects